North Mississippi National Wildlife Refuges Complex

Comprehensive Conservation Plan

USFWS Photo

Comprehensive Conservation Plans provide long-term guidance for management decisions; set forth goals, objectives, and strategies needed to accomplish refuge purposes; and identify the Fish and Wildlife Service's best estimate of future needs. These plans detail program planning levels that are sometimes substantially above current budget allocations and, as such, are primarily for Service strategic planning and program prioritization purposes. The plans do not constitute a commitment for staffing increases, operational and maintenance increases, or funding for future land acquisition.

North Mississippi National Wildlife Refuges Complex

Comprehensive Conservation Plan

U.S. Department of the Interior
Fish and Wildlife Service
Southeast Region

November 2005

Submitted by: _____   Date: 9/20/05
Steve Gard, Project Leader
North Mississippi National Wildlife Refuges Complex

Concur: _____   Date: 9/27/05
Ricky Ingram, Refuge Supervisor
Southeast Region

Concur: _____ *Acting*   Date: 9-28-05
Jon Andrew, Regional Chief
Southeast Region

Approved by: _____   Date: 9-29-05
Sam Hamilton, Regional Director
Southeast Region

COMPREHENSIVE CONSERVATION PLAN

NORTH MISSISSIPPI NATIONAL WILDLIFE REFUGES COMPLEX
GRENADA, MISSISSIPPI

U.S. Department of the Interior
Fish and Wildlife Service
Southeast Region
1875 Century Boulevard
Atlanta, Georgia 30345

November 2005

TABLE OF CONTENTS

SECTION A. COMPREHENSIVE CONSERVATION PLAN

LIST OF FIGURES

LIST OF TABLES

I. Background

INTRODUCTION

The U.S. Fish and Wildlife Service has developed this Comprehensive Conservation Plan (CCP) to provide a foundation for the management and use of the North Mississippi National Wildlife Refuges Complex (Complex), headquartered in Grenada, Mississippi. The North Mississippi National Wildlife Refuges Complex is comprised of Coldwater River, Dahomey, and Tallahatchie National Wildlife Refuges and the Farm Service Agency tracts of land in the area. The Complex provides habitat for large concentrations of wintering waterfowl and numerous species of neotropical migratory birds. This comprehensive conservation plan is intended to serve as a working guide for the Complex's management programs and actions over the next 15 years.

The plan was developed in compliance with the National Wildlife Refuge System Improvement Act of 1997 and Part 602, National Wildlife Refuge System Planning, of the Fish and Wildlife Service Manual. The actions described within this plan also meet the requirements of the National Environmental Policy Act (NEPA) of 1969. Compliance with NEPA was met with public involvement throughout the CCP process and the development of an environmental assessment. When fully implemented, this plan will strive to achieve the vision and purposes of each refuge within the Complex.

The plan's overriding consideration is to carry out the purposes for which each refuge was established. Fish and wildlife are the first priority in refuge management, and public use (wildlife-dependent recreation) is allowed and encouraged as long as it is compatible with, or does not detract from, each refuge's mission and purposes.

The plan has been prepared by a planning team composed of representatives from each of the refuges in the Complex; the Service's Jackson, Mississippi, Ecological Services field office; with the assistance of an environmental contractor. In developing this plan, the planning team and refuge staff incorporated the input of the Mississippi Department of Wildlife, Fisheries, and Parks, other agencies, non-governmental organizations, local citizens, the public, and stakeholders. This public involvement and the planning process itself are further described in Chapter III. Plan Development.

This plan represents the Service's preferred alternative and is being put forward after considering three other alternatives, as described in the draft EA. After reviewing public scoping comments and management needs, the planning team developed these alternatives in an attempt to determine how to best meet the goals and objectives of the Complex. The preferred alternative is the Service's recommended course of action for the future management of the Complex.

PURPOSE AND NEED FOR PLAN

The purpose of this comprehensive conservation plan is to identify the role that the North Mississippi National Wildlife Refuges Complex will play in support of the mission of the National Wildlife Refuge System, and to provide long-term guidance to the refuges' management programs and activities. The plan is needed to:

- Provide a clear statement of direction for the future management of the Complex;

- Provide neighbors, visitors, non-governmental partners, and government officials with an understanding of the Service's management actions on and around the Complex;
- Ensure that the Service's management actions, including land protection and recreational and educational programs, are consistent with the mandates of the National Wildlife Refuge System Improvement Act of 1997;
- Ensure that the management of the Complex considers federal, state, and county plans; and
- Provide a basis for the development of budget requests for the Complex's operational, maintenance, and capital improvement needs.

A critical management consideration for the Service is to communicate with the public and include public participation in its efforts to carry out the mission of the National Wildlife Refuge System. Many agencies, organizations, institutions, businesses, and private citizens have developed relationships with the Service to advance the goals of the Refuge System.

This comprehensive conservation plan supports the Partners-in-Flight Initiative, Lower Mississippi Valley Migratory Bird Wetland Conservation Initiative, North American Waterfowl Management Plan, Western Hemisphere Shorebird Reserve Network, National Woodcock Management Plan, and the National Wetlands Priority Conservation Plan.

THE U.S. FISH AND WILDLIFE SERVICE

The U.S. Fish and Wildlife Service is the primary federal agency responsible for the conservation, protection, and enhancement of the nation's fish and wildlife populations and their habitats. Although the Service shares some conservation responsibilities with other federal, state, local, tribal, and private entities, it has specific trustee obligations for migratory birds, threatened and endangered species, anadromous fish, and certain marine mammals. In addition, the Service administers a national network of lands and waters for the management and protection of these resources.

"The mission of the U.S. Fish and Wildlife Service, working with others, is to conserve, protect, and enhance fish and wildlife and their habitats for the continuing benefit of the American people."

As part of its mission, the Service manages the 96-million-acre National Wildlife Refuge System, comprised of more than 540 national wildlife refuges, thousands of small wetlands, and other special management areas throughout the nation, including Puerto Rico and the U.S. Virgin Islands. It also operates 66 national fish hatcheries, 64 fishery resource offices, and 78 ecological services field stations. The agency enforces federal wildlife laws, administers the Endangered Species Act, manages migratory bird populations, restores nationally significant fisheries, conserves and restores wildlife habitat, such as wetlands, and helps foreign governments with their conservation efforts. It also oversees the Federal Aid Program that distributes hundreds of millions of dollars in excise taxes on fishing and hunting equipment to state fish and wildlife agencies.

THE NATIONAL WILDLIFE REFUGE SYSTEM

The National Wildlife Refuge System is the largest collection of lands and waters specifically managed for fish and wildlife. The mission of the Refuge System, as defined by the National Wildlife Refuge System Improvement Act of 1997, is:

"... to administer a national network of lands and waters for the conservation, management, and where appropriate, restoration of the fish, wildlife and plant resources and their habitats within the United States for the benefit of present and future generations of Americans."

The National Wildlife Refuge System Improvement Act of 1997 established, for the first time, a clear mission of wildlife conservation for the National Wildlife Refuge System. The Act states that the Service will manage each refuge to:

- Fulfill the mission of the Refuge System;
- Fulfill the individual purposes of each refuge;
- Consider the needs of fish and wildlife first;
- Fulfill the requirement of developing a comprehensive conservation plan for each unit of the Refuge System, and fully involve the public in the preparation of these plans;
- Maintain the biological integrity, diversity, and environmental health of the Refuge System; and
- Recognize that wildlife-dependent recreation activities, including hunting, fishing, wildlife observation, wildlife photography, and environmental education and interpretation, are legitimate and priority public uses.

Following passage of the Act in 1997, the Service immediately began efforts to carry out the direction of the new legislation, including the preparation of comprehensive conservation plans for all refuges. The development of these plans is now ongoing nationally. Consistent with the Act, the Service is preparing all refuge comprehensive conservation plans in conjunction with public involvement, and is requiring each refuge to complete its plan within a 15-year schedule.

Approximately 38 million people visited the country's national wildlife refuges in 2002, mostly to observe wildlife in their natural habitats. As this visitation continues to grow, significant economic benefits are being generated to local communities that surround the refuges. Economists have reported that national wildlife refuge visitors contribute more than $400 million annually to the local economies. In 2001, 82 million U.S. residents, 16 years and older, fished, hunted, or observed wildlife, which generated $108 billion. In a study completed in 2002 on 15 refuges in 14 states around the nation, visitation had grown 36 percent in seven years. At the same time, the number of jobs generated in surrounding communities grew to 120 per refuge, up from 87 jobs in 1995, pouring more than $2.2 million into local economies. Other findings also validate the belief that communities near refuges benefit economically. Expenditures on food, lodging, and transportation grew to $6.8 million per refuge, up 31 percent from $5.2 million in 1995. For each federal dollar spent on the Refuge System, surrounding communities benefited with $4.43 in recreation expenditures and $1.42 in job-related income (Caudill and Laughland, unpubl. data).

Volunteerism continues to be a major contributor to the successes of the Refuge System. In the Southeast Region for 2004, 6,349 volunteers supported 125 stations and contributed 293,937 hours, a service valued at $5,052,777.

The wildlife and habitat vision for national wildlife refuges stresses the following principles:

- Wildlife comes first.
- Ecosystems, biodiversity, and wilderness are vital considerations in refuge management.
- Ecological integrity must be maintained.
- Growth of refuges must be strategic.
- The National Wildlife Refuge System serves as a model for habitat management with broad participation from others.

NORTH MISSISSIPPI NATIONAL WILDLIFE REFUGES COMPLEX COMPREHENSIVE CONSERVATION PLAN

This Comprehensive Conservation Plan for the North Mississippi National Wildlife Refuges Complex, consisting of three national wildlife refuges – Coldwater River, Dahomey, and Tallahatchie – as well as a number of smaller fee title properties and floodplain and conservation easements, is being prepared as mandated by the National Wildlife Refuge System Improvement Act of 1997, to guide management actions and direction for the Complex over the next 15 years. Fish and wildlife conservation will receive first priority in refuge management; wildlife-dependent recreation will be allowed and encouraged as long as it is compatible with, or does not detract from, the legislated purposes of the three refuges that make up the Complex.

LEGAL POLICY CONTEXT

Administration of national wildlife refuges is guided by the mission and goals of the National Wildlife Refuge System, congressional legislation, Presidential executive orders, and international treaties. Policies for management options of refuges are further refined by administrative guidelines established by the Secretary of the Interior and by policy guidelines established by the Director of the Fish and Wildlife Service. Refer to Appendix F for a complete listing of relevant legal mandates.

By law, lands within the National Wildlife Refuge System are closed to public use unless specifically opened. All programs and uses must be evaluated based on mandates set forth in the National Wildlife Refuge System Improvement Act of 1997. Those mandates are to:

- Contribute to ecosystem goals, as well as refuge purposes and goals;
- Conserve, manage, and restore fish, wildlife, and plant resources and their habitats;
- Monitor the trends of fish, wildlife, and plants;
- Manage and ensure appropriate visitor uses, as those uses benefit the conservation of fish and wildlife resources and contribute to the enjoyment of the public (these uses include hunting, fishing, wildlife observation, wildlife photography, and environmental education and interpretation); and
- Ensure that visitor activities are compatible with refuge purposes.

RELATIONSHIP TO THE MISSISSIPPI DEPARTMENT OF WILDLIFE, FISHERIES, AND PARKS

A provision of the National Wildlife Refuge System Improvement Act of 1997, and subsequent agency policy, is that the Service shall ensure timely and effective cooperation and collaboration with other federal agencies and state fish and wildlife agencies during the course of acquiring and managing refuges. This cooperation is essential in providing the foundation for the protection and sustainability of fish and wildlife throughout the United States.

The Mississippi Department of Wildlife, Fisheries, and Parks (MDWFP) (http://www.mdwfp.com) is a state-partnering agency with the Service. It is charged with enforcement responsibilities for migratory birds and endangered species, as well as managing the state's natural resources. The total area owned or managed by the State of Mississippi in support of wildlife, recreation, and fisheries is 828,408 acres, including 42 wildlife management areas (WMA's), 29 state parks encompassing 823,297 acres; and 21 lakes totaling 5,111 acres.

The MDWFP directs the state's wildlife conservation program and provides public recreation opportunities, including an extensive hunting and fishing program, on several WMAs and parks located near the Complex. The MDWFP's participation and contribution throughout this comprehensive conservation planning process has been valuable. It is continuing its work with the Service to provide ongoing opportunities for an open dialogue with the public to improve the condition of fish and wildlife populations in Mississippi. Not only has the MDWFP participated in biological reviews, public meetings, and field reviews as part of the planning process, it is also an active partner in annual hunt coordination, planning, and various wildlife and habitat surveys. Two of the three refuges in the Complex, Dahomey and Tallahatchie, have an active hunting and fishing program conducted in cooperation with the MDWFP. A key part of the planning process is the integration of common objectives between the Service and the MDWFP.

ASSISTANCE TO PRIVATE LANDOWNERS

Service policy for involvement with private landowners in developing and implementing habitat improvement projects was outlined in the National Wildlife Refuge System Improvement Act (NWRSIA) of 1997, and the Partners for Fish and Wildlife (PFW) Program. Additional authorities reside within the Fish and Wildlife Act (1956) and the Fish and Wildlife Coordination Act (1934).

Section 5, Item (4) (E) of the National Wildlife Refuge System Improvement Act of 1997 specifically states that the Service shall "ensure effective coordination, interaction, and cooperation with owners of land adjoining refuges and the fish and wildlife agency of the States in which the units of the Refuge System are located."

The PFW Program Policy states that in ranking and selecting private lands projects for funding and technical assistance, the highest priority shall be placed on those projects that would provide important and direct benefits to the goals and objectives of any nearby units of the National Wildlife Refuge System.

Most of the land within the Complex work area is privately owned. These privately owned lands should play an important role in the restoration and reestablishment of native habitats needed to support the diverse fish and wildlife resource for which this geographic area was historically known. Existing or potential habitat on private lands is essential for achieving the goals and objectives of national and regional plans.

The Service has several existing programs that are dedicated to providing technical assistance and funding for priority habitat projects on private lands. The Service's primary project delivery mechanism for habitat projects on private lands currently resides within the PFW Program. Additional funding and technical assistance for private lands are also available through several other Service-funded programs, including the Challenge Cost-Share Program (CCS), the Mississippi Partners for Wildlife Program, Migratory Birds Program, and several grant programs within the Threatened and Endangered Species Program.

Under the PFW Program, landowners may receive up to $25,000 for on-the-ground project implementation. Exceptions to the $25,000 limit per private landowner may be requested in unique or special circumstances. PFW projects typically receive a minimum 50 percent in-kind cost share and require a minimum 10-year commitment from the landowner. Typically, landowner agreements are for more than 20 years. Since the PFW Program was initiated in 1988, approximately 87,000 acres of bottomland hardwood forest wetlands have been planted, and over 20,000 acres of other habitat projects have been completed within the Lower Mississippi River Valley (LMRV). Over the past several years, the PFW Program has provided from between $350,000 to $400,000 in project funds each year for projects within the entire LMRV.

The Mississippi Partners for Wildlife Program is funded separately from the PFW Program, receiving funding primarily through the Service's Refuge Challenge Cost-Share Program. This program also requires at least a 50 percent cost-share from other partners. In Mississippi, this partnership involves private landowners, Ducks Unlimited, and the MDWFP. Approximately $50,000 in Service funds are made available each fiscal year through this partnership agreement. These funds are used to provide water-control structures to private landowners to flood harvested cropland during the fall and winter (November 15-February 28). This partnership provides significant benefits for wintering waterfowl, other migratory birds, and water quality.

The Farm Bill Conservation Programs, available through the U.S. Department of Agriculture (USDA) under the 2002 Farm Bill, provide significant opportunities for the development and implementation of habitat improvement projects on private lands. These programs include the Wetland Reserve Program (WRP), the Conservation Reserve Program (CRP), the Wildlife Habitat Incentives Program, and the Environmental Quality Incentives Program. Many millions of dollars are available to eligible private landowners for habitat conservation under these programs. For example, under the WRP, administered by the Natural Resources Conservation Service (NRCS), over 100,000 acres of permanent and 30-year easements, directed to restore natural wetlands and native vegetation, have been implemented in Mississippi since 1990. The 2002 Farm Bill provides authorization for over 1,000,000 additional acres at a rate of approximately 250,000 acres per year. Much of the enrolled acreage for the WRP (over 45 percent) has previously come from the LMRV.

All of the various conservation programs under the Farm Bill have specific eligibility and other important project selection criteria. This information is readily available through the Internet or from USDA, and Service biologists assigned to work with private landowners are very knowledgeable about these programs.

LOWER MISSISSIPPI RIVER VALLEY ECOSYSTEM

OVERVIEW

The North Mississippi National Wildlife Refuges Complex lies within a physiographic region known as the Lower Mississippi River Alluvial Valley (LMRV; Figure 1). The LMRV was once a 25-million-acre complex of forested wetlands that extended along both sides of the Mississippi River from Illinois to Louisiana. Historically, the extent and duration of seasonal flooding from the Mississippi River fluctuated annually, recharging the LMRV's aquatic systems and creating a rich diversity of dynamic habitats that supported a vast array of fish and wildlife resources.

ECOLOGICAL THREATS AND PROBLEMS

Forest Loss and Fragmentation

The LMRV has changed markedly over the last 100 years as civilization spread throughout the region. Since European settlement, it has been estimated that 20 million acres of bottomland hardwood forested wetlands have been lost (Figure 2). The greatest changes to the landscape have been in the form of land clearing for agriculture and flood control projects.

Although these changes have allowed people to settle and earn a living in the area, they have had a tremendous effect on biological diversity, biological integrity, and environmental health of the Lower Mississippi River Alluvial Valley. Immense areas of bottomland hardwood forests have been reduced to forest fragments ranging from very small tracts just a few acres in size, with limited functional value, to a few large areas of more than 10,000 acres that have maintained many of the original functions and values of bottomland hardwood forests. Species endemic to the LMRV that have become extinct, endangered, or threatened include the red wolf, Florida panther, ivory-billed woodpecker, and Louisiana black bear.

Breeding bird surveys show continuing declines in species and species populations. The avian species most adversely affected by fragmentation include those that are area-sensitive (dependent on large continuous blocks of hardwood forest); those that depend on forest interiors; those that depend on special habitat requirements, such as mature forests or a particular food source, and/or those that depend on good water quality.

More than 70 species of breeding migratory songbirds are found in the region. Some of these species, including Swainson's warbler, prothonotary warbler, wood thrush, and cerulean warbler, have declined significantly and need large forested blocks to recover, survive, and thrive.

Fragmentation of bottomland hardwood forests has left many of the remaining forested tracts as biological oases surrounded by inhospitable agricultural lands. Intensive agriculture has removed most of the forested corridors along sloughs that formerly connected forest patches. The loss of connectivity between the remaining forested tracts hinders the movement of wildlife between tracts and reduces the functional values of many remaining smaller forest tracts. The lost connections also result in a loss of gene flow needed to maintain genetic viability and diversity within wildlife populations. Restoring the connections to allow gene flow and reestablish travel corridors is particularly important for some wide-ranging species.

Alterations to Hydrology

In addition to the loss of vast acreage of bottomland forested wetlands, there have been significant alterations in the region's hydrology due to urban development, river channel modification, flood control levees, reservoirs and deforestation, as well as degradation to aquatic systems from excessive sedimentation and contaminants.

The natural hydrology of a region is directly responsible for the connectedness of forested wetlands and indirectly responsible for the complexity and diversity of habitats through its effects on topography and soils. Natural resource managers recognize the importance of dynamic hydrology to forested wetlands and waterfowl-habitat relationships (Fredrickson and Heitmeyer 1988).

Instead of natural hydrology, large-scale, man-made hydrological alterations have changed the spatial and temporal patterns of flooding throughout the entire LMRV. In addition, these alterations have reduced both the extent and duration of annual seasonal flooding (with some conspicuous exceptions, like most of the Coldwater River Refuge). The loss of this annual flooding regime has had an enormous impact on the forested wetlands and their associated wetland-dependent species.

In view of the hydrologic changes, it is very difficult – if not impossible – to fully emulate and reconstruct the structure and functions of a natural wetland. Because wetlands depend on a dynamic interface of hydrologic regimes to maintain water, vegetation, and animal complexes and processes, restoration is especially difficult (Mitsch and Gosselink 1993).

Figure 1. Lower Mississippi Alluvial Valley

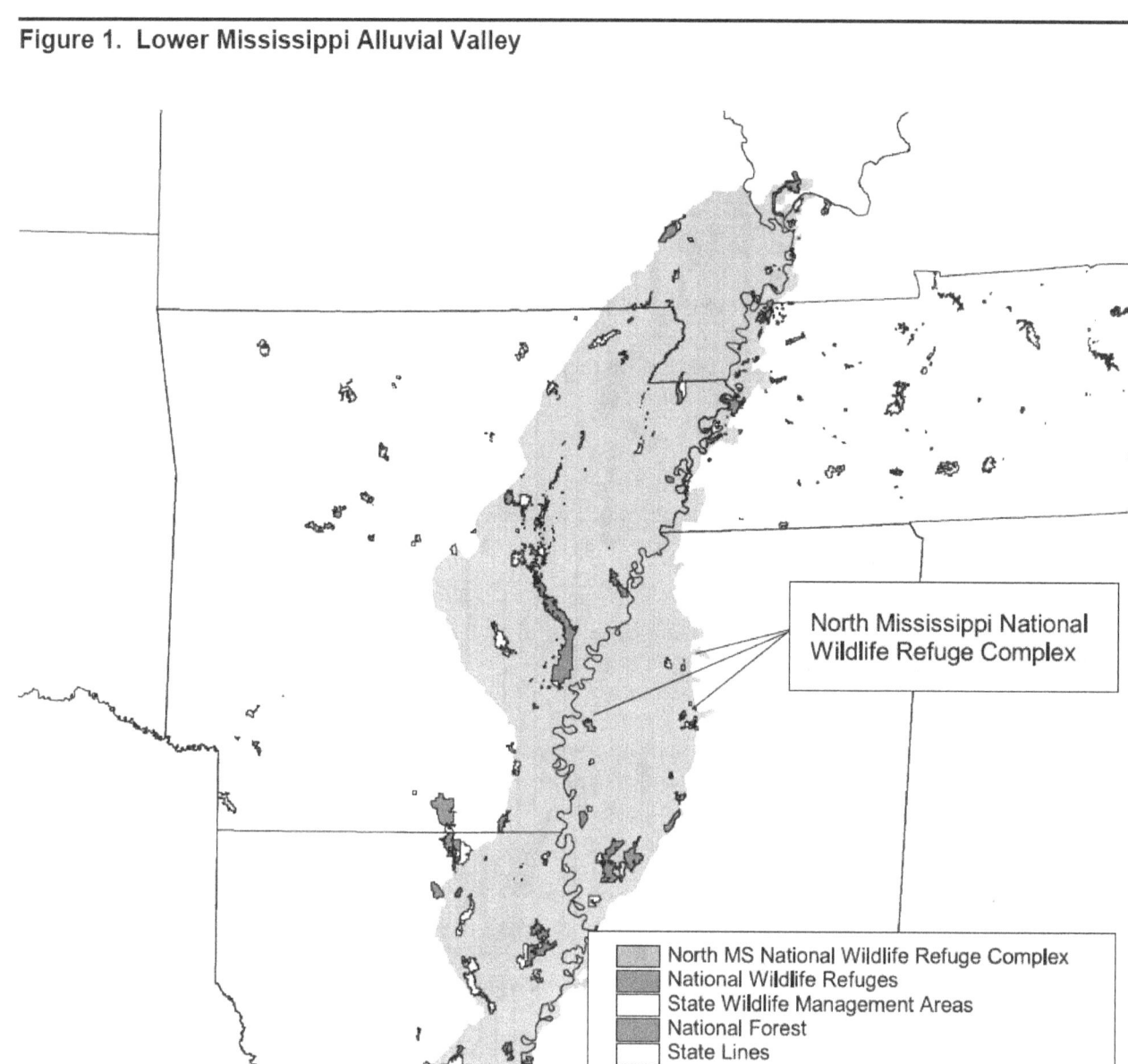

North Mississippi National Wildlife Refuge Complex

North MS National Wildlife Refuge Complex
National Wildlife Refuges
State Wildlife Management Areas
National Forest
State Lines
MS Alluvial Valley Physiographic Boundary

N

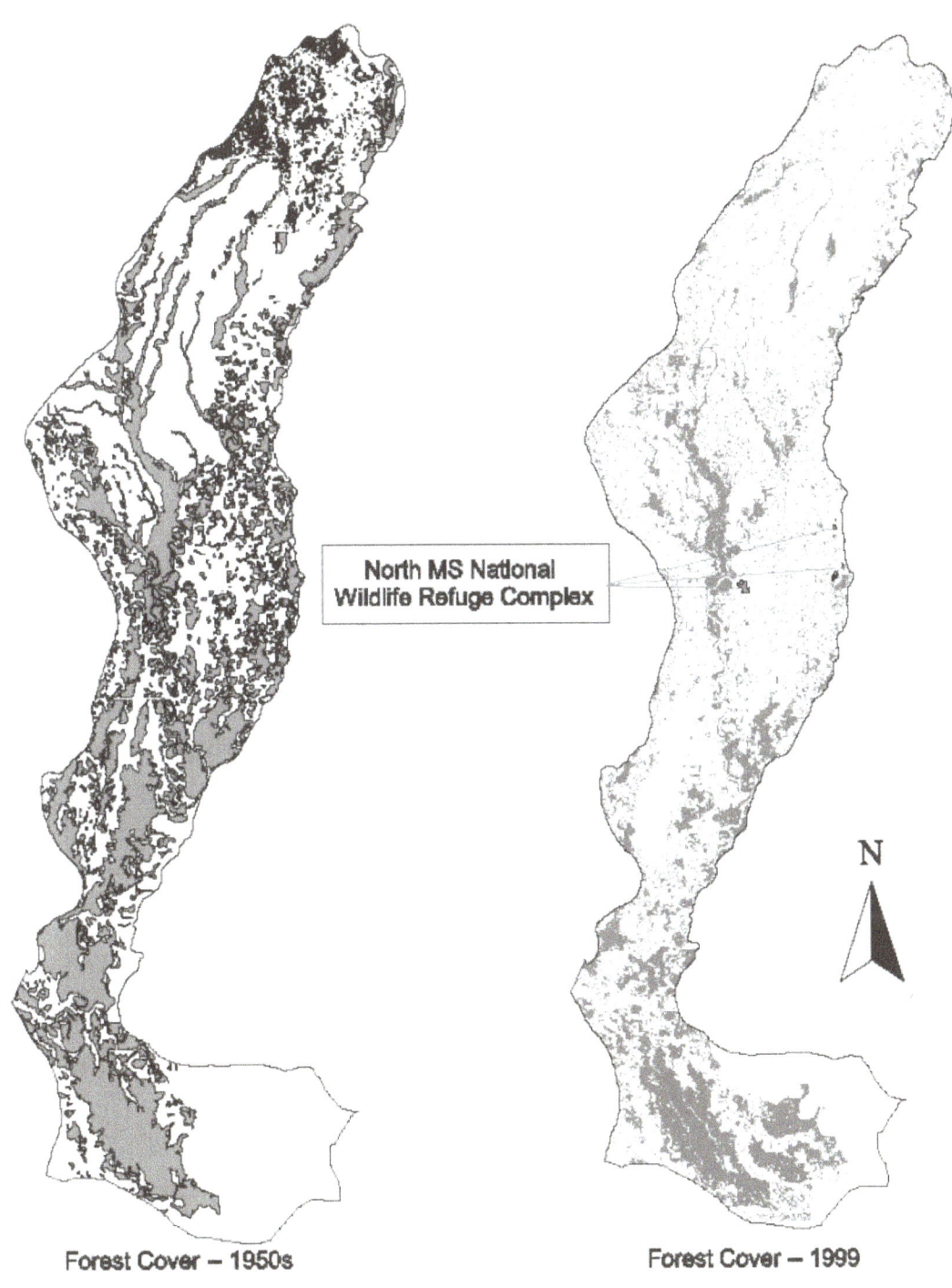

North MS National
Wildlife Refuge Complex

N

Forest Cover – 1950s

Forest Cover – 1999

Siltation of Aquatic Ecosystems

Aquatic systems, including lakes, rivers, sloughs, and bayous, have been degraded as a result of deforestation and hydrologic alteration. Clearing of bottomland hardwood forests has led to an accelerated accumulation of sediments and contaminants in all aquatic systems. Many water bodies are now filled with sediments, greatly reducing their surface area and depth. Concurrently, the non-point source runoff of excess nutrients and contaminants is threatening the area's remaining aquatic resources.

Hydrologic alterations have basically eliminated the geomorphological processes that created oxbow lakes, sloughs, and river meander scars. Consequently, the protection, conservation, and restoration of these aquatic resources take on an added importance in light of the alterations associated with flood control and navigation.

Proliferation of Invasive Aquatic Plants and Animals

Compounding the problems faced by aquatic systems is the growing threat from invasive aquatic vegetation like coffeeweed and willows. Static water levels caused by the lack of annual flooding and reduced water depths resulting from excessive sedimentation have created conditions favorable for the establishment and proliferation of several species of invasive aquatic plants. Additionally, the introduction of exotic (non-native) vegetation capable of aggressive growth is further threatening viability of aquatic systems. These invasive aquatic species threaten the natural aquatic vegetation important to aquatic systems, and choke waterways to a degree that often prevents recreational use.

Furthermore, non-native wildlife and fish have been successfully introduced or released in this temperate climate. Animals like the nutria compete with native wildlife for limited resources and many, like feral hogs, have caused extensive habitat damage and alterations.

CONSERVATION PRIORITIES AND INITIATIVES

Declines in the LMRV's bottomland hardwood forests and their associated fish and wildlife resources have prompted the Service to designate this forest system as an area of special concern. A collaborative effort involving private, state, and federal conservation partners is now underway to implement a variety of tools to restore the functions and values of wetlands in the LMRV. The goal is to prioritize and manage wetlands to most effectively maintain and possibly restore the biological diversity in the LMRV. Some areas are prioritized as focus areas for reforestation.

It is widely recognized, however, that most of the 20+ million acres of forested wetlands that have been cleared and converted to other uses in the LMRV will not be reforested. Some areas would have lower value for reforestation and are targeted for intensive management for non-forest-dependent species, such as waterfowl and shorebirds. Through cooperative efforts, apportioning resources, and the focusing of available programs, the LMRV's biological diversity can be improved.

North American Waterfowl Management Plan
Lower Mississippi Valley Joint Venture

Several coordinated efforts have been initiated to set priorities and establish focus areas to overcome the impacts of hydrologic changes and forest fragmentation. A cooperative private-state-federal partnership known as the North American Waterfowl Management Plan, Lower Mississippi Valley Joint Venture (LMRVJV), was established in 1986 to help provide sufficient wintering waterfowl habitat throughout the LMRV. LMRVJV partners have helped to establish step-down management objectives (expressed in duck-use-days and number of acres of flooded habitat) for public and private lands throughout the LMRV.

The initial LMRVJV effort has expanded to also establish population objectives for shorebirds and neotropical migratory forest-nesting birds. The LMRVJV is working with the U.S. Shorebird Conservation Working Group to establish step-down objectives for shorebird foraging habitat for the fall migration period throughout the LMRV.

Partners in Flight

Growing concern about declines in many land bird species not covered by existing conservation initiatives led to the launching of Partners-in-Flight (PIF) in 1990. PIF is an international, cooperative effort of government agencies, philanthropies, professional organizations, conservation groups, industry, academia, and private individuals. Its initial focus was on neotropical migratory birds – species that breed in North America and winter in Central and South America – but its emphasis has now expanded to encompass most land birds and other species requiring terrestrial habitats. PIF has a number of initiatives underway, including a North American Landbird Conservation Plan.

Migratory Bird Conservation Zones

Another cooperative private-state-federal partnership involving the North American Waterfowl Management Plan, PIF, and the LMRVJV has identified a number of Migratory Bird Conservation Zones. LMRV Forest Bird Conservation Areas are shown in Fig. 3. The three refuges in the Complex are identified in these zones and are core areas. The purpose of identifying these zones is to focus a number of private, state, and federal restoration programs into specific areas in an effort to provide maximum benefits for neotropical migratory forest interior-nesting birds.

The goal of this collaborative restoration effort is to provide islands or blocks of forested habitat in an otherwise highly fragmented landscape. The targeted block sizes range from 10,000 to 100,000 acres. Such areas are large enough to support viable populations of various suites of neotropical migratory songbirds. These areas will also support other species, like the Louisiana black bear, that prefer and thrive in large forested blocks.

Most MBCZs encompass an existing or proposed wildlife management area or national wildlife refuge. These public lands serve as anchors of biodiversity that are enhanced and supported by the expansion of forested blocks, either through public or private management.

One of the biggest challenges to the restoration efforts underway in the LMRV, and one that affects refuges in particular, is the need to meet long-term management objectives that address comprehensive ecosystem needs, including those of wintering migratory waterfowl, neotropical migratory birds, shorebirds, wading birds, bears, and other wide-ranging species. Oftentimes, management for one species or species group conflicts with the management objectives for another species or species group. The tendency is to pursue short-term priorities that frequently change as scientific knowledge expands and interests in special resources shift. Caution must be exercised to prevent the start-up of restoration actions that are difficult to reverse and fail to meet the long-term, comprehensive management needs of the ecosystem or a specific area within the ecosystem. An example might be a tendency to totally reforest Dahomey National Wildlife Refuge in an effort to reduce fragmentation and create acreage to meet an objective for forest interior-nesting birds. Such an approach would overlook the critical habitat needs of waterfowl and shorebirds that require a complex of seasonally flooded croplands, moist-soil areas, and forested wetlands.

The habitat goals of the Lower Mississippi Valley Joint Venture can only be met through active management of croplands, moist-soil areas, and forested wetlands on both public and private land (Reinecke and Baxter 1996). Active management (i.e., vegetation manipulation and hydrology restoration) is required to compensate for the spatial and temporal habitat changes that have been caused by deforestation and hydrologic alterations throughout the LMRV. The North Mississippi National Wildlife Refuges Complex uses a system of levees, water control structures, pumps, and wells to provide dependable seasonally flooded croplands and moist-soil areas as part of its waterfowl and shorebird habitat step-down objectives. If totally reforested, the Complex would not be able to meet its waterfowl/shorebird habitat step-down objectives. Setting habitat and species objectives from the perspective of the LMRV is advantageous because it looks at the regional context (i.e., the "big picture") and enables managers to plan and provide habitat for a diversity of species throughout their range.

Although reforestation is probably the best solution for restoring the vast forests that have been converted to row-crop agriculture, it must be remembered that the flooding and drying regime drives the ecosystem in the LMRV. The plant and animal communities throughout the LMRV are dependent upon the hydrologic cycle. It is incumbent upon land managers to manage hydrology in an effort to restore the ecological diversity that once characterized the LMRV. Ditches can be plugged and structures installed to control and manage water in an effort to mimic historic flood cycles and to meet waterfowl/shorebird habitat objectives.

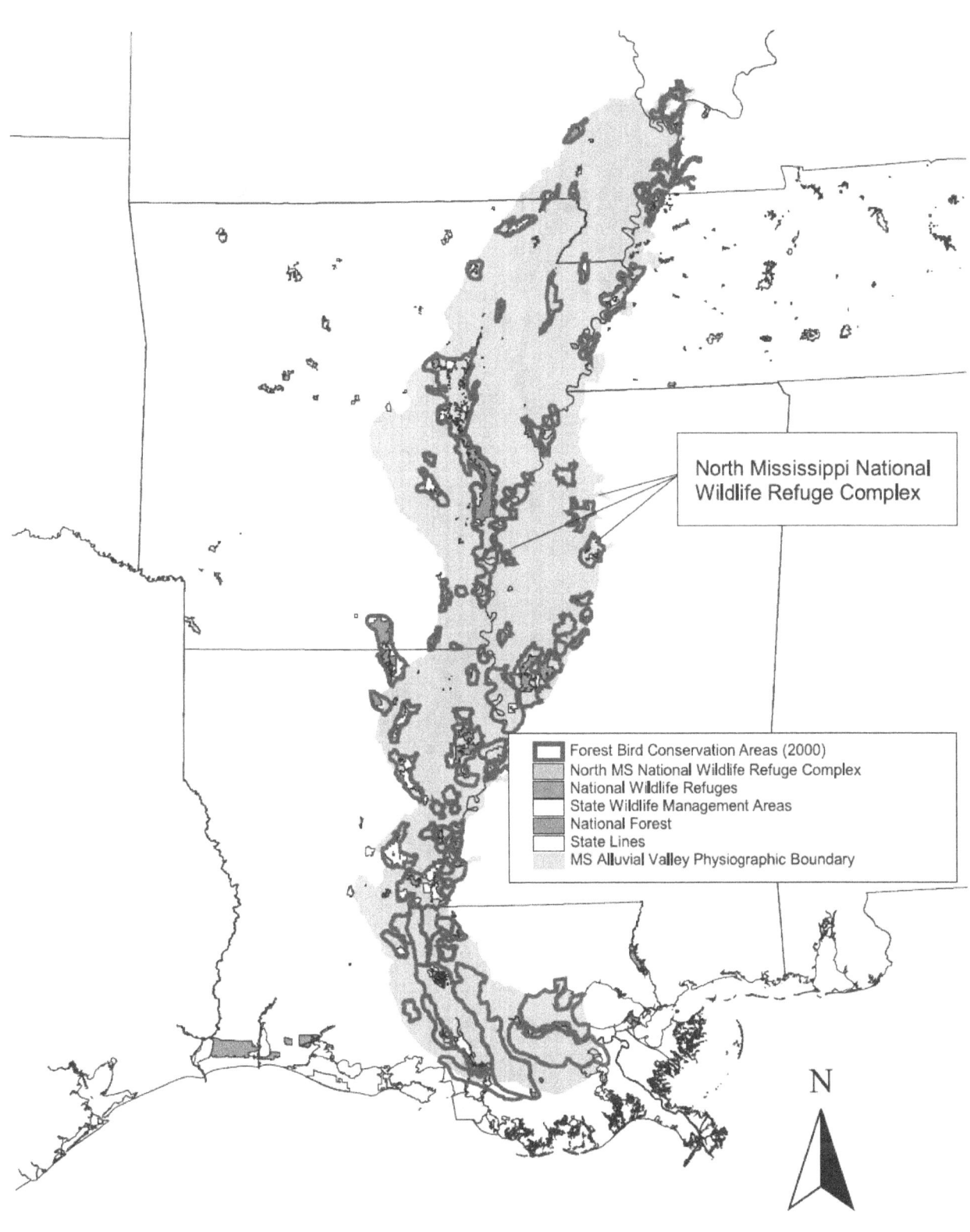

II. The Complex

INTRODUCTION AND HISTORY

The North Mississippi National Wildlife Refuges Complex, formerly the Mississippi Wetland Management District, is comprised of three distinct work areas. Each contains a national wildlife refuge and all Farm Service Agency tracts within that area. The three refuges plus 128 Farm Service Agency properties total 33,746 acres, with the Complex headquartered in Grenada (Figure 4). Since the Complex was established in 1989 and assigned administrative responsibility for Coldwater River, Dahomey, and Tallahatchie National Wildlife Refuges, the overriding collective thrust has been the creation, restoration, and enhancement of wetlands on public and private lands. The Complex provides habitat for large concentrations of wintering waterfowl and numerous species of neotropical migratory birds (Public Use Review, 1, 3).

The Complex has a staff of ten full-time permanent employees (Table 1). In 2004, 42 volunteers contributed approximately 1,000 hours towards wildlife and maintenance projects for Dahomey refuge and Tallahatchie refuge. There are also active Youth Conservation Corps (YCC) and internship programs.

PURPOSE AND ECOSYSTEM CONTEXT

Although the Complex has an overriding purpose of providing for the habitat needs of migratory birds, with an emphasis on waterfowl, each refuge within the Complex has a unique purpose and establishing legislation. For this plan, we are combining the refuges due to their proximity to each other, the similarity of issues and habitats, shared management and personnel, and in order to address the value of managing these refuges as a true complex of lands within the LMRV. The collective goals, objectives, and strategies of the complex will not detract from, but rather support the individual purposes guiding each refuge in the Complex.

WINTERING HABITAT FOR WATERFOWL

The LMRV is a critical ecoregion for wintering North American migratory waterfowl (Reinecke et al., 1989). The Complex provides important foraging and resting (refuge) habitats within the LMRV for migratory ducks and geese and thus fits into the large-scale, collaborative planning and habitat management initiative called the North American Waterfowl Management Plan (NAWMP), described in Chapter I of this CCP. NAWMP selected the LMRVJV as one of the wintering habitat focus areas. One of the LMRVJV's first tasks was to find a model or decision tool for determining how much habitat was needed and a way to relate this objective to the population goals of NAWMP. The solution was to view wintering areas as responsible for contributing to the spring breeding population goals of NAWMP proportional to the percentage of ducks historically counted in wintering areas (Loesch et al., 1994, Reinecke and Loesch 1996).

Figure 4. Regional vicinity map of North Mississippi National Wildlife Refuges Complex

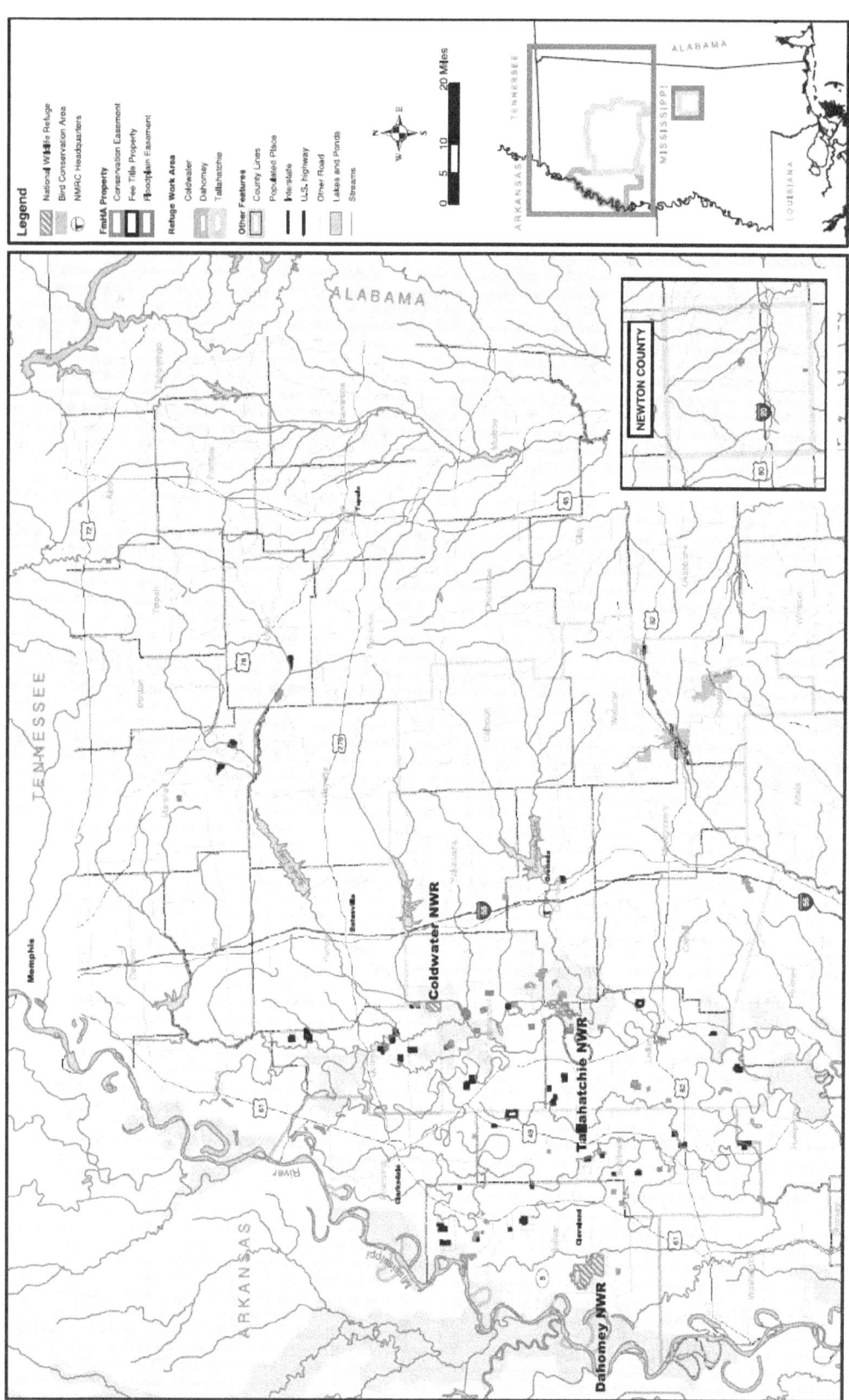

Table 1. Acres managed by current staffing, North Mississippi National Wildlife Refuges Complex

Refuge Headquarters	Refuges Managed	Acres Managed	Complex/Refuge Staff
Complex Headquarters (located in Grenada, MS)	Coldwater River NWR (2,374 acres) Dahomey NWR (9,431 acres) Tallahatchie NWR (4,199 acres)	16,004 acres in refuges (fee title) + 260 acres (school board lease) + 17,212 acres in 128 Farm Service Agency tracts = 33,476 total acres managed by complex	Project Leader (GS-13) Refuge Manager (GS-12) Dahomey: Refuge Manager (GS-12) Private Lands Biologist (GS-12) Wildlife Biologist (GS-12) Refuge Operations Specialist (GS-9) Park Ranger (GS-9)-vacant Office Automation Assistant (GS-7) Equipment Operator x2 (WG-10)
Complex Staff TOTAL			10

Sources: Biological Review (2003), Public Use Report (2002) and 2002 Annual Narrative

There is currently no staff based at Coldwater River or Tallahatchie National Wildlife Refuges. Development/management there is handled by the North Mississippi National Wildlife Refuges Complex.

Table 2. Land acquisition history, North Mississippi National Wildlife Refuges Complex

YEAR	Coldwater River NWR (acres)	Dahomey NWR (acres)	Tallahatchie NWR (acres)
2003			116
2001	306		
1997			1,656
1996	298	260	
1995	40		
1993		9,269	
1992			1,870
1991	1,730	162	557
TOTAL	**2,374**	**9,691**	**4,199**

Source: USFWS – Realty

Table 3. Location of each refuge, North Mississippi National Wildlife Refuges Complex

Refuge	County	Location
Coldwater River	Quitman/Tallahatchie	5 miles south of Crowder, MS, on Dummy Line Road
Dahomey	Bolivar	10 miles southwest of Cleveland, MS, and 22 miles northeast of Greenville
Tallahatchie	Grenada/Tallahatchie	9 miles west of Holcomb, MS, on U.S. Highway 8

Table 4. Establishment date, legislation, and purpose of each refuge within the North Mississippi National Wildlife Refuges Complex

Refuge	Year Established	Establishment Legislation	Refuge Purpose
Coldwater River	1991 as Black Bayou unit of Tallahatchie NWR 2000 as "stand alone" refuge	Migratory Bird Conservation Act; Consolidated Farm and Rural Development Act	"...for use as inviolate sanctuary, or for any other management purpose, for migratory birds," and for conservation purposes, under the Consolidated Farm and Rural Development Act
Dahomey	1992	Migratory Bird Conservation Act; Fish and Wildlife Act of 1956; Emergency Wetlands Resource Act of 1986	"...for use as inviolate sanctuary, or for any other management purpose, for migratory birds," "...for the development, advancement, management, conservation, and protection of fish and wildlife resources..." and "for the conservation of the Wetlands of the Nation in order to maintain the public benefits they provide and to help fulfill international obligations contained in various migratory bird treaties and conventions."
Tallahatchie	1991	Migratory Bird Conservation Act, Consolidated Farm and Rural Development Act	"...for use as inviolate sanctuary, or for any other management purpose, for migratory birds," and for conservation purposes, under the Consolidated Farm and Rural Development Act

To contribute ducks to spring populations, wintering areas have to provide sufficient habitat to ensure adequate winter survival. To quantify winter habitat requirements, the LMRVJV had to identify limiting factors and the LMRVJV assumed foraging habitat was most likely to limit waterfowl populations in the LMRV (Reinecke et al., 1989). The methodology for doing so is discussed more thoroughly in the 2002 Biological Review for the Complex.

The LMRVJV has established habitat objectives for the LMRV. These objectives were based on food production and acres by habitat type for the complex of habitats, including harvested and unharvested cropland, moist-soil areas, and flooded forest land. Each of these habitats is required to provide an important part of the food resources (e.g., native weed seeds, small grains, and invertebrates) required by waterfowl wintering in the LMRV. Agricultural grains are high in carbohydrates (i.e., "hot foods") needed by waterfowl to maintain body temperature during cold periods in winter. Acorns and other native weed seeds (moist-soil seeds) and invertebrates provide higher levels of protein and other nutrients used by waterfowl to complete other important functions during the winter period, such as molting and improving body condition for return migration to the breeding grounds, as well as egg-laying. These objectives have been stepped down for private and public lands throughout the LMRV, including the North Mississippi National Wildlife Refuges Complex. They are shown in Table 5.

Table 5. Migrating and wintering waterfowl foraging habitat objectives established by the LMRVJV for the Complex (acres)

Habitat	Objective (Acres)	Current Capability (Acres)	(+/-Acres)
Coldwater River NWR			
Forested wetland	700	0[1]	-700
Scrub/shrub	0	31	+ 31
Moist-soil	190	190[2]	0
Unharvested cropland	0	0	0
Dahomey NWR			
Forested wetland	750	440	-310[3]
Moist-soil	318	200[4]	-118
Unharvested cropland	218	84[5]	-134
Harvested cropland	0	253[5]	+253
Tallahatchie NWR			
Forested wetland	80	0	-80[6]
Moist-soil	852	690	-162
Unharvested cropland	212	50	-162
Farm Service Agency			
Forested wetlands	0	0	0
Moist-soil	3,000	0[7]	-3,000
Unharvested crop	0	0	0

[1] 700-acre reforested area with water management capability (currently not functional) could serve as a greentree reservoir in the future.

[2] Current capability is actually 415 acres of which 225 acres are devoted to fall migrating shorebird habitat.

[3] Ducks Unlimited MARSH Agreement assumes 800 acres flooded, refuge estimates 750 acres are flooded, actual acres flooded is estimated to be 440 acres.

[4] Assumes one of two 100-acre impoundments on the south end of the refuge is in moist-soil every year.

[5] Assumes that agricultural grain crops are cooperatively farmed at a 75:25 exchange rate, with the refuge receiving 25 percent unharvested crop that is left in the field and 75 percent of the crop harvested; all is flooded in winter.

[6] 100-acre reforested area with water management capabilities could possibly serve as a greentree reservoir in the future.

[7] Foraging habitat capabilities on these properties are unknown due to the lack of accurate information.

Despite being highly fragmented, the productive hardwood forests of the Mississippi Delta play an important role in providing migration and breeding habitat for forest-breeding birds, as well as those dependent on forests for other activities, such as foraging or wintering. By increasing block size and improving timber stand structure, this habitat has the potential to provide much greater benefit for this wide variety of non-game birds, many of which are listed in Table 6.

Table 6. Forest-dependent birds in the Complex work area

Species	Priority	Use	Preferred habitat
Swainson's warbler	Extremely high	Nesting Foraging	Dense understory Open moist ground
Cerulean warbler	Extremely high	Breeding, nesting and foraging	Canopy of sawtimber trees (mature timber)
Swallow-tailed kite	Extremely high	Breeding and nesting	Superemergent trees, possibly cypress
Prothonotary warbler	High	Breeding	Cavity nester – usually in trees above open water
Red-headed woodpecker	High	Breeding	Cavity nester
Northern parula	High	Breeding	Canopy, usually with Spanish moss
Kentucky warbler	High	Breeding	Nests in patches of dense ground cover
Yellow-billed cuckoo	High	Breeding	Midstory and canopy
Wood thrush	High	Breeding Foraging	Midstory Moist ground
American woodcock	High	Foraging	Open moist ground but under very dense understory cover
Black duck	High	Wintering	Open water
Wood duck	Moderate	Breeding	Cavity nesting over or near open water
Acadian flycatcher	Moderate	Breeding	Open midstory
Eastern wood-pewee	Moderate	Breeding	Open canopy
Carolina chickadee	Moderate	Breeding	Cavity nester
Mississippi kite	Moderate	Breeding	nests in trees along edges in open country
Baltimore oriole	Moderate	Breeding	Scattered hardwoods in open country
Ruby-throated hummingbird	Moderate	Breeding	Woody vegetation in moist habitats, usually near tubular flowers
Blue-gray gnatcatcher	Moderate	Breeding	Mature and moist hardwood forests

Species	Priority	Use	Preferred habitat
Hooded warbler	Moderate	Breeding	Dense understory
Bald eagle	Moderate	Breeding	Nests in superemergent trees large enough to support massive nests
Rusty blackbird	Moderate	Wintering	Winter roost in canopy; forages on the ground
Yellow-throated warbler	Local/regional interest	Breeding	Canopy, usually with Spanish moss
American redstart	Local/regional interest	Breeding	Hardwood forests, usually near water
Yellow-throated vireo	Local/regional interest	Breeding	Open canopy
Summer tanager	Local/regional interest	Breeding	Open canopy
Pileated woodpecker	Local/regional interest	Breeding	Mature and extensive forest, with dead trees for nesting

As it has with setting waterfowl habitat objectives, the LMRVJV has undertaken a coordinated effort to identify Bird Conservation Areas (BCA's) throughout the LMRV for restoration of forest blocks that support sustainable breeding populations of area-sensitive, high priority forest-breeding bird species. There are seven BCA's in the Complex work area with established forest block size objectives (Table 7). Selective reforestation through private land programs or expansion of existing refuges would contribute toward forest block objectives.

Overall future desired condition of mature wetland forests would be to emphasize (1) increasing stand structural diversity by favoring retention of largest trees (removing surrounding potentially competing trees), (2) opening up stands to allow light to reach the ground in support of better understory structure, and (3) group selection-sized openings to further structural complexity and support regeneration of shade-intolerant tree species (oaks) where needed.

Table 7. Bird Conservation Area (BCA) forest core acreages and deficit in the Complex work area

BCA Name	Core goal	Core acreage	Deficit
Coldwater Creek (Coldwater River NWR)	2,100	0	-2,100
Coahoma	8,106	14,216	Achieved
O'Keefe	2,100	472	-1,628
Tunica	5,200	15,383	Achieved
Malmaison (Tallahatchie NWR)	5,200	6,654	Achieved
Dahomey (Dahomey NWR)	2,100	521	-1,579
Whittington	7,300	37,215	Achieved

A core forest area is that contiguous block of interior forest that is 1.6 miles from all forest edges. This protective core forest habitat is essential to many of the highest priority bird species, such as the cerulean warbler and swallow-tailed kite. Based on this definition, Dahomey is the only refuge of the three in the Complex to have sufficient acreage to refer to its core forest habitat. Research has shown that up to 20-30 percent of a study tract can be degraded by fragmentation before neotropical migratory songbirds begin treating a contiguous tract as separate patches. If a mile buffer (in which there have been substantial encroachments) within the BCA surrounding Dahomey refuge is included in this calculation, the 20-30 percent figure has already been surpassed. Managed early successional openings of between 1 and 5 acres that serve as habitat for resident and migratory wildlife game species are not considered to impact the block nature of the forest tract [BioReview, 37-38].

One species of interest, the American woodcock, is showing significant long-term declines in the eastern United States. Habitat loss, including the loss of preferred, safe, nocturnal wintering habitats, is likely a key factor. The Complex may be important in helping the Service to meet its objectives in the North American and Regional Woodcock Management Plans. Woodcock/quail management is an explicit goal of Coldwater River refuge [BioReview, 43].

SCRUB/SHRUB HABITAT

Scrub/shrub (or early successional) associated birds are another group of vulnerable avian species within the southeast (see Table 8). These species are generally considered a lower priority than mature forest species within the LMRV, but some species may benefit temporarily during the early years of reforestation, especially the white-eyed vireo, painted bunting, orchard oriole, and Bell's vireo. However, good opportunities exist for overall effective bird conservation through the establishment and maintenance of scrub/shrub sites throughout the Complex, including edges and small blocks within existing refuges and Farm Service Agency tracts. Many of these tracts are generally isolated from larger forest blocks.

Table 8. Scrub/shrub associated birds in the Complex work area

Species	Priority	Use	Preferred habitat
Breeding			
Painted bunting	High	Breeding	Dense thickets of shrubs, saplings, or second-growth trees
White-eyed vireo	High	Breeding	Dense and usually moist thickets
Bell's vireo	High	Breeding	Streamside thickets or upland scrub oaks
Orchard oriole	High	Breeding	Scattered hardwood trees in open country
Yellow-breasted chat	Moderate	Breeding	Dense cover of shrubs or saplings
Northern bobwhite	Moderate	Breeding	Ground-nester
Field sparrow	Moderate	Breeding? Wintering	
Transients			
Golden-winged warbler	Extremely high		
Cerulean warbler	High		

Species	Priority	Use	Preferred habitat
Transients			
Blue-winged warbler	High		
Bay-breasted warbler	High		
Canada warbler	High		
Blackburnian warbler	High		
Palm warbler	High		
Bobolink	High		
Veery	High		
Philadelphia vireo	High		
Black-billed cuckoo	Moderate		
Olive-sided flycatcher	Moderate		
Willow flycatcher	Moderate		
Least flycatcher	Moderate		
Chestnut-sided warbler	Moderate		
Black-throated green warbler	Moderate		
Mourning warbler	Moderate		

Scrub/shrub species apparently are able to withstand cowbird and depredation problems better within smaller blocks of habitat (i.e., 50-100 acres, possibly as small as 25-acre patches) than mature forest priority species, many of which require thousands of contiguously forested acres. With better information, the project leader and his staff may want to consider targeting certain sites for this habitat phase. Sites selected for long-term maintenance of scrub/shrub will require periodic disturbances. One option for minimizing the frequency of disturbance (to set back succession) necessary to maintain scrub/shrub habitat would be to plant areas with native fruit-producing, shrub species such as plum, swamp dogwood, devil's-walking-stick, deciduous holly, and various species of hawthorn.

GRASSLAND HABITAT

The emphasis on "grassland" habitat conditions used by high priority species on the Complex is likely restricted to forest restoration sites actually more often dominated by "brushy" annuals. Priority grassland species are mostly found at the Complex during migration and winter, but a few species may breed in small numbers (Table 9). Recently planted reforestation sites constitute the primary habitats on the refuges. However, higher sites with sandy soils (i.e., poorer quality sites) dominated by broomsedge (*Andropogon* spp.) should be maintained in particular for wintering LeConte's sparrows. Priority grassland species include sparrows (principally LeConte's, but also grasshopper and possibly lark), sedge wren, bobolink, and raptors (most notably bald eagle, northern harrier, short-eared owl, and loggerhead shrike).

Table 9. Grassland-dependent birds in the Complex work area

Species	Priority	Use	Preferred habitat
Henslow's sparrow	High	Wintering	
LeConte's sparrow	High	Wintering	
Sedge wren	High	Wintering	
Short-eared owl	High	Wintering	
Dickcissel	Moderate	Breeding	Herbaceous cover where vegetation is at least 2 feet high
Northern bobwhite	Moderate	Breeding	Ground-nester
Loggerhead shrike	Moderate	Breeding Foraging	Tree or shrub nesting Forages on ground
Field sparrow	Moderate	Breeding Wintering	scattered saplings, shrubs, and tall herbaceous cover; wintering - dense cover of herbs, particular tall composites
Northern harrier	Moderate	Wintering	
Grasshopper sparrow	Moderate	Wintering	
Field sparrow	Moderate	Breeding? Wintering	

HABITAT FOR MIGRATING SHOREBIRDS

Throughout the LMRV, habitat for spring (northward) shorebird migration is probably provided in most years with normal rainfall and evaporation rates. Peak migration is expected April to mid-May (but extends from mid-March to late May). Southbound migration starts in early July, peaks August through September, and ends by mid-October.

Disruption of normal evaporation patterns over the last 50 years in the LMRV and the lack of rainfall in this highly modified hydrological environment have led to a severe shortage of fall habitat for shorebirds. Opportunities do exist, however, to provide good quality habitat for southbound migrants in fall. A focus on providing shorebird habitat is considered the highest non-game bird priority for the Complex. The LMRVJV-coordinated shorebird (fall migration) habitat objective for Coldwater River refuge is 225 acres of mudflats and for former FmHA tracts is currently listed as an additional 100-200 acres.

Within the larger context, about 1,500 acres of habitat have been tentatively identified for Mississippi towards supporting a tentative LMRV population objective of 500,000 shorebirds during southbound migration.

High priority shorebird species include the stilt sandpiper, buff-breasted sandpiper, western sandpiper, short-billed dowitcher, and Wilson's phalarope. Those of moderate priority are the semipalmated sandpiper, sanderling, greater yellowlegs, dunlin, common snipe, least sandpiper, willet, American avocet, and killdeer.

HABITAT FOR MARSHBIRDS AND COLONIAL WATERBIRDS/WADING BIRDS

Secretive marshbirds, including rails and bitterns, are mostly found on the Complex during migration and winter, but may breed in small numbers. Ricefields, moist-soil units, and unmanaged herbaceous marsh dominated by cattail, rushes, and other perennials constitute the primary habitats on the Complex. Management for these species coincides well with ongoing wetland restoration practices on many of the former FmHA sites and, to a lesser degree, management practices targeting waterfowl. Included in this group are "secretive marshbirds" (e.g., rails, bitterns, grebes, moorhens, and coots) and raptors (most notably bald eagle and northern harrier).

Complex holdings support several colonial wading bird rookeries. Shallow water areas found on the refuge during late summer and fall provide critical foraging opportunities for long-legged wading birds such as wood storks, herons, egrets, and ibis. The primary management tools are to 1) protect rookeries from disturbance and, where possible, maintain standing water under nest trees throughout the nesting season to minimize nest predation by raccoons, and 2) incorporate water level management for wading birds into shallow water management for waterfowl and shorebirds. In the shallow water provided for wading birds, they will be searching for foraging habitat rich in small fish and crustaceans, a much different food source than is targeted in waterfowl and shorebird management.

High priority species are the least tern (interior population-foraging on open water), white ibis (breeding?, migrant), and the American white pelican (wintering). Species of local or regional interest include the wood stork (migrant), roseate spoonbill (migrant), glossy ibis (migrant), double-crested cormorant (breeding, wintering), anhinga (breeding), great blue heron (breeding), great egret (breeding), snowy egret (breeding), little blue heron (breeding), cattle egret (breeding), green heron (breeding), yellow-crowned night-heron (breeding).

MONITORING RAPTORS

The Complex has two records (from August 1999) of one extremely high priority raptor: the swallow-tailed kite (migration, breeding - nest in superemergent trees, possibly cypress). However, these individuals appear to have been dispersing juveniles rather than residents. The Complex also has several species of moderate priority, including the Mississippi kite (breeding - nest in trees along edges in open country), loggerhead shrike (breeding - nest in tree or shrub, forages on ground, wintering), northern harrier (wintering), and bald eagle (wintering, nesting possible - nests in superemergent trees large enough to support massive nests). The Complex will identify and monitor year-round occurrence and abundance of raptors.

REPLICATING HISTORIC FOREST CONDITIONS

About 80 percent of the forestlands in the LMRV has been cleared and converted to other land uses, leaving only remnant, fragmented forested tracts. Fish and wildlife resources have been similarly impacted, leaving remnant populations that must be managed to meet refuge purposes and to achieve their maximum potential. Some of the most unique forested habitats remaining in the delta are forested ridges. Because of the importance of the remaining delta forests to the wildlife resources on the Complex and conservation priorities set forth in various plans, forest resources should be managed to mimic old growth forests and increase vertical vegetative structure.

Several species of waterfowl heavily utilize flooded forested habitat in winter for resting and foraging for acorns, other fruits, various seeds, and invertebrates. Wood ducks seek these areas almost exclusive of other habitats. Mallards, gadwall, and wigeon all utilize flooded forested habitat as one of the complex of preferred habitats.

Flooding of forest habitat in winter should mimic or enhance natural flood conditions. Typically, flooding should occur only during the dormant period for deciduous hardwoods common in each impoundment. Flooding should never occur before the dormant period starts in late fall (mid-November to late-December) and only rarely after green-up in the spring. Flooding dates and duration should be varied annually and in some years given stands should not be flooded.

LEGAL POLICY

The administration of the Complex is guided by a variety of international treaties, federal laws, and Presidential executive orders. Management options under each refuge's establishing authority and the National Wildlife Refuge System Improvement Act of 1997 (the legal and policy guidance for the operation of national wildlife refuges) are contained in the documents and acts listed in Appendix F.

RESOURCE AND MANAGEMENT DESCRIPTIONS

COLDWATER RIVER NATIONAL WILDLIFE REFUGE

Coldwater River National Wildlife Refuge, formerly the Black Bayou Unit of the Tallahatchie National Wildlife Refuge, consists of 2,469 acres of fee title lands (see Figure 5). Over half of this acreage is abandoned old fields of poorly drained soils that flood most winters.

A 495-acre portion of Coldwater River refuge contains 25 ponds that were previously managed as a commercial catfish operation. These ponds range in size from 9 to 21 acres, and are now managed for shorebirds, migratory waterfowl, and marsh birds. A Water Management Plan guides the active management on the 16 ponds with wells and water control structures. Coldwater River refuge's unique mix of habitats and proximity to the migration corridors of the Little Tallahatchie River and the Panola-Quitman Floodway attract a high diversity of migrant waterbirds all year round.

About 300 acres of old-field habitat on the west side of the refuge are managed for grassland birds. A natural sump of 250 to 300 acres along the east side and a similar area in the west central portion of the refuge have been reforested with hardwoods, but due to the wetness, *Baccharis*, willow, and button bush thickets now dominate many acres. This area holds thousands of mallards during annual winter flooding. Another approximately 750 acres have been reforested with native hardwoods with varying degrees of success. No cooperative farming is used on Coldwater River refuge.

Figure 5. Coldwater River National Wildlife Refuge land cover types

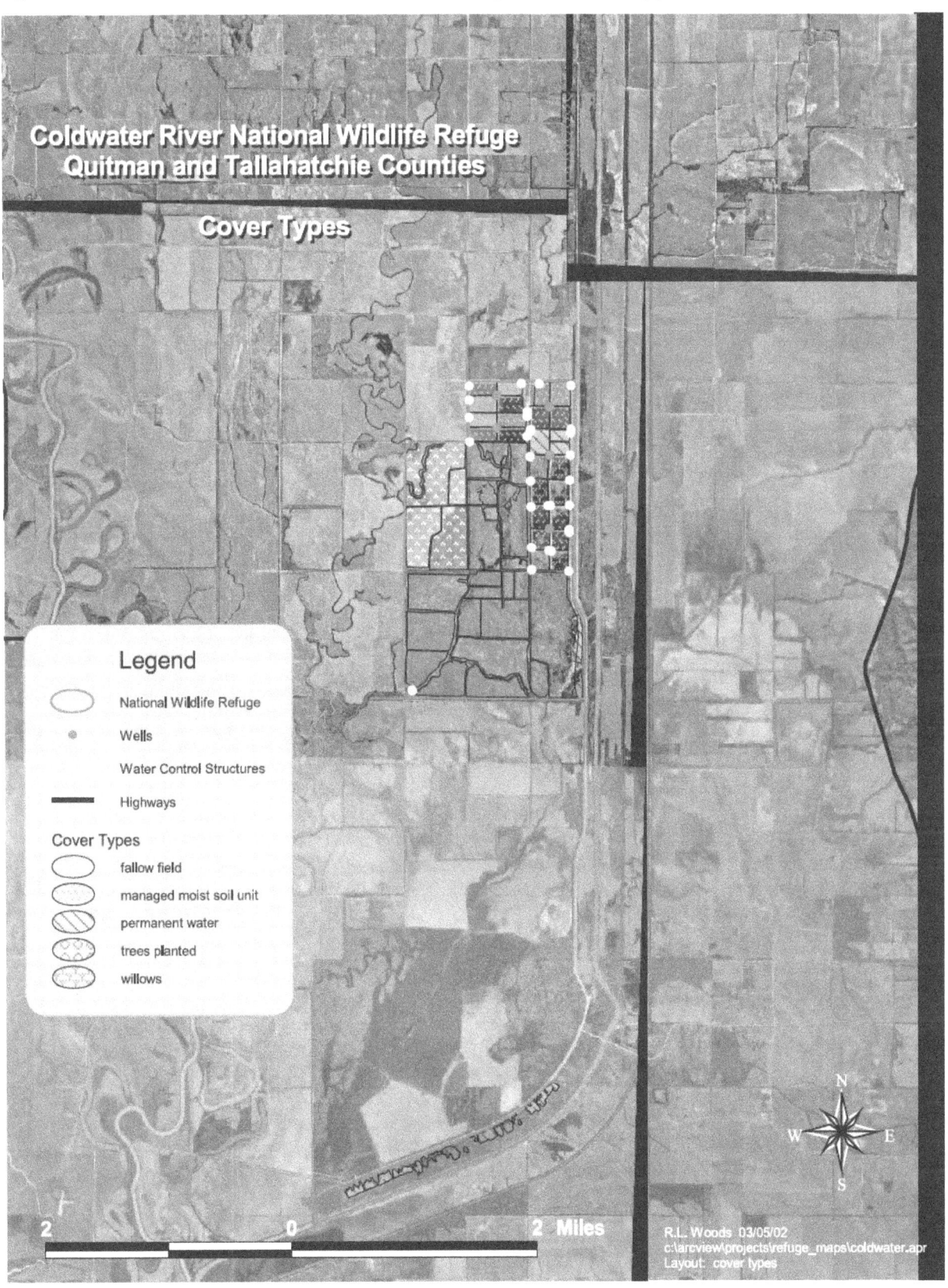

DAHOMEY NATIONAL WILDLIFE REFUGE

Dahomey National Wildlife Refuge is located in Bolivar County in the western part of the Complex near the Mississippi River (see Figure 6). Dahomey refuge's woodlands are the largest contiguous tract of bottomland hardwood habitat occurring outside the Mississippi River main line levee in northwest Mississippi. The refuge's forestland is a relic of a habitat type that once predominated throughout the Lower Mississippi Delta. Unfortunately, stream channelization and levee construction activities in the vicinity of the refuge have reduced historical flooding regimes to the point that a significant portion of the habitat within the refuge is no longer subject to periods of seasonal inundation.

In 1994, the Complex installed levees, pipes, and water control structures in two streams occurring within the refuge, creating an approximately 600-acre greentree reservoir. During 1999, the Complex converted an 85-acre agricultural field into four moist-soil impoundments. In 2001, Ducks Unlimited constructed two levees on the southern portion of the refuge to create two moist-soil units totaling 223 acres.

Dahomey refuge consists of 8,126 acres of mature bottomland hardwood forest (596 of which are occupied by the greentree reservoir), 104 acres of fallow fields, 308 acres of moist-soil units, 297 acres of agricultural fields, 849 acres of early successional reforestation areas, and 7 acres of permanent water (in a lake and numerous drainage ditches). The moist-soil units are managed primarily for wintering waterfowl.

TALLAHATCHIE NATIONAL WILDLIFE REFUGE

Until 2000, Tallahatchie National Wildlife Refuge consisted of the Bear Lake and Black Bayou Units. In 2000, Black Bayou Unit became a separate refuge – Coldwater River National Wildlife Refuge. The Bear Lake unit retained the name Tallahatchie. Today, the refuge is a 4,199-acre patchwork of cultivated farmlands, old fields, reforested lands, and small, scattered plots of bottomland hardwood forest bisected by the meandering Tippo Bayou, its centerpiece. The refuge is located in Grenada and Tallahatchie counties (see Figure 7). Its lands, like those of Coldwater River and Dahomey refuges, lie within the Mississippi River Alluvial Valley, referred to locally as the "Delta," where topography is flat and much of the soil is of the heavy clay, hydric variety that has been subject to extensive clearing and drainage efforts. The old oxbows and low-lying fields along Tippo Bayou are permitted to flood each winter and hold large concentrations of waterfowl. Most of the agricultural land (628 acres) on the refuge is devoted to corn, soybeans, and rice. This represents about 15 percent of the refuge land use. Twenty-five percent of the crops produced are left on the ground for wildlife through the Service's cooperative farming program. Most of the remainder of the refuge has been reforested through planting efforts by Complex staff.

CLIMATE

The area's climate is a humid, warm-temperate, continental type characteristic of the southern United States. The average yearly rainfall is 52 inches; March is the wettest month with an average of 5.6 inches and August the driest with 2.4 inches. Tropical storms or hurricanes coming from the Gulf of Mexico may occasionally bring several days of heavy rain. Thunderstorms, which usually bring the heaviest rains, are occasionally accompanied by hail and tornados. Drought conditions during the summer may increase the danger of fire. Average annual snowfall is less than an inch.

Figure 6. Dahomey National Wildlife Refuge land cover types

Figure 6. Dahomey National Wildlife Refuge land cover types

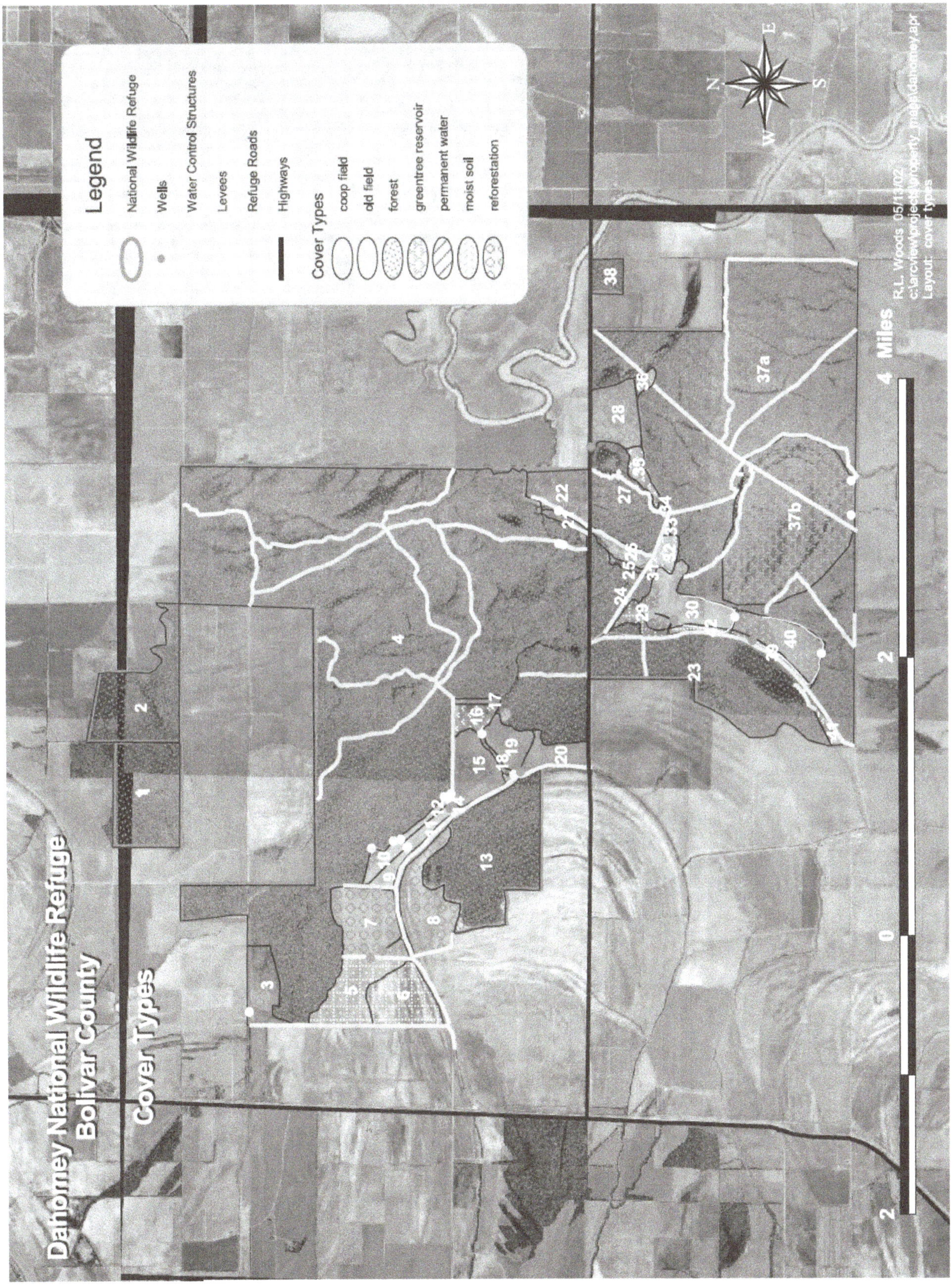

Figure 7. Tallahatchie National Wildlife Refuge land cover types

Figure 7. Tallahatchie National Wildlife Refuge land cover types

Tallahatchie National Wildlife Refuge
Grenada and Tallahatchie Counties

Cover Types

Legend

National Wildlife Refuge

Cover Types
coop fields
old field
moist soil
permanent water
reforestation

January is usually the coldest month, while July is normally the hottest. Winters are mild, with temperatures seldom remaining below freezing for long. Summers are hot and humid with heat indexes commonly reaching 110-115°F. The average growing season is 219 days, from March 25 to October 30.

PHYSIOGRAPHY, GEOGRAPHY, AND SOILS

Within the region, the Mississippi Delta is an alluvial plain of the Mississippi River reaching from Memphis, Tennessee, to Vicksburg, Mississippi. It is 75 miles wide at the widest point near the middle, tapering on each end. The river flows along the western edge, while the eastern edge is bordered by steep bluffs that rise 200 feet above the elevation of the Delta. The Delta is composed of alluvial soils deposited primarily by the Mississippi River with surface features resulting from the meandering of the Mississippi and lesser streams like the Tallahatchie River. Old channels, oxbow lakes, brakes, sloughs, and other features developed in areas that bordered the main river channels, while slackwater areas farther from the channel resulted in broad flats. These features intermixed as the Mississippi meandered across the Delta.

The alluvial soils in the lower Mississippi Delta range from silts and clays in the more poorly drained areas to sandier, coarser-grained soils on natural levees and ancient sandbars. Due to the location of waterfowl-oriented refuges in wetland areas, most of the soils within the Complex are silts and clays, which have fine texture, low permeability and high shrink-swell potential. The surface layer is often hard when dry, friable when moist, and plastic when wet, making moisture content an important consideration when working the soil. There are lighter soils in limited areas, but most of the broad natural levees adjacent to major streams are privately owned cotton production areas.

HYDROLOGY

The water table is very shallow in the Delta. Irrigation wells are drilled to a depth of 100-120 feet, reaching an aquifer connected to the Mississippi River.

Historically, the refuges were subject to winter/spring flooding by the Mississippi River. The Lower Delta was completely flooded five times between 1882 and 1927, despite the river levee. Since then, the mainline Mississippi River levee has been substantially upgraded, preventing widespread flooding from the river.

Within the vicinity of, and in Dahomey refuge, stream channelization and levee construction activities have reduced historical flooding regimes to the point that a significant portion of the habitat within the refuge is no longer subject to periods of seasonal inundation. This has had a striking impact on the refuge's vegetation community, a remnant of a habitat type that was once dominant throughout the Lower Mississippi Valley. Therefore, one of the Complex's objectives for Dahomey refuge is to restore and manage seasonal hydro-periods within its wetland habitat.

In 1994, the Complex installed levees, pipes, and water control structures in two streams occurring within Dahomey refuge, creating an approximately 600-acre greentree reservoir. During 1999, the Complex converted an 85-acre agricultural field into 4 moist-soil impoundments. In 2001, Ducks Unlimited constructed two levees on the southern portion of the refuge to create two moist-soil units totaling 223 acres.

Tippo Bayou bisects the portion of the Tallahatchie refuge north of State Highway 8 and generally forms the eastern boundary of the refuge south of State Highway 8. Normally highly turbid, Tippo Bayou depends primarily on rice field runoff for base flow. Except for high water periods, the bayou is shallow and has low dissolved oxygen levels. Out-of-bank flooding of Tippo Bayou occurs on an annual basis and may cause portions of the refuge to be inaccessible from December to April. Eight water control structures have been installed and one levee has been constructed.

Coldwater River refuge is located 4.5 miles north of the confluence of the Panola-Quitman Floodway and the Tallahatchie River. Bounded by those two water bodies, the refuge experiences heavy flooding. Typically beginning in November, water begins to accumulate north of the confluence and backs northward to the refuge. A large portion of Coldwater River refuge is under water from November to April.

WATER QUALITY

Agricultural runoff from any source in the Delta carries organochlorine pesticides, which are bound to soil particles. These pesticides, heavily used for years in the Delta, have persisted in the soil for over 15 years since their use was banned, and likely will exist for many more. Pesticide contamination is an issue to be confronted on all stations of the Complex. Fish and wildlife species are subject to contain OC compounds that may exceed predator protection levels or human consumption concern levels.

North Carolina State University completed the Lower Mississippi River Ecosystem Study, which determined chemical contamination at 26 national wildlife refuges in the LMRV. Field sampling for the study spanned a 6-year period from 1995 to 2000. Dahomey and Tallahatchie refuges were included in the study.

Results of the sample analyses indicate that contaminant/water quality problems occur on both Dahomey and Tallahatchie refuges. Concentrations of DDTM were above concern levels in sediment samples. DDTM, toxaphene, and current use pesticide concentrations in water samples exceeded the Environmental Protection Agency's chronic water quality criteria for those contaminants. It also appears that several of the waterbodies contain high levels of suspended solids, turbidity, and nutrients, and that dissolved oxygen levels are at or near zero for extended periods.

Contaminated runoff from agricultural land is likely causing the contaminant/water quality problems. To reduce contaminated runoff entering the refuge, best management practices (BMPs) such as drop inlet structures, minimum till practices, vegetative field borders, and grassed waterways should be installed on agricultural land in the watersheds, and some of the agricultural land with high erosion rates should be revegetated. In addition, concentrations of DDTM, toxaphene, and current use pesticides should be monitored in fish and wildlife, and investigations should be undertaken to determine organochlorine pesticides concentrations in fish, and aquatic oriented wildlife such as wood ducks, raccoons, and fish eating birds and mammals. Also, temperature and pH, along with concentrations of suspended solids, nutrients, and turbidity should be determined for the streams and lakes.

BMPs can also be implemented through the Service's Private Lands Program, the Natural Resources Conservation Service's Wetland Reserve and Conservation Reserve Programs, and the Mississippi Soil and Water Conservation Commission's Clean Lakes Program. These federal and state agency programs pay about 75 percent of the cost of the BMPs, and the landowner pays the remainder.

Siltation, whether pesticide-laden or not, is a concern throughout the Complex, particularly wetlands that receive agricultural runoff such as those on Dahomey refuge, and the Tippo Bayou area in Tallahatchie refuge. These areas not only have diminished water quality, but are filling in, resulting in a loss of aquatic habitat.

FLORA

The cover type for the Delta was primarily bottomland hardwood forest prior to the clearing, which began with settlement by Europeans around 1820. The dominant forest type was oak-gum-cypress. Canebrakes originally covered the broader flats of slightly higher ground. They were very extensive on the natural levees forming almost pure stands. Most of the surviving forests now occupy lower ground too wet for agriculture, and are dominated by wet-site species. These wetlands have a fluctuating water level and are semi-dry part of the year. The lowest areas contain cypress and buttonbush throughout the Complex. Cypress is complemented or somewhat replaced in some low areas by swamp tupelo on all the stations. Other woody species in permanent or semi-permanent flooded areas include swamp privet, water elm, black willow, and water locust. At slightly higher elevations are green ash, red maple, cottonwood, sugarberry, honey locust, sycamore, bitter pecan, overcup oak, American elm, and Nuttall oak. Extensive flats support scattered deciduous holly (possum haw) in the mid-story, while higher elevations grow extensive stands of dwarf palmetto (*Sabal minor*). Hardwoods on still higher sites include willow oak, pecan, sweet gum, black locust, and water oak. Prominent vines include poison ivy, cross-vine, Virginia creeper, muscadine grape, and false grape in forested areas, and ladies' eardrops, peppervine, and trumpet creeper in more open situations.

Vegetation associations vary between refuges. Coldwater River refuge has distinctly wetter conditions, with fewer areas to support species found on well-drained soils. Since the refuge was acquired, over 1,300 acres of marginal agricultural fields have been reforested with bottomland hardwood tree species such as Nuttall oak, willow oak, water oak, bald cypress, green ash, and others [5-page gloss on Coldwater]. Black willows are prevalent along all internal drainages [Bio rev, iii]. Similarly, over 1200 acres of marginal agricultural fields have been reforested with bottomland hardwood tree species on Tallahatchie refuge.

Vegetation also varies within refuges, according to topography. The distribution of bottomland hardwood species across floodplains is primarily a function of a soil moisture gradient in which a couple of feet can be telling [FMPH, 80]. On Dahomey refuge, red oak-gum is the principle forest type. Cruise observations reveal a transition to elm-ash-sugarberry forest type [FHMP, 87].

FAUNA

Mammals

Mammals occurring on the Complex represent most species extant in the Delta. Large mammals include the whitetail deer, which are abundant on all stations, the feral hog (an invasive species), especially on Tallahatchie, and the American black bear, which occasionally is seen on Dahomey refuge (though not a permanent resident).

Medium-sized mammals include opossum, armadillo, eastern cottontail, swamp rabbits, beaver, muskrat, mink, nutria, coyote, red fox, gray fox, raccoon, striped skunk, river otter, and bobcat. The nutria was introduced from South America and is a noteworthy invasive species. Beavers have a tremendous potential impact on bottomland hardwoods. They interfere with wildlife control activities by plugging culverts, ditches, and water control structures [2002 annual review, 12]. Problems associated with the impounding of water by beaver are proving to be the single greatest threat to timber resources within the Complex [FHMP, 86].

Armadillos extended their range into this part of Mississippi some time during the latter half of the 20th century. Their impact here has not been investigated. Coyotes are also a recent arrival, with first sightings recorded in the 1980s. Their presence is thought to be responsible, among other things, for the scarcity of foxes. River otters seem to have made a comeback in recent years. Raccoons are abundant and tend to overpopulate.

Small mammals have not been surveyed on the Complex, but potentially include (number of species in parentheses) shrews (3), bats (12), chipmunk (1), squirrel (3), new world rats and mice (7), voles (1), old world rats and mice (3), weasel (1), rabbits(2) [FHMP, 17], and mink (1).

Birds

Over 225 species of migratory birds use the Complex, of which some 77 species breed here. Ten species with Partners-in-Flight concern scores of 20 or more are common or abundant, including prothonotary warbler, painted bunting, red-headed woodpecker, yellow-billed cuckoo, wood thrush, white-eyed vireo, yellow-breasted chat, Carolina chickadee, loggerhead shrike, and dickcissel.

The most abundant wintering waterfowl species is the mallard followed variously by green-winged teal, northern pintail, northern shoveler, and gadwall, among the ducks, and snow and blue geese, and greater white-fronted geese among the geese. Wood ducks and hooded mergansers are common nesters in the spring and summer.

The Complex provides excellent habitat for breeding colonial wading birds. Nesting species include the great blue heron, great egret, snowy egret, little blue heron, cattle egret, yellow-crowned night heron, anhinga, green heron, and more recently, double-crested cormorants. White ibis have occupied rookeries in the past, but have not nested on the refuges for several years. They are considered a priority species under the colonial waterbird objective for the Complex.

About 20 species of shorebirds use the refuge complex, especially where habitat is managed intensively. Some of the most numerous species are least sandpipers, pectoral sandpipers, semipalmated plovers, greater yellowlegs, and stilt sandpipers.

Reptiles

A survey of reptiles has not been done on any of the refuges. In 2001, the refuge staff initiated calling frog surveys to monitor refuge frog populations, as well as beginning an overall inventory of amphibians and reptiles on the three traditional refuge properties (Coldwater River, Dahomey, and Tallahatchie refuges.) [BioReview, 44] A list has been prepared based on species ranges and personal encounters by the refuge staff; including alligators (1 species), turtles (15 spp.), lizards (8 spp.), and snakes (31 spp.).

Various species of water snakes are common or abundant, especially the broad-banded and diamond-backed water snakes. Poisonous snakes include the copperhead, cottonmouth, and timber (canebrake) rattlesnake. Rat snakes of mixed or uncertain subspecies are a serious nest predator, climb well, and are abundant on the Complex. Racers and western ribbon snakes are also common.

The most commonly seen turtle species is the red-eared slider, whose range spans the three refuges in the Complex. Alligator snappers have been trapped on the Tallahatchee refuge, while common snappers and western spiny softshell turtles are known to inhabit all three refuges [annual nar. 2002, 4].

The ground skink and the five-lined skink are two of the most common lizard species.

Amphibians

Calling frog surveys and searches for salamander breeding sites were begun in 2001 throughout the Complex. The numbers of species that may occur on the refuge include: salamanders (12), toads (3), treefrogs (9), narrow-mouthed toad (1), spadefoot toads (1) and true frogs (5). Cricket frogs, green treefrogs, bullfrogs, bronze frogs, and southern leopard frogs are abundant. Salamanders, although present, are rarely encountered with the exception of the marbled salamander, which can frequently be found in the spring at Dahomey refuge. When completed, the results from the reptile and amphibian inventory, as well as the calling frog surveys, will be incorporated into a GIS-based database. The calling frog survey data will be submitted to the North American Amphibian Monitoring Program, a national database.

Fish

Fish populations consist mostly of rough fish that can withstand hot, murky water with low oxygen content such as long-nosed gar, buffalo, carp, bowfin and shad. Sport fish such as largemouth bass, bream (panfish), and channel catfish have been stocked in suitable waters. A wide variety of fish species exists in the larger streams and bayous, including largemouth bass, various bream, and crappie.

THREATENED AND ENDANGERED SPECIES

Animals

Several federally listed threatened and endangered animals may occur on the Complex. Numbers of the threatened bald eagle (*Haliaeetus leucocephalus*) are on the rise locally and this large raptor is more frequently sighted throughout the Complex than it used to be. Nesting has been documented at nearby lakes. The endangered least tern (*Sterna antillarum*) is an occasional visitor to managed moist-soil units and open water wetlands in search of foraging habitat mostly during summer months. The interior population of the least tern breeds in isolated areas along the Missouri, Mississippi, Ohio, Red, and Rio Grande river systems. From late April to August, terns use barren to sparsely vegetated sandbars along rivers, sand and gravel pits, or lake and reservoir shorelines. Dams, reservoirs, channelization, and other changes to river systems have eliminated most historic least tern habitat. The endangered wood stork (*Mycteria americana*) is provided excellent habitat for breeding within the Complex. Shallow water areas found on the Complex during late summer and fall provide long-legged wading birds with critical foraging opportunities.

The peregrine falcon (*Falco peregrinus*), an occasional visitor to the Complex, was listed as an endangered species in 1970, but was de-listed in 1999, as a result of recovery of its populations from successful efforts at captive breeding and reintroductions. The paddlefish (*Polyodon spathula*) can reach nearly 7 feet in length and 200 pounds. It is a former candidate species for federal listing and is still considered a species of management concern. It was once abundant in the Mississippi, Missouri, and Gulf Coast drainages, so much so that it was commercially harvested as a source of eggs for caviar. There is evidence that Tippo Bayou is a staging ground for spawning by the paddlefish. To date, however, spawning has not been documented.

The black bear was once distributed throughout Mississippi. However, because of excessive harvest and habitat loss, black bear populations have been severely reduced. The Complex is located entirely within the historic range of the state-listed endangered American black bear (*Ursus a. americanus*). It also borders, to the south, the range of the federally listed threatened Louisiana black bear (*Ursus a. luteolus*). Though no breeding population has been documented in Mississippi, several individual bears, including females with cubs, have been sighted on the Complex, most notably along the Mississippi River in Bolivar County.

Efforts by the Black Bear Conservation Committee and its member agencies are currently underway to restore bears to their historic range, with current focus on the Louisiana black bear within the State of Louisiana. However, bear sightings in the lower Mississippi Delta have increased dramatically over the last few years, suggesting a possible expansion of these bears across the Mississippi River from existing natural and repatriated bear populations in Louisiana.

Also, a breeding population of black bears currently exists in the White River National Wildlife Refuge in southeast Arkansas, to the west and across the Mississippi River from the Complex. Individual bears have been documented crossing the river into Mississippi. Consequently, there is a possibility that more White River refuge bears could immigrate into the Complex. It should be noted that the subspecific status of the White River refuge bear population is unresolved.

Plants

The endangered pondberry (*Lindera melissifolia*) is a rarely seen deciduous shrub that grows in seasonally flooded wetlands and on the edges of sinks and ponds. Much of the lands where pondberry was historically found have been ditched and converted to agricultural fields. The drainage and flooding of wetlands, cattle grazing, domestic hog foraging, and timber cutting have also adversely affected pondberry abundance. Pondberry has been found on Service property in Bolivar County. Its presence on Dahomey refuge in Bolivar County has not yet been verified; however, an ecological assessment conducted there concludes that suitable habitats for pondberry do exist and that its presence there is very likely (Stewart 1990). It has not yet been documented on other properties administered by the Complex. [FHMP, 18]

CULTURAL RESOURCES

Cultural resources include historic properties as defined in the National Historic Preservation Act (NHPA), cultural items as defined in the Native American Graves Protection and Repatriation Act, archaeological resources as defined in the Archaeological Resources Protection Act (ARPA), sacred sites as defined in Executive Order 13007, *Protection and Accommodation of Access To "Indian Sacred Sites,"* to which access is provided under the American Indian Religious Freedom Act and collections. As defined by the NHPA, a historic property or historic resource is any prehistoric or historic district, site, building, structure, or object included in, or eligible for inclusion in, the National Register of Historic Places (NRHP), including any artifacts, records, and remains that are related to and located in such properties. The term also includes properties of traditional religious and cultural importance (traditional cultural properties), which are eligible for inclusion in the NRHP as a result of their association with the cultural practices or beliefs of an American Indian tribe. Archaeological resources include any material of human life or activities that is at least 100 years old, and that is of archaeological interest.

Section 106 of the NHPA provides the framework for federal review and consideration of cultural resources during federal project planning and execution. The implementing regulations for the Section 106 process (36 CFR Part 800) have been promulgated by the Advisory Council on Historic Preservation. The Secretary of the Interior maintains the NRHP and sets forth significant criteria (36 CFR Part 60) for inclusion in the register. Cultural resources may be considered "historic properties" for the purpose of consideration by a federal undertaking if they meet NRHP criteria. The implementing regulations at 36 CFR 800.16(v) define an undertaking as "a project, activity, or program funded in whole or in part under the direct or indirect jurisdiction of a Federal agency, including those carried out by or on behalf of a Federal agency; those carried out with Federal financial assistance; those requiring a Federal permit, license or approval; and those subject to state or local regulation administered pursuant to a delegation or approval by a Federal agency." Historic properties are those that are formally placed in the NRHP by the Secretary of the Interior, and those that meet the criteria and are determined eligible for inclusion.

Like all federal agencies, the Service must comply with Section 106 of the NHPA. Cultural resources management in the Service is the responsibility of the Regional Director and is not delegated for the Section 106 process when historic properties could be affected by Service undertakings, for issuing archaeological permits, and for Indian tribal involvement. The Regional Historic Preservation Officer (RHPO) advises the Regional Director about procedures, compliance, and implementation of the several cultural resources laws. The Refuge Manager assists the RHPO by early informing the RHPO about Service undertakings, by protecting archaeological sites and historic properties on Service managed and administered lands, by monitoring archaeological investigations by contractors and permittees, and by reporting violations.

The Complex follows these procedures to protect the public's interest in preserving its cultural/historic legacy that may potentially occur on the Complex. Whenever construction work is undertaken that involves any excavation with heavy earth-moving equipment like tractors, graders, and bulldozers, such as for the development of moist-soil units, the Complex contracts with a qualified archaeologist/cultural resources expert to conduct an archaeological survey of the subject property. The results of this survey are submitted to the RHPO, as well as the State Historic Preservation Officer (SHPO), which in Mississippi is an official within the Historic Preservation Division of the Mississippi Department of Archives and History. The SHPO reviews the surveys and determines whether cultural resources will be impacted, that is, whether any properties listed in or eligible or eligible for listing in the NRHP will be affected. If cultural resources are actually encountered during construction activities, the Complex is to notify the SHPO immediately. To date, no properties on the Complex have been determined to be eligible for the NRHP.

This region of Mississippi has long been settled and used by humans, in good part because of its mild winters and abundant fish and wildlife resources. Prior to European settlement, a number of Indian tribes inhabited the Delta. In the northern part of the Complex, the Quizquiz tribe was a predecessor of the historic Tunica. Only one village of Quapaw was identified in 1763, with the rest in Arkansas. The first Europeans to travel through the Delta were the Spaniards of De Soto's expedition of the 1540s. Next were the French, who arrived in the mid-1600s. The Europeans had a devastating effect on the Indians of this area. A number of tribes are mentioned by the French as living in the Delta, but almost all had disappeared from the area by 1750, as a result of disease, warfare, and migration. In 1802 the land was sold to the United States as part of the Louisiana Purchase (Heisler, 1978).

The Lower Mississippi River is noted for its prehistoric earthen mounds, erected by the area's indigenous inhabitants. Although the first people entered what is now Mississippi about 12,000 years ago, the earliest major phase of earthen mound construction in this area did not begin until some 2,100 years ago. Mounds continued to be built sporadically for another 1,800 years. Of the mounds that remain today, some of the earliest were built to bury important members of local tribal groups. These mounds were usually rounded, dome-shapes. Later mounds were rectangular, flat-topped earthen platforms upon which temples or residences of chiefs were erected.

Eight hundred years ago, the lower Mississippi Delta was home to highly organized societies. There were roads, commerce, and cultural centers anchored by large and impressive earthen monuments. Wonders of geometric precision, these earthworks were the centers of human life. However, mound construction was already in a period of decline in the 1500s, when the first Europeans arrived in the region and brought with them epidemic diseases that decimated native populations across the southeast. As a result, by the time sustained contact with European colonists began about 1700, the long tradition of mound building was reaching its end. Surviving mounds are protected because they are owned by state or federal agencies committed by law to their preservation. Most of the mounds in Mississippi, however, are on privately owned land. As a result, many mounds have been irreparably damaged or completely destroyed by modern development and looting. Indian mounds, therefore, are critically endangered cultural sites (Indian Mounds of Mississippi, NPS 2002). The Complex includes at least one documented mound on the Pennington Farm Service Agency property.

RECREATION AND VISITOR SERVICES

The Complex contains abundant populations of fish and wildlife, including a number of game species. The opportunity for consumptive and non-consumptive wildlife-dependent recreation attracts many members of the public to the refuges and Farm Service Agency properties; in recent years the Complex has received about 100,000 visits annually. Hunting and fishing are the most popular public uses on the Complex's three refuges and many Farm Service Agency properties, and are provided in accordance with federal, state, and refuge regulations.

Hunting is the most popular recreational activity throughout the Complex. This includes hunting on some of the Farm Service Agency fee title properties where the activity had existed prior to acquisition by the Complex [public use review,1]. The hunting program is monitored and partially funded through general hunt permits, currently $12.50 each, and valid for most types of game. Deer, rabbits, squirrels, raccoons, waterfowl, feral swine, and turkey may be taken on the Complex during the appropriate seasons. In 2003, approximately 1,500 hunters received hunting permits for the Complex. That same year, only a very limited number of fishing permits were issued. On Dahomey refuge, an 8-acre lake was constructed in 1999 and stocked with bass, bream, and catfish. It was subsequently opened to fishing by the public.

Wildlife observation and photography are other public uses at the Complex. Coldwater River refuge is closed to the general public because of its critical importance as a wildlife sanctuary, but wildlife may be observed from public roads on the eastern and western boundaries of the refuge. On Dahomey and Tallahatchie refuges, many of the refuge roads are open to the public and several Special Use Permits are issued annually to photographers. Nonetheless, most of the participation in these activities is incidental, as there are no formal programs to encourage expanding and participating in these activities.

Environmental education and interpretation are also provided on an as-needed basis. The staff has responded to requests for interpretive programs, but there are no refuge-specific programs and no dedicated staff to develop and conduct an effective education and outreach program.

SOCIOECONOMIC ENVIRONMENT

The traditional refuges administered by the Complex lie within the counties of Tallahatchie, Bolivar, Grenada, and Quitman. In addition, complex-administered Farm Service Agency properties occupy these, as well as eleven surrounding counties. The westernmost counties are found within what is referred to as the Mississippi Delta while the easternmost counties are located in the Mississippi Hill Country. The entire Complex region is largely rural, and the Delta area containing the three refuges has an economy based on manufacturing and agriculture; principle crops are cotton, soybeans, corn, rice, and catfish. Much or most of the counties' land bases are used for agriculture (see Table 10).

Table 10. Percent of the Tallahatchie, Grenada, Bolivar and Quitman counties' land base used for agricultural production

County	Total Area (square miles)	Area used for agriculture 2002* sq. miles (%)
Tallahatchie	652	331 (51%)
Grenada	449	99 (22%)
Bolivar	906	578 (64%)
Quitman	406	207 (51%)

* Includes cultivated and grazing land (pasture) but not forestry/timberland
(Source: Agricultural Statistical Service, USDA, conversion of head of cattle to acres performed by Jack Curry, Mississippi Development Authority, 2/02, 2/03, 2/24, 2004)

Mississippi is the most economically depressed state in the nation, with lower than average household and per capita income and educational attainment levels. However, with the exception of Bolivar County (8.3 percent unemployment in the 2000 U.S. Census), the counties surrounding the Complex actually have unemployment rates below the national average. Tables 11 and 12 provide additional demographic and geographic information about Tallahatchie, Grenada, Bolivar, and Quitman counties.

Table 11. County employment data

County	Leading Industry	Sources of Earnings	Unemployment Rate (MS state, 5.7%)
Tallahatchie	Manufacturing	23.3%	4.9%
Grenada	Manufacturing	27.7%	3.4%
Quitman	Educational, health and social services	19.6%	4.4%
Bolivar	Educational, health and social services	26.2%	8.3%

Source: *Census 2000 Summary File 3 (SF 3) - Sample Data*, American Fact Finder, U.S. Census Bureau

OUTDOOR RECREATION ECONOMICS

The fish and wildlife of the Mississippi Delta, including those of the Complex, are economically important (Table 13). In addition to commercial fishing on the Mississippi River, hunting, recreational fishing, wildlife viewing, and wildlife photography are economically important to local businesses. Resident and nonresident hunting and fishing revenues for the state total $13.7 million dollars for 525,479 licenses (MS Development Authority 2002). These hunters and anglers spend an estimated $1.8 billion in the state annually (Gillette 2000).

Unfortunately, a general lack of regard for the preservation of fish and wildlife resources, combined with wetland clearing and draining, has led to the loss of valuable fishery spawning grounds and the loss of habitat for many wildlife species. In the attempt to restore and protect some of these resources, the Complex serves an important role, not only by providing habitat for a diversity of plant and wildlife species, but also as a place where people can go to enjoy these resources, either through observation or more directly through hunting or fishing.

The refuges of the Complex have become vital to the rural communities economies' in which they reside, not only with the activities they provide, but through employment opportunities to individuals who themselves contribute to the local economy. With improved access, facilities and staffing, these refuges can serve as pivotal attractions providing a much needed and important commodity in the economic life of these communities. Hunting and fishing and more recently, eco-tourism, including wildlife observation and photography, and environmental interpretation, are increasingly being seen as desirable industries. As the population increases and the number of places left to enjoy wildlife decreases, the Complex may become even more important to the local community. It can benefit the community directly by providing recreational and employment opportunities for the local population, and indirectly by attracting tourists from outside the area to generate additional dollars to the local economy.

TOURISM

Overall, tourism within the counties of Tallahatchie, Bolivar, Grenada, and Quitman does not contribute significantly to the local economy (Table 14). Music, festivals, casinos, historical sites, and outdoor recreation are some of the tourism opportunities available in northern Mississippi. It has been recognized that there are tourism opportunities in these counties, but there is a lack of infrastructure and expertise to effectively position these areas as heritage and cultural tourism destinations. The State of Mississippi has initiated plans to develop the "Mississippi Millennium Blues Trail," which would pass through the counties surrounding the Complex. A study was commissioned by the Mississippi Department of Tourism to determine the baseline and potential development of new and existing attractions that may draw tourists to this area. It was identified that the potential was here, but that for the most part, had yet to be developed and promoted. The local chapter of the Audubon Society is currently developing a Mississippi River birding trail, which would follow Highway 1 (Old River Road) along the Mississippi River mainline levee.

Table 12. Geographic and demographic statistics for the four counties including refuges within the Complex

County	Land Area (sq. miles)	Population	% population change (1990-2000)	Median Age	Per capita Income ($)	**% below poverty	% White	% Black	% Hispanic	% Asian	% Native American
Tallahatchie	652	14,903	-2.0	33.3	10,749	26.8	39.4	59.4	0.9	0.4	0.1
Bolivar	906	40,633	-3.0	29.8	12,088	27.9	33.2	65.1	1.2	0.5	0.1
Grenada	449	23,263	7.9	35.7	13,786	17.6	57.9	40.9	0.6	0.3	0.1
Quitman	406	10,117	-3.6	30.8	10,817	28.6	30.5	68.6	0.5	0.2	0.1

Sources: U.S. Census 2000, Demographic Profiles, U.S. Census Bureau; Fact Finder, U.S. Census Bureau; Center for Population Studies, University of Mississippi;

Table 13. Activities by participants, 16 years old and older, throughout Mississippi

Activity	# of Participants	Activity Days	Average Days/participant	Total Expenditures ($1,000)	Trip-related Expenditures ($1,000)	Equipment and Other ($1,000)	Average $/participant	Average trip Expenditure/ day
Fishing	*586,000	9,500,000	16	$211,000	$118,000	$93,000	$363	$13
Hunting	**357,000	8,500,000	24	$360,000	$132,000	$227,000	$969	$16
Wildlife Watching	***631,000	NA	NA	$303,000	$36,000	$267,000	$481	NA

*136,000 nonresidents, 450,000 residents
**111,000 nonresidents, 245,000 residents
***55,000 nonresidents, 576,000 residents

Source: 2001 National Survey of Fishing, Hunting, and Wildlife-Associated Recreation in Mississippi

Table 14. Estimated county tourism & recreation (T&R) revenues/employment

County	Total T&R Revenues	Total T&R Employment	Total Establishment Based Employment	T&R Employment Percentage
Tallahatchie	$1,904,596	24	2,410	1
Bolivar	$22,475,718	382	13,300	2.9
Grenada	$34,162,697	615	11,270	5.5
Quitman	$2,258,241	25	1,830	1.4

(Mississippi Development Authority, Division of Tourism 2003)

III. Plan Development

OVERVIEW

In preparation for developing this comprehensive conservation plan, the Complex conducted a biological review and a public use review in the summer of 2002. Initial planning began in September 2003 with a meeting of planning team members. Early in the process of developing this plan, the planning team identified a list of issues and concerns that were likely to be associated with the conservation and management of the North Mississippi National Wildlife Refuges Complex. Formal public involvement began with the scoping process in November 2003, through which interested stakeholders were able to register their concerns, thereby ensuring that they would be considered in developing the comprehensive conservation plan.

Planning team members reviewed the results of this internal and external scoping and used them, along with supporting goals, objectives and strategies, to develop four different management alternatives for the Complex. The four alternatives were evaluated in an environmental assessment, and the preferred alternative forms the basis of this plan. The draft comprehensive conservation plan and environmental assessment were released to the public for review and comment. The Service considered all comments and suggestions received in the preparation of this final plan, which will become the general plan guiding management decisions and actions on the Complex for the next 10-15 years.

Refuge planning policy requires a Wilderness Review concurrent with the comprehensive conservation planning process. The Service inventoried refuge lands within the planning area and found no areas that meet the eligibility criteria for a Wilderness Study Area, as defined by the Wilderness Act. Therefore, the suitability of refuge lands for wilderness designation is not analyzed further in this plan. The results of the wilderness inventory are included in Section B, Appendix I.

PLANNING PROCESS AND PUBLIC INVOLVEMENT

Prior to starting the planning process, the Complex conducted a biological review and a public use review in 2002 (finalized in 2003), which provided detailed analysis of resources and existing programs in these fundamental areas, and offered recommendations for future management in the form of goals, objectives, and strategies.

The biological review was held during the week of June 3-7, 2002. The team was comprised of biologists, managers, foresters, and non-Service managers/biologists whose combined expertise represented some of the premier wildlife and habitat management experience found in the state. The biological review team provided a critical examination of current programs, culminating in a range of alternatives identifying data needs, habitat objectives, opportunities for improvement, and so forth, all while emphasizing future partnership opportunities on mutual interests. The October 2003 final Biological Review report summarizes the recommendations submitted by the biological review teams.

The public use review team (comprised of Complex and Regional Office staff) also met in 2002. After reviewing existing public use programs, facilities and opportunities, the team prepared a Public Use Review Report that outlines recommendations on public use at the Complex. Emphasis was placed on the main six, generally compatible wildlife-dependent public use opportunities, namely hunting, fishing, wildlife observation, wildlife photography, and environmental education and interpretation.

Initial planning began in September 2003 with a meeting of planning team members. At and following this meeting, an initial list of issues was identified by the planning team and refuge staff. The team also developed a mailing list of the public, landowners, state and tribal agencies, non-profit organizations, local governments, and other interested stakeholders. Letters were then sent notifying these parties of the planning process that was just getting underway, encouraging their participation, and informing them of two upcoming open house-style scoping meetings that would be held in November 2003 at the Complex headquarters in Grenada, Mississippi, and at Delta State University in Cleveland, Mississippi. That letter and notices published in local newspapers also stated that even if a person or group was unable to attend either of these meetings, they could send in written comments to the Complex headquarters.

On November 11, 2003, at the Complex headquarters, and on the following day at Delta State University, the public scoping meetings were conducted to obtain information and concerns from the public. The open house sessions each lasted from 5 to 9 p.m. with brief presentations at 7 p.m. by members of the planning team. The presentations touched on the need to prepare a comprehensive conservation plan, its purpose, how the public could participate, and an overview of the resources and programs of the Complex. Planning team staff had prepared maps and exhibits and placed these around the room for the public to view.

Six people attended the first open house in Grenada and about fifteen people attended the second open house at Delta State University. After the presentations, participants were invited to make oral comments or ask questions, which a number did. A comment form was also made available to attendees, which asked questions prompting written responses about what they saw as the main issues facing Coldwater River, Dahomey, and Tallahatchie refuges. Overall, the Complex received about a dozen sets of written comments, both comment forms and letters. A total of approximately 25 individuals provided oral and/or written comments. Input obtained from all of these meetings and correspondence was considered in developing this plan.

The period of public review and comment began on September 9, 2004, and ended on October 21, 2004. Public comments and Service responses are addressed in Appendix H.

The following comments were received via the public scoping process:

Recreation and Visitor Services

- Upgrade and maintain the refuges so that they are accessible (especially to the inner-most parts of the refuges) as well as visitor-friendly (especially for handicapped persons) (x3).

- Long-range plans should include facilities for bird watching, photography, and wildlife observation. Incorporate Dahomey refuge into Audubon birding trail.

- Should develop new programs for public use, thereby attracting more tourists to the Delta.

- Road system is good.

- ATVs should be allowed on specified gravel paths for retrieving of game, with due restrictions placed on their use (x2).

- Better enforce closed areas on refuges from encroaching hunters.

- Allow for a limited amount of rifle and muzzle-loading hunting on Dahomey refuge.

- The Complex offers some of the only public hunting opportunities in the vicinity.

- Should use available resources/funds to try to acquire more land.

Wildlife Management

- Increase the populations of game species, especially deer, on Dahomey refuge (x4).

- Increase the deer population by limiting the number of does harvested for several years.

- Remove size restriction on bucks for the youth hunt. Increase the size restriction on bucks for general hunts (X2).

- Determine impacts of wild hogs and coyotes on deer and other game species (x2).

- Forest management should take hunters more into consideration.

- Increase number of food plots.

- Habitat management is right on track. No changes necessary (x3).

- Repair levees (x2).

- There seem to be fewer pintail and canvasback ducks than in the past.

Staff and Staffing

- More staff needed (x3).

- Staff should be more considerate of visitors/ hunters with health problems.

- Partners for Fish and Wildlife.

- The Partners for Wildlife program is very successful and appreciated (x2).

- CRP (Conservation Reserve Program) good for this area.

ISSUES AND CURRENT CONDITIONS

A result of these biological and public use reviews and scoping meetings was the development of a list of significant issues that needed to be addressed in the comprehensive conservation plan. Alternatives for addressing these issues were developed in the environmental assessment. The preferred alternative formed the basis for the objectives and strategies to achieve the goals developed by the planning team. This process ensures that the most significant issues are resolved or given priority over the life of this plan. Below is a summary of these significant issues along with some discussion of their impacts to the resources.

Threatened and Endangered Species

Recovery and protection of threatened and endangered plants and animals is an important responsibility delegated to the Service and its national wildlife refuges. Several federal threatened and endangered species are thought to use, or could use, the North Mississippi National Wildlife Refuges Complex, including the bald eagle, wood stork, Louisiana black bear, and the least tern [FHMP, 122]. The bald eagle and Louisiana black bear are threatened (the bald eagle is proposed for delisting), while the wood stork and least tern are both endangered.

Pondberry, the only threatened or endangered plant species believed to occur on the Complex, has been found on Service property in Bolivar County. Its presence on Dahomey refuge in Bolivar County has not yet been verified; however, an ecological assessment conducted there concludes that suitable habitats for pondberry do exist and that its presence there is very likely (Stewart 1990). It has not yet been documented on other properties administered by the Complex. [FHMP, 18]

Invasive Species

An "invasive species" is defined as a species that is 1) non-native (or alien) to the ecosystem under consideration, and 2) whose introduction causes or is likely to cause economic or environmental harm or harm to human health. (Executive Order 13112). Invasive species can be plants, animals, and other organisms (e.g., microbes). Deliberate or inadvertent human actions are the primary means of invasive species introductions.

Several invasive species occur on the Complex. Some of the more prominent and obvious are feral hogs, coyote, nutria, and armadillo. These wildlife species were either accidentally released and became acclimated to living in the wild, were intentionally released for sport or trade, or have expanded their range. These animals have been sporadically controlled by lethal means.

Invasive plants, insects, and smaller organisms are more difficult to recognize and monitor. The Complex does not have an invasive species monitoring program to detect not only their initial introduction, but rate of spread and their impacts. However, we know several invasive plants, such as Johnson grass and kudzu, which have spread across the Complex, overtaking and displacing native vegetation. Control of these invasive plant species has been opportunistic and sporadic, using both biological and chemical means.

The Complex does not have an "Invasive Species Management Plan". There are no structured programs or funding specifically provided for an invasive species management program.

Resident Wildlife

The mission of the National Wildlife Refuge System is:

"To administer a national network of lands and waters for the conservation, management, and where appropriate, restoration of the fish, wildlife and plant resources and their habitats within the United States for the benefit of present and future generations of Americans."

While the Service and the Refuge System's priority is the protection of federal trust species (migratory birds, threatened and endangered species, interjurisdictional fishes and marine mammals), this mission clearly states that these refuges should also provide for other wildlife, such as resident species. In other words, by acquiring refuge lands, we also assume responsibility for managing the resident wildlife that may be dependent on refuge resources, but not to the exclusion or detriment of the purpose for which the refuge was established. A variety of wildlife species indigenous to the LMAV inhabit the Complex. Some of the more notable are those easily seen by the general public, such as white-tailed deer, wild turkey, and cottontail rabbits. Many of these species are also available to the public for hunting opportunities, which elevates their importance to the public and land managers.

The Northern bobwhite quail historically and traditionally has been one of the most important and cherished of game birds in the south. However, for the last several decades, bobwhite quail and many other small game species associated with early successional stages and grasslands have declined at an average of 3 percent per year, and in the last 10 years the rate of decline has escalated to about 6 percent per year. While many factors have contributed to this decline – including predators, pathogens, and pesticides – the primary cause of decline is deteriorating habitat quality. This is due to advanced natural succession, intensive monoculture farming, more intensive timber management, reduced use of prescribed burning, and the extensive use of exotic grasses, including fescue and Bermuda grass. Bobwhite quail prefer an interspersion of woodlands, brush, grass, and croplands. Although early successional habitat is present on the Complex properties, it does not meet the annual needs of the target species. Quail and other wildlife have little or no accessible protective cover adjacent to feeding/nesting areas [BioReview, 39].

Agricultural farming practices have become more mechanized, and chemical control of pests has increased dramatically. Small patchwork farms that once provided nesting, brood rearing and protective cover have been replaced by large monoculture farm operations that have eliminated thousands of miles of weedy ditch banks and fence rows.

Another upland game species, wild turkey, can be found on every refuge in the Complex. Predation and habitat loss have caused dramatic population declines in the past, causing the closure or limiting of hunting seasons. Hunted populations should continue to be monitored to ensure they are not over-harvested. Management actions for quail and grassland birds would also benefit turkey production and survival.

Beaver, another resident wildlife species, have become pests, building dams that hold water on trees, causing die-offs of mature bottomland hardwoods. Incidental trapping by Special Use Permit has been ineffective in the past. However, this issue must be addressed or many more acres of critical forests will be lost and will take decades to recover.

Migratory Birds

Ducks

All refuges within the Complex have a purpose that gives priority to migratory birds over all other wildlife species. This purpose guides a majority of the operation and management actions on the refuges. Management actions include providing agricultural hot foods, moist-soil areas, and forested wetlands to meet the feeding, resting, and breeding needs of migratory and resident waterfowl. Comments from the biological review teams and the public provided overwhelming support to continue or expand these programs with specific stipulations for improving and focusing efforts. In support of the North American Waterfowl Management Plan, the LMVJV office assigned each refuge minimum habitat objectives needed to provide sufficient water, food, sanctuary, and resting/loafing areas to meet the needs of wintering waterfowl. The objectives are based on the best available information available. There currently are a number of research projects studying the available resources and habitat on private lands, the results of which will likely alter objectives in the future.

The amount of refuge croplands and moist-soil areas needed to meet the habitat objectives and the numbers of waterfowl that these areas can support merit particular attention. Lands currently in agricultural crops that exceed that needed to meet the objectives would be evaluated for conversions to moist-soil, early successional habitats or reforestation to address the needs of other species of migratory and non-migratory birds and mammals. Providing undisturbed waterfowl sanctuaries while providing quality hunting opportunities is another significant issue.

Geese

Geese were addressed separately due to their unique habitat needs compared to ducks. Goose species, including snow, white-fronted, and Canada geese, prefer feeding and resting in more open fields with little or no standing water. Thousands of geese winter on the Complex. Goose use on the Complex tends to be sporadic and primarily restricted to Coldwater River and Tallahatchie refuges and only a few Farm Service Agency tracts. Concentrations are generally restricted to less than 5,000 birds at any one time.

Any management actions for snow geese should support the "Arctic Tundra Habitat Emergency Conservation Act" to reduce the snow/Ross' goose populations that have experienced rapid population growth reaching levels such that they are damaging habitats on their arctic and sub-arctic breeding areas in Canada. This degradation may be irreversible and has negatively impacted other bird populations. Natural marsh habitats on some migration and wintering areas also have been impacted. In addition, goose damage to agricultural crops has become a problem. There is increasing evidence that lesser snow and Ross' geese act as reservoirs for the bacterium that causes avian cholera. The threat of avian cholera to other bird species likely will increase as these goose populations expand.

Non-game birds

Neotropical migratory birds are a species group of special management concern. Broad species groups include breeding forest landbirds, breeding scrub/shrub landbirds, transient song(land) birds, marsh and grassland birds, shorebirds (addressed below), colonial waterbirds/wading birds, and raptors. The Partners-in-Flight Bird Conservation Plan for the Mississippi Alluvial Valley has habitat objectives for all these groups of birds, but all of these groups can be accommodated on existing and restored habitats throughout the Complex. Habitat needed for the most area-sensitive species, namely interior forest-dependent birds, has been evaluated and habitat objectives established. The plan identifies Dahomey refuge as the only refuge within the Complex currently having the necessary size for creating a block of interior forest habitat that meets minimum critical standards. The other two refuges will need to be expanded first. Large interior forest blocks are extremely rare along the entire LMRV due to clearing of lands, primarily for agriculture. Nevertheless, the birds continue to follow historical migratory pathways along the Mississippi Flyway. This has resulted in a direct correlation between the decline of the forests and the decline of the populations of bird species, particularly those with sensitive habitat needs. Balancing the needs of waterfowl, which requires more open habitat, with the needs of these imperiled songbirds, is a significant issue that generated much discussion during the biological review.

Another issue is lack of baseline information on all groups of birds throughout the Complex. There have been limited surveys on specific areas on the Complex (mostly presence/absence data for species occurrence), as well as aerial winter waterfowl surveys of the Complex's refuges and properties since 1996, but comprehensive and standardized surveys of all of the refuges and for all habitat types are lacking.

Shorebirds

Habitat for spring (northbound) shorebird migration in the LMRV is not considered to be limited. The acreage of open, bare-soil areas, flooded by spring rains, at this point, provides ample habitat. Peak migration occurs from March to mid-May.

Southbound migration starts in early July, peaks August through September, and tapers off toward winter, usually lasting until at least the end of October. The lack of shallow-flooded or mudflat habitats in late summer/fall results in a severe shortage of shorebird habitat. Given that a focus on providing shorebird habitat is considered one of the highest non-game bird priorities for the Complex, it is important that existing shorebird management practices be continued and improved upon.

A 1500-acre habitat target has been identified for the entire State of Mississippi as necessary to support a tentative LMRV population objective of 500,000 shorebirds during southbound migration. This migration figure is based on conservative assumptions, and experts believe that the objective figure may need to be as much as twice that amount. An information need in connection with this effort is to document overall use of the Complex and determine peak passage of the various shorebird species.

Managing moist soil for both waterfowl and shorebirds can be done provided managers have full water level management capabilities enabling them to ensure drawdown and flooding of impoundments at critical times. The Complex has been focusing its shorebird management efforts on Coldwater River refuge. There is good water level control, as well as data on the success of these impoundments, providing for both waterfowl and shorebirds. It was recognized by the biological review team that there are also other opportunities within the Complex, including former catfish ponds at the Henson and Kimbrough Farm Service Agency Tracts, to conduct similar successful programs.

HABITATS

Bottomland Hardwood Management and Restoration

The Complex is situated within the physiographic region known as the Lower Mississippi Valley (LMRV). The LMRV was once a 25-million-acre forested wetland complex that extended along both sides of the Mississippi River from Illinois to southern Louisiana. The extent and duration of annual flooding of the Mississippi River fluctuated annually, and served to recharge aquatic systems and create rich, dynamic habitats that supported a vast array of fish and wildlife resources.

As civilization pushed westward, the highest, least flood-prone lands were cleared and converted to rich farmland. With success in agriculture and an expanding human population, more land was being cleared and additional flood control measures were implemented. Today, the LMRV is bisected by levees and a myriad of flood control projects and supports less than five million acres of bottomland hardwood forests. The fish and wildlife resources have mirrored the decline in the forests.

Although reforestation is the obvious "fix" for the vast forests that have been converted to row-crop agriculture, it must always be remembered that hydrology (flooding) drives the ecological system in the LMRV. It is imperative that managers remember that reforestation is only part of the solution. Restoring or mimicking a natural hydrologic cycle in conjunction with reforestation is needed.

Large areas have been reforested on the Complex. In many areas, fragmentation has decreased and structure and food sources have been generated. Federal programs, such as carbon sequestration, have driven some of these efforts. Nevertheless, little is known about managing these reforested bottomland hardwood habitats. There is little historical information on "what was here" and "how it was structured" prior to European settlement. Only recently have studies addressed this issue. It has been assumed, in many cases, that all trees are good, no matter where they are planted. Further, we have come to realize that some of the smaller, isolated reforested lands, such as Farm Service Agency properties, serve to perpetuate the hostile "edge effect" for some species. These smaller reforested sites provide little habitat for neotropical migratory species of special concern. Hindsight tells us that leaving some of these areas in a scrub/shrub habitat would have been more conducive to the priority bird species using these small areas.

The other issue related to reforestation is the discussion on diverse structure and stands that are attractive to commercial harvest. Commercial harvests have been a valuable tool in managing existing hardwood stands, often the only tool. Scheduled harvests are essential to maintaining a healthy forest that is diverse and provides structure and desirable tree species. While nature will eventually alter forest conditions, this slow process on the limited remaining acres will not provide the most desirable habitat in the interim.

As lands are removed from row crop agriculture and previously converted agricultural lands are acquired, the potential for reforestation in conjunction with water management capabilities will expand.

Agricultural Crops for Waterfowl

Farming operations within the Complex are conducted in support of specific waterfowl objectives set for each refuge. Specific agricultural crops provide cover and supplement more nutritional "natural foods" with high calorie "hot foods" for migratory waterfowl. In addition, farming can be used to set back succession and control weeds in moist-soil units. The main cooperative farming crops on the Complex are rice, corn, milo, and soybeans.

All farming operations are conducted cooperatively with local farmers (except at Coldwater River refuge, where co-op farming is not practiced). Cooperative farming is a mutually beneficial arrangement where the farmer is allowed to farm refuge land under certain guidelines and restrictions, including location of crops, techniques, crops planted, and chemicals used. Title 50, Part 29, of the Code of Federal Regulation and Service policies require that the value of a refuge's share of cooperatively grown crops be set at rates that reflect the fees and charges received by private landowners in the vicinity for similar privileges. The value can be established through the use of competition in selecting cooperators or through an analysis of local market conditions to establish the prevailing rates in the nearest comparable area. Cooperative farmers are authorized through the current Farm Bill to receive direct and counter-cyclical payments.

Approximately 1,200 acres of the Complex are farmed by 3 cooperative farmers. Under the current cooperative farm program guidelines of crop sharing and rotation, this amount of production is needed to meet the current 430-acre objective for the Complex.

Cooperative farming has been a long-standing practice throughout the Refuge System nationwide, and has been a mutually beneficial program for both refuge programs and for farmers. However, due to more restrictive regulations regarding approved chemicals, agricultural burning, and the encouraged use of "Best Management Practices," the use of cooperative farming to achieve objectives needs to be reviewed. Furthermore, due to the steady declines in crop prices in recent years, cooperative farming may no longer be a profitable endeavor for the average farmer. It is becoming more challenging to find farmers who are willing to alter their familiar farming techniques to meet Service agricultural policies. As restrictions are implemented in the name of environmental protection and wildlife conservation, we run the risk of losing our current corps of willing farmers due to hardship and loss of profit.

If Fish and Wildlife Service resources were used to fully meet the habitat objectives, there would need to be a significant increase in funding following initial one-time costs. As cooperative farming on the Complex does not place emphasis on growing crops for maximum yield, the use of chemicals to control weeds and insects would be reduced and Best Management Practices (BMP's) could be fully implemented. However, the 430-acre objective would need to be adjusted for this reduced production, BMP programs (such as buffer strips), and crop rotation. Additional staff and equipment would be needed to meet the stated objectives.

Acres that could be flooded or that have been historically used by waterfowl would be given the highest priority for meeting this objective. Most of the surplus acres would be converted to early successional habitats, such as grassland, scrub/shrub, and moist-soil. Many of these lands are adjacent to similar early successional habitats. Reforesting most of these lands would not contribute to interior forest objectives due to their size and distribution. There may be opportunities to reforest lands that would create buffers to human disturbance along roadsides and trails. In addition, the LMRVJV is reevaluating unharvested crop objectives based on new studies that are determining the value of harvested agricultural fields on private lands. Preliminary results indicate that earlier harvest dates and more efficient harvest techniques have significantly reduced the waste grain available when wintering waterfowl arrive in the Delta. Based on this new information, unharvested crop objectives may increase. Acres maintained in early successional habitat would be more easily converted back to agricultural production.

Moist-Soil Management

The LMJV has established moist-soil objectives in support of the North American Waterfowl Management Plan for the North Mississippi National Wildlife Refuges Complex. Moist-soil management refers to management that provides moist-soil conditions during the growing season to promote the natural production of beneficial plants. Seeds produced by these plants often attract and concentrate waterfowl and other wetland wildlife species. The decomposing vegetative parts of moist-soil plants also provide substrate for invertebrates, which are critical food for many wetland wildlife species. Factors that determine the success of moist-soil management include the timing and rate of the dewatering, soil disturbance, the stage of plant succession, and the timing and rate of reflooding. Best success is achieved when water levels can be controlled, although good results can be obtained under natural conditions when artificial draining and flooding are not possible.

Waterfowl depend on nutrient-rich seeds and invertebrates for various parts of their lifecycles. While high-calorie agricultural crops "hot foods" provide the needed energy for wintering migratory waterfowl, it is equally important they receive the nutrients needed to remain healthy and reproduce. "Hot foods" must be in close proximity to natural wetlands and moist-soil units to facilitate waterfowl access to aquatic invertebrates and other natural foods that are comparatively scarce in croplands.

ECOLOGICAL INTEGRITY

Maintenance of the ecological integrity of the Refuge System is required by the National Wildlife Refuge System Improvement Act of 1997. If we are to truly understand the ecological integrity of these lands, we must gather baseline information on all wildlife and their habitats to document their existence, monitor trends, and understand the impacts of refuge programs on biodiversity. It has been the history of the Refuge System and most land managers, often due to lack of expertise, to focus their efforts on the more common, sometimes recreational, wildlife species. Nevertheless, the mission of the Refuge System, with the exclusion of federal trust species, does not give preference to any one group.

The biological review team recognized that the North Mississippi National Wildlife Refuges Complex is lacking specific data on many resident wildlife species, but in particular, non-game wildlife, such as reptiles, amphibians, mussels, insects, small mammals, and their habitats. Most efforts have focused on studying and managing game species like white-tailed deer. While it is recognized that this is an important animal, especially to the hunting public, dozens of other wildlife species and associated habitats still need to be studied. Directing staff and resources to address these data gaps will be critical.

Contaminants and sedimentation have impacted every refuge within the Complex. Agricultural row crops are grown on much of the lands that surround refuges within the Complex. As a result, drainage from watershed lands brings agricultural chemicals into the refuges waters, which are bioaccumulating in fish. Historical use of organochlorine pesticides (DDT, PCB's, toxaphene, dieldrine, lindane, etc.), which contain heavy metals (mercury) were commonly used in farming operations, particularly cotton, prior to being banned in the 1970s. Unfortunately, these chemicals do not readily break down and still remain in the substrate of the sediment that was deposited in waters within and surrounding the refuges. These chemicals continue to contaminate fish and other aquatic-dependent resources such as fish-eating birds, wood ducks, and raccoons.

Contaminant levels are particularly extreme on Tallahatchie refuge. Due to levels of current use pesticides, DDTM and toxaphene, found in sampled fish, stream water, and sediment, the MDEQ has issued a limit fish consumption advisory for both benthic and predatory fish at the refuge. All of the refuges are dependent on watersheds and streams and rivers to provide some of the water resources to manage water-dependent habitats. Principal drainage on Dahomey refuge, for example, consists of four bayous in addition to man-made ditches and canals. On Coldwater River refuge, where 90 percent of the unit is inundated each spring, floodwaters come from the Tallahatchie, the Yocona, and Little Tallahatchie rivers, as well as the Panola-Quitman Floodway. Studies have shown that runoff from agricultural fields and upstream gravel mining operations has resulted in excessive siltation and turbidity in water bodies throughout the Complex. Wetlands have been filled in, hydrology has been altered, trees have been killed by deepening deposits, and open water habitats have become shallow due to silt-laden waters traversing these areas. This has resulted in loss of important wildlife habitat, including migratory bird habitat, and has increased densities of undesirable fish populations (e.g., common carp, buffalo, gar, bowfin, and freshwater drum). This is supported by studies conducted by the U.S. Geological Survey. In order to maintain ecological integrity on the refuges, water quality issues, both on and off refuges, need to be addressed.

Priority Public Use

The National Wildlife Refuge Improvement Act of 1997 has established six priority public uses on refuge lands when they are compatible and desirable for that specific refuge. These priority uses are hunting, fishing, wildlife observation, wildlife photography, and environmental education and interpretation. The visitor services program of the Complex has always focused on "traditional" recreational uses, primarily hunting, with little emphasis on interpretive and educational activities due to the lack of staff. This lack of effective outreach is evidenced by the general public, either misunderstanding the purposes of the North Mississippi National Wildlife Refuges Complex and the National Wildlife Refuge System, or simply being unaware of their existence. It is the intent of the Complex to expand its visitor services to include these historically "non-traditional" uses (e.g., wildlife observation, wildlife photography, and environmental education and interpretation) without alienating the more "traditional" visitors. The challenge will be to what degree these expanded activities can be provided while minimizing conflicts among user groups.

Hunting

Dahomey and Tallahatchie refuges allow hunting for squirrel, rabbit, bobwhite quail, raccoon, deer, turkey (Dahomey only), waterfowl, snipe, woodcock and feral hogs. In addition, there are youth hunts for deer, turkey (Dahomey only), waterfowl and squirrel. Special facilities are available for mobility-impaired hunters. Each hunter must obtain from one of the Hunter Information Stations a user information card. The card must be filled out before hunting and displayed on the vehicle dash. Prior to leaving the refuge, the reverse side of the card must be completed and deposited at one of the Hunter Information Stations. There is a $12.50 permit required to hunt on Dahomey refuge, Tallahatchie refuge, and select Farm Service Agency tracts (small game only).

At present, hunting is not allowed on Coldwater River refuge, and one issue is whether or not this policy should be maintained. Another issue is whether to allow off road vehicles (ORVs) for hunting. The Complex does not currently permit the use of ORVs for hunting (retrieving game) due to their disruption of wildlife and damage to habitat. Overall, there appears to be broad appreciation among the public that the refuges in the Complex offer some of the best hunting opportunities in the vicinity, a sentiment expressed during public scoping meetings for the CCP.

Fishing

Coldwater River, Dahomey, and Tallahatchie refuges are currently open to fishing at certain periods throughout the year. There are, however, very few fishing opportunities on the Complex. The Complex does not support a high-quality fishery. Only a very limited number of permits for fishing was issued in 2003.

The Fisheries and Aquatic Resources Strategic Plan for the Southeast Region is a Service management document completed in 1997. The plan recognizes fisheries and aquatic resource management as important. Service activities, both on and off refuges, list several goals in pursuit of these endeavors. Goal 5 directs the Service to "Provide for sustainable recreational fishing opportunities in the southeast adequate to meet public needs." Objective F under this goal states, "Provide and maintain recreational fishing opportunities on FWS (Service) lands" and lists several tasks in conjunction with this pursuit, including "…establish new recreational fishing opportunities," "increase access to recreational fishing sites on and across FWS (Service) lands," and "develop methods for integrated management of migratory bird populations, other animals and plants, and recreational fisheries on FWS (Service) lands."

Sedimentation, contaminants, and access have been some of the issues hindering the development of a quality fishing program. Most waterways within the Complex have been altered or are artificial, such as former catfish ponds, preventing or impeding natural stocking of desirable gamefish into these waters. This has resulted in larger concentrations of "rough fish." In addition, the Mississippi Department of Environmental Quality (MDEQ) has issued a health recommendation to not eat bottom feeders more than two times per month, due to their contaminant concentrations. There is a need for consistent notices at boat launching ramps and other places where fisherman can be contacted about MDEQ warning.

Fishing opportunities at the Complex can be maintained and expanded by developing kids fishing days, parking areas, one or more handicapped-accessible piers, and maintaining bank fishing areas.

Wildlife Observation and Photography

Currently, there are limited wildlife viewing opportunities on the Complex. Coldwater River refuge has the greatest potential for wildlife observation. The number and variety of shorebirds, wading birds, and waterfowl there create a spectacular sight. The proximity of this north-most refuge to Memphis, and to Interstate 55 provide a potentially larger population base from which to attract visitors. The Audubon Society is proposing to develop a Great River Road Birding Trail that would include Dahomey refuge.

The Complex has two photo-blinds available for wildlife photographers that can be used on a first-come, first-serve basis. There are a number of opportunities for expanding wildlife observation and photography on the Complex, including development of trails and observation decks at some of the more opportune sites on all three refuges. For example, a walking trail around the impoundments at Coldwater River refuge and an accompanying observation deck would offer wildlife watchers and photographers great views of shorebirds, wading birds, and waterfowl. Efforts to increase such opportunities appear to have the broad support of surrounding communities and the public.

Environmental Education and Interpretation

Previously, the Complex had a staff person who developed a significant environmental program that included providing programs to schools and developing kits on endangered species and wetlands for teachers to use. While demand was high for these programs, the Complex lost this position. Groups that are interested in partnering with the Complex to develop environmental education opportunities include Delta State University and the Audubon Society. There are four universities within a 1-hour drive of Grenada, each of which has an annual conservation festival. Environmental education could be expanded in a number of ways, such as staging events like career days, developing an educational natural trail, and using seasonal hires and volunteers to develop and implement environmental education programs, camps, and kits/trunks.

Currently, there is limited interpretation on the three refuges. Through a partnership with Ducks Unlimited, an interpretive trail (Hasserway Trail) was developed at Grenada Lake Recreation Area. There are no interpretive panels at any of the refuges. These can be developed and installed at all three refuges. Interpretation can be organized by themes that reinforce important messages for visitors. Examples of such themes include migratory birds (both waterfowl and neotropical), reforestation, history of Farm Service Agency lands, culture, and history of the area, bottomland hardwoods, and the wildlife that depend on this diminished habitat.

The Complex already engages in a significant amount of outreach. Staff persons are members of local civic groups like the Chamber of Commerce. They help judge the local science fairs and have participated in community events at the Grenada Lake Recreation Area. When staff is available, the refuge conducts some special events, such as Migratory Bird Day or National Wildlife Refuge Week. Opportunities for improving outreach include developing a more extensive website, placing general brochures in the State's Welcome Center on Interstate 55, and placing a portable display in appropriate locations and a permanent display at the Grenada Lake Visitor Center, which is operated by the Corps of Engineers.

Interior Roads and Trails

All roads within the Complex that are currently open to the public are in fair to good shape and usually provide all weather access with a minimal clearance two-wheel drive vehicle (except when flooded during the winter months). Federal, state or county highways and U.S. Army Corps of Engineers levees currently run adjacent to or bisect portions of all refuges within the Complex. Coldwater River refuge is presently not open to the public. Many of the current interior roads were constructed to facilitate farming and/or timber harvest. As refuge programs were developed, only certain roads and trails were maintained for public and refuge use.

Two Executive Orders govern off-road vehicle (ORV) use on federal public lands: Executive Order 11644, signed by President Nixon in 1972, and Executive Order 11989, signed by President Carter in 1977. Together these orders require that ORVs on public lands must be managed to "protect the resources of those lands, to promote the safety of all users of those lands, and to minimize conflicts among the various uses of those lands." The orders also require that when ORV routes are designated, federal land managers must minimize damage to soils, watershed, vegetation, and other land resources, minimize wildlife harassment and impacts to wildlife habitat, and minimize conflicts between ORV use and other uses of the land. These policies and orders have a direct effect on our ban of ORVs on the refuges of the Complex. Studies have shown that the excessive off-trail use of ORVs can have a detrimental effect on habitats. These impacts can include soil erosion, altering natural water flow, destroying the root systems of plants, and spreading noxious and invasive weeds. Thus, we have prohibited their use on the Complex. Also, due to the small size of the refuges within the Complex and several good access points, there is little to no need for ORV use. Most Complex users have no problem with this policy, though some hunters have requested the use of ORVs to retrieve game.

Visitor Facilities

Currently, the Complex has two offices. The first office is located in Grenada, Mississippi, on Highway 7 and is the headquarters for the Complex. This office receives about 11,000 visitors annually. The second office is located at Dahomey refuge in Boyle, Mississippi, on Hwy 446. Both offices serve the purpose of providing office space for staff and general information for visitors. At present, no refuge of the Complex, or the Complex itself, has a visitor center. Furthermore, neither Tallahatchie nor Coldwater River refuges have manned offices.

Although Tallahatchie and Dahomey refuges offer several miles of hiking trails through the use of gravel roads and abandoned logging roads, the Complex is significantly lacking designated interpretive trails and signage.

Recreation Opportunities on Farm Service Agency Fee Title Tracts

The Complex contains 128 separate Farm Service Agency tracts, totaling over 17,000 acres and dispersed throughout the Complex work area. The public use on these tracts is largely confined to small game hunting on a limited number of properties. These tracts of land are scattered throughout northern Mississippi and most are blocks of land smaller than 200 acres.

CULTURAL RESOURCES MANAGEMENT

With the enactment of the Antiquities Act of 1906, the Federal Government recognized the importance of cultural resources to the national identity and sought to protect archaeological sites and historic structures on those lands owned, managed, or controlled by the United States. The body of historic preservation laws has grown dramatically since 1906. The National Historic Preservation Act of 1966 and its Section 104 have a particular bearing on all federal agencies. Several themes recur in the laws and the promulgating regulations. They include: 1) each agency is to systematically inventory the "historic properties" on their holdings and to scientifically assess each property's eligibility for the National Register of Historic Places; 2) federal agencies are to consider the impacts to cultural resources during the agencies' management activities and seek to avoid or mitigate adverse impacts; 3) the protection of cultural resources from looting and vandalism are to be accomplished through a mix of informed management, law enforcement efforts, and public education; and 4) the increasing role of consultation with groups, such as Native American tribes and African American communities, to address how a project or management activity may impact specific archaeological sites and landscapes deemed important to those groups.

Several targeted cultural resource inventories have been completed at different sites throughout the Complex. Whenever the Complex proposes an action that will result in excavation or substantial ground disturbance, like constructing a moist-soil unit, it conducts a cultural resources survey. However, no overall inventory of the Complex's cultural resources has been carried out to date, and the Complex currently has no Cultural Resources Management Plan.

PRIVATE LANDS AND FOREST FRAGMENTATION

The three refuges that comprise the North Mississippi National Wildlife Refuges Complex are truly islands in a sea of privately owned agricultural lands, particularly Dahomey refuge. The refuges, along with other federal- and state-owned tracts, are some of the best examples of the bottomland habitat that once dominated the landscape of the Mississippi Delta. In fact, Dahomey refuge's 8,126-acre bottomland hardwood forest is the largest contiguous tract of bottomland hardwood habitat outside the Mississippi River main line levee in northwest Mississippi [2002 Annual Narrative, p. vii]. Continual threats to these remaining habitats and the fish and wildlife that inhabit them are fragmentation and destruction through intensive agriculture, one-time high-grade timber harvests, federal flood control projects, and certain catfish farming practices.

It is recognized by all federal land managers that there will never be enough land owned to meet the habitat needs of resident and migratory wildlife with which managers have been entrusted. The vast majority of these needed lands is in private ownership. While many landowners are actively managing their lands for wildlife, many would benefit from assistance, both in knowledge and resources, to provide the optimal benefit to some of the more imperiled wildlife species, including forest-interior songbirds and endangered and threatened species. With limited resources, it is necessary to identify a management "Focus Area" in which to concentrate efforts. This area would also be studied for those lands that would be suitable and beneficial for inclusion in the Refuge System to meet the goals and objectives of the Complex, and national, state, and regional plans to preserve and protect wildlife, fisheries, and their habitats.

Funding and Staffing

Funding has been insufficient to support current refuge programs. Lack of staff and inadequate facilities has prevented the Complex from realizing its purposes and management objectives. While this is true for all the refuges within the Complex, it is especially noteworthy at Coldwater River refuge, where intensive management of the former catfish pond moist-soil management complex is highly recommended; there is simply not adequate staffing. Overall, at the Complex, the lack of adequate staff has had a negative impact on biological, maintenance, and visitor services programs, including degrading facilities, limiting wildlife and habitat projects, and restricting the development of a visitor services program.

Biological and public use review teams, as well as the public, identified a need for additional staff. The biological review identifies a need to add two or three biologists, a forester, and three or four biological/forestry technicians/equipment operators to the current staff. The top recommendation in the public use review is for a full-time public use staff person.

Three full-time employees departed in 2002. There is currently no staff based at Coldwater River or Tallahatchie refuges. Development/management there is handled by the North Mississippi National Wildlife Refuges Complex.

Monitoring, Inventory, Research, and Adaptive Management

Management decisions are currently based on the best available data and past personal experiences. In preparing for the biological review and further evidenced by comments received by the review team, it is apparent that there are vast data gaps with regard to the habitat, wildlife, fisheries, and biodiversity within the Complex.

Issues addressed by the review team and identified by refuge staff include lack of baseline information on many of the fish, plants, insects, and wildlife dependent on these refuge lands. The review team also recognized the lack of scientifically sound inventory and monitoring methods which, in turn, hinders the setting of Complex and national objectives. In addition, a lack of information on the current population, rate of spread, and structured control measures of invasive species has resulted in random control methods that may not be the most effective techniques in the long term.

There is a tremendous opportunity to cooperate with partners, including other federal agencies, state agencies, non-governmental organizations, and universities to conduct research on the various resources and habitat restoration programs being carried out on the Complex. There are several projects that have been completed and contributed to our understanding of the Complex resources. However, there are many more opportunities to actively pursue partnerships that not only can benefit the Complex, but also further other management and restoration efforts throughout the LMRV.

IV. Comprehensive Conservation Plan

INTRODUCTION

This proposed plan contains the goals, objectives, and strategies that will be used to achieve the refuge vision over the next 15 years.

Three other alternatives for managing the Complex were considered and the planning team chose Alternative D (Enhanced Wildlife Management and Public Use Program) as the preferred alternative or proposed action. The other alternatives evaluated were Alternative A - No Action (Current Management Direction), Alternative B, Public Use Emphasis, and Alternative C, Wildlife Management Emphasis. All of these alternatives are described and evaluated in the Environmental Assessment.

Implementing the preferred alternative will result in a diversity of habitats for a variety of wildlife and fish species while meeting the Complex's primary purpose of providing habitat for wintering waterfowl. Specific results will include increased waterfowl and songbird use and production; increased habitat for forest interior-dependent wildlife; enhanced resident wildlife populations; restored wetlands and hydrology; and greater opportunities for a variety of compatible wildlife-dependent public use.

An overriding concern reflected in this CCP is that wildlife conservation is the first priority in refuge management. Public use is allowed if compatible and appropriate with wildlife and habitat conservation. Wildlife-dependent public uses – hunting, fishing, wildlife observation, photography, environmental education and interpretation – will be emphasized. Each of these activities is specifically mentioned in the National Wildlife Refuge System Improvement Act of 1997 as being a generally appropriate use of the National Wildlife Refuge System. Of course, for any given refuge, managers must still determine the compatibility of a particular use given specific circumstances.

VISION

The vision for the North Mississippi National Wildlife Refuges Complex is as follows:

Based on sound science, the North Mississippi National Wildlife Refuges Complex will protect, manage, and, where appropriate, restore a system of lands and waters to provide for wildlife, fisheries, and plants and their habitats within northern Mississippi for the benefit of present and future generations of Americans. These refuges contain some of the most important migratory bird habitats in the National Wildlife Refuge System and will continue to be focal points for the protection, management, restoration, and enjoyment of resident wildlife, migratory birds, and other federal trust resources within the Lower Mississippi River Alluvial Valley and Central Gulf ecosystems.

The Complex will expand its role in land protection efforts by acquiring, within approved acquisition boundaries, additional habitats for migratory birds and other federal trust species and by working with all interested parties to promote conservation efforts on non-refuge lands. The Complex will play a critical role in reducing forest fragmentation and lead in reforestation and restoration of bottomland hardwoods and other wetlands. The Complex will provide and promote research opportunities that address an understanding of the resource management needs of the Lower Mississippi River and Central Gulf Ecosystems.

The Complex will build partnerships to promote the ecological health of the landscape, wildlife-dependent recreation, and the historical and cultural resources of the region. When compatible, wildlife-dependent recreational opportunities for hunting, fishing, wildlife observation, wildlife photography, and environmental education and interpretation will be provided while promoting the public's understanding of the purposes for the Complex and the mission of the Refuge System.

COMPREHENSIVE CONSERVATION PLAN

GOALS, OBJECTIVES, AND STRATEGIES

The goals, objectives, and strategies outlined below are the Service's response to the issues, concerns, and needs expressed by the planning team, the refuge staff, and the public. These goals, objectives, and strategies reflect the Service's commitment to achieve the mandates of the National Wildlife Refuge System Improvement Act of 1997, the mission of the Refuge System, the North American Waterfowl Management Plan, the Partners-in-Flight Plan, the vision for the North Mississippi National Wildlife Refuges Complex, and the purposes of Coldwater River, Dahomey, and Tallahatchie refuges. Depending upon the availability of funds and staff, the Service intends to accomplish these goals, objectives, and strategies during the next 15 years.

Goal 1 – Promote the conservation and management of migratory birds within northern Mississippi in a manner that supports treaties and national and international plans and initiatives.

Background: The paramount purpose of the Complex is to provide habitat for migratory birds. Each of the three refuges has been nominated as an "Important Bird Area," based on significant numbers of birds found on the refuges at different times of the year.

The Complex has a variety of habitats, including flooded timber, grasslands, ponds, and moist soil, as well as management programs including croplands and waterfowl sanctuary areas, that provide feeding, resting, and loafing habitat for tens of thousands of wintering ducks and geese each year and nesting habitat for wood ducks and hooded mergansers.

Non-game waterbird groups include shorebirds, marsh and wading birds, and colonial waterbirds. The most important foraging habitats for these groups consist of former commercial catfish ponds converted to moist-soil management units. Breeding colonial/wading birds find nesting habitat in brakes, swamps, and a few wooded impoundments throughout the Complex.

Objective 1-1: Migratory Waterfowl
Over the next 15 years, provide habitat to increase current objectives for migrating and wintering waterfowl as shown in Table 15 below. Annually monitor waterfowl response to management actions.

Discussion: Concern over waterfowl population declines in the 1980s resulted in the establishment of the North American Waterfowl Management Plan, which focused the attention of federal, state, and private conservation groups on critical wintering and breeding areas. The LMRVJV was selected as one of the wintering focus areas. In setting habitat objectives for the LMRVJV, it was agreed that foraging habitat was the limiting factor and objectives were set based on food production and acres by habitat type for the complex of habitats, including harvested and unharvested cropland, moist-soil areas, and flooded forest land. Each of these habitat types is required to provide the variety of food resources (i.e., native seeds, small grains, and invertebrates) required by waterfowl wintering in the LMRV. Step-down objectives were established by state for public and private lands. Each segment of habitat must be provided if the wintering waterfowl needs in the LMRVJV area are to be met. These step-down objectives are shown in Table 5 of this CCP.

Table 15. Habitat objectives for migratory waterfowl (acres)

Habitat	Current Objective	Increased Objective
Coldwater River NWR		
Forested wetland	700	2520
Moist-soil	190	684
Dahomey NWR		
Forested wetland	750	900
Moist-soil	318	382
Unharvested crop	218	262
Tallahatchie NWR		
Forested wetland	80	528
Moist-soil	852	5623
Unharvested crop	212	1399

Strategies:

Prepare a Biological Inventory/Monitoring Plan by 2008, which includes refuge-specific waterfowl inventory and monitoring protocols, standardized routes, and computerized databases.

Conduct waterfowl inventories at least twice monthly (October to mid-March). Couple aerial counts with ground counts on the more visible areas of the refuge to establish a correction factor for aerial surveys.

Continue the long-term process of seeking willing sellers of lands with value or potential value as waterfowl habitat within the authorized acquisition boundaries of each refuge.

Objective 1-2: Wood Duck Nest Boxes

Per the biological review, provide year-round habitat and maintain a program of 600 well-maintained nest boxes throughout the Complex necessary to enhance wood duck populations.

Discussion: Wood ducks are common year-round residents of the LMRV and the Complex. Preferred habitats include forested wetlands, wooded and shrub swamps, tree-lined rivers, streams, sloughs, and beaver ponds. Wood ducks seek food in the form of acorns, other soft and hard mast, weed seeds, and invertebrates found in shallow flooded timber, shrub swamps, and along stream banks. They loaf and roost in more secluded areas and dense shrub swamps. Wood ducks are cavity nesters, seeking cavities in trees within a mile of water. Brood survival is higher in situations where nests are close to water. Due to loss of bottomland hardwoods and over-harvest, wood ducks were almost extirpated in the early 1900s. Even today, forestry practices and competition for nest sites from a host of other species limit reproduction. Nest boxes are commonly used to supplement natural cavities and increase local production of wood ducks. Box programs are not a panacea. They must be maintained – requiring time to clean and repair at least annually. Production can be increased by more frequent checks and cleaning of boxes, but this must be weighed with other time constraints.

Currently there are approximately 75 nest boxes on the Complex. Adequate habitat is available to support 2-3 times as many on existing lands in the refuges. The numerical target of 600 nest boxes assumes both intensification of efforts on existing habitats and expansion of lands within the refuges up to the authorized boundaries.

Strategies:

Place a minimum of 50 new boxes per year for the next 10 years as habitat and staffing limitations allow.

Replace and relocate boxes to meet regional guidelines as existing wood duck nest boxes deteriorate.

Place boxes such that they are not visible from one box to the next or at least 100 yards apart.

Place boxes in areas that are readily accessible for semiannual inspections.

Check boxes at least twice annually (once pre-season and once at the end of the first peak of nesting).

Place predator guards on all box structures.

Place boxes no more than one mile from a water source and close to available scrub/shrub habitat. Where feasible and where dump nesting does not occur, place boxes over standing water.

Maintain all cull trees that have or may develop natural nesting cavities and are within one mile of a water source. This will also benefit many other cavity nesting species (woodpeckers, mergansers, squirrels, etc.).

Place boxes above mean high water mark to prevent them from being flooded and to facilitate management of the program (i.e., maintenance, box checks, etc.).
Evaluate nest efficiency and nesting success in boxes and adjust the program accordingly.

Evaluate duckling survival in and use of various habitats on each refuge.

Objective 1-3: Wood Duck Banding
Increase the preseason (July-September 15) flyway and state banding objective by eight times (corresponding to the increase in nest boxes), with increased emphasis on the entire Complex contributing to these data.

Discussion: Because wood ducks are secretive, it is difficult to monitor their population status and survival using visual counts similar to the method used for most other species of waterfowl. Pre-season wood duck banding is the only method used for estimating wood duck populations, survival, and possibly other population parameters. State banding quotas by sex and age have been established by the Mississippi and Atlantic flyways and the state quotas have been allocated to various state and federal facilities around Mississippi. The Complex contributes toward achieving the annual Mississippi pre-season banding quota. The pre-season period extends from July through September and, for statistical purposes, it is assumed that all ducks that are in the same age and sex class and banded during this 3-month period, have the same survival rate. In Mississippi and several other southern states with a special wood duck or teal season, the pre-season banding period is stopped September 15 to prevent any potential conflicts (i.e., baiting) with hunters.

All wood duck quotas assigned to the Complex are for the preseason (July - September 30) banding period. In the past, the Complex banded quite a few adult hens in boxes prior to July 1. These ducks are more vulnerable to predation during periods of nesting and brood rearing and have survival rates lower than those banded later in summer. Breeding season banding may occur when staff is available to assess survival rates and return of nesting hens.

Strategies:

Expand banding program to include more sites throughout the Complex, particularly as the wood duck box program is expanded.

As funding becomes available, hire two, GS-5, six-month seasonal biological technicians to monitor and maintain wood duck boxes and conduct preseason trapping and banding program throughout the Complex.

Continue to examine the most effective means of trapping and banding wood ducks; ensuring the objective is met with minimal effort and resources.

Objective 1-4: Marsh and Wading Birds
Within three years of the plan's approval, determine marsh and wading bird use of wetland habitats, with special emphasis on the black rail, yellow rail, king rail, American bittern, least bittern, and wood stork. Annually conduct management activities that will enhance marsh bird habitat.

Discussion: In addition to wetlands such as the former catfish ponds, rice fields and moist-soil units would be the primary habitat for this group on the Complex. Included in this group are "secretive marshbirds" (e.g., rails, bitterns, grebes, moorhens, gallinules, and coots).

No specific population objectives have been established for these species at this time within the LMRV, but survey/monitoring protocols (secretive marshbird surveys) can be used for tracking peak movements in and out of the Complex and to document responses to habitat management.

"Secretive marshbird surveys" employ a taped playback-response protocol along a designated route for pied-billed grebes (breeding), rails and bitterns. The protocols developed were intended to survey breeding birds, but these should also be useful for surveying birds during migration (and winter) as most rails vocalize all year.

Priority species include the following: High – black rail, yellow rail; Moderate – American bittern, king rail, bald eagle, northern harrier; Local or Regional Interest – least bittern.

Strategies:

Collect baseline data on marshbird populations, use of impoundment habitats and responses to various water management regimes, with special emphasis on black and yellow rails and least bitterns.

Track bird use by date, location, and habitat type (vegetated, flooded moist-soil areas, flooded rice fields, and permanent impoundments containing a significant amount of rank emergent vegetation in shallow water).

By 2007, establish a route along levee roads most likely to support marsh habitats for summer, migration, and winter secretive marshbird counts, with summer counts focusing on black rail, king rail, and least bittern. Surveys can be set up as a random sample of stops across the refuge or may be targeted on actively managed versus unmanaged units to judge responses to management practices.

By 2007, establish an additional roadside route within each refuge's acquisition boundary along wetlands which potentially support marshbirds.

Conduct surveys three times per month, with priority on mid-March to mid-April and mid-August to late November. The direction of the survey should be alternated from one survey to the next.

Through the effective use of moist-soil management, maintain a diversity of marsh plant communities among impoundments to support an equally diverse marsh associated avifauna.

<u>Objective 1-5: Colonial Waterbirds</u>
Within two years of the plan's approval, identify, map, and develop monitoring protocol for colonial waterbird rookeries and provide foraging habitat.

Discussion: Complex provides excellent habitat for breeding colonial wading birds. For example, Coldwater River refuge has a rookery dominated by great blue herons and great egrets. Shallow water areas found on the refuge during late summer and fall provide critical foraging opportunities for long-legged wading birds such as wood storks and herons, egrets, and ibis. The primary management tools are to 1) protect rookeries from disturbance and, where possible, maintain standing water under nest trees throughout the nesting season to minimize nest predation by raccoons, and 2) incorporate water level management for wading birds into shallow water management for waterfowl and shorebirds. (In the shallow water habitat provided for wading birds, they will be searching for foraging habitat rich in small fish and crustaceans, a much different food source than is targeted in waterfowl and shorebird management.)

Priority species include the following: High - least tern (interior population-foraging on open water), white ibis (breeding?, migrant), American white pelican (wintering); Local or Regional Interest - wood stork (migrant), roseate spoonbill (migrant), glossy ibis (migrant), anhinga (breeding), great blue heron (breeding), great egret (breeding), snowy egret (breeding), little blue heron (breeding), cattle egret (breeding), green heron (breeding), yellow-crowned night-heron (breeding).

Strategies:

By 2009, provide additional nesting structures to expand rookeries.

By 2010, provide data on nesting success to the state coordinator.

Locate, geo-reference, protect from disturbance, and monitor (nesting population by species) colonial waterbird rookery sites in the Complex work area, especially on refuge properties.

Conduct aerial survey of work area to locate rookeries in April and determine potential disturbance factors. Survey active rookeries in June following existing Colonial Waterbird Monitoring Program guidelines established through the Mississippi Museum of Natural Science and coordinate data transfer to the Museum of Natural Science (contact Museum Ornithologist for information). This monitoring program may be modified to meet regional or national standards.

Record white pelican use on refuges to determine periods of use and peak annual populations. Make contact with local aquaculture facilities to gain information on the presence and numbers of pelicans in the area.

Where possible, provide foraging habitat by maintaining shallow ponds and "run-out" sites in summer and fall. Attempt to integrate waterbird foraging habitat management into waterfowl and shorebird habitat management.

Work with the LMRVJV Office to update colonial waterbird step-down objectives for the Complex.

Objective 1-6: Shorebirds (including Woodcock)
By 2014, provide 653 acres of high quality migration habitat for shorebirds, including woodcock. Annually monitor shorebird use and contribute data to the International Shorebird Survey.

Discussion: Throughout the LMRV, habitat for spring (northward) shorebird migration is probably provided in most years with normal rainfall and evaporation rates. Peak migration is expected April to mid-May (but extends from mid-March to late-May).

Southbound migration starts in early July, peaks August through September, and ends by mid-October. Disruption of normal evaporation patterns over the last 50 years in the LMRV and the lack of rainfall in this highly modified hydrological environment lead to a severe shorebird habitat shortage. Opportunities do exist, however, to provide good quality habitat for southbound migrants in fall. A focus on providing shorebird habitat is considered the highest non-game bird priority for the Complex. The current LMRVJV coordinated shorebird (fall migration) habitat objective for Coldwater River refuge is 225 acres of mudflats and for Farm Service Agency tracts is an additional 100-200 acres.

Within the larger context, about 1,500 acres of habitat have been tentatively identified for Mississippi towards supporting a tentative LMRV population objective of 500,000 shorebirds during southbound migration. Habitat objectives for shorebirds are tentative with the assumptions that 1) an average shorebird weighs 45 grams; 2) stays at a site for 10 days; 3) requires about 8 grams of food per day; 4) chironomids are the primary food source; and that 5) they must gain 1 gram of biomass per day to continue their migration.

Priority species include the following: High - stilt sandpiper, buff-breasted sandpiper, western sandpiper, short-billed dowitcher, Wilson's phalarope; Moderate - semipalmated sandpiper, sanderling, greater yellowlegs, dunlin, common snipe, least sandpiper, willet, American avocet, and killdeer.

Shorebird habitat should be a combination of mudflats and shallow water (0-4") with a dense invertebrate population available July 15–October 31. Monitoring shorebird responses to habitat management would include a greater focus on habitat conditions, including a weekly survey of water levels, vegetative response to water regimes, invertebrate food productivity, and whether shorebirds, in general, are present or not.

American woodcock populations in this region have declined an average of 1.6 percent per year from1968 – 2002 (Kelley 2002). Population declines are thought to be the result of land use changes associated with land conversion and the maturing of forest habitats. Woodcock numbers appear low on the Complex because of insufficient nesting and brood habitat types. Woodcock and quail need exposed soil and patchy cover for optimum foraging. In addition, the woodcock needs moist thickets containing high understory stem basal area (BA) with little or no ground litter.

Wintering habitat includes moist bottomland hardwood forests with dense brush and understory, especially when found in close association with agricultural fields and old field habitat. These sites are typically wet thickets with a high density of plant stems with the ground open and clear. Typical cover includes privet, cane, and briars that result from openings in the canopy. The scrub/shrub and dense habitats found in certain portions of the refuges provide good daytime cover for woodcock. These habitats result from reforestation, old field succession, and ice storms.

At dusk, woodcocks move to open or brushy fields to forage and conduct courtship activities. These habitats include agricultural fields that were not fall disked and sparse grasslands that may have received a cool fall burn to create patchy openings of exposed soil interspersed between grass clumps 1 to 3 feet in height. Woodcock are closely tied to earthworms, which are their major food resource. The grassland areas provide habitat preferred by other priority species (e.g., Northern bobwhite and winter grassland birds).

Strategies:

Conduct annual shorebird surveys following the International Shorebird Survey (ISS) protocol to document shorebird use of the Complex overall and peak passage of the various shorebird species. The ISS is essentially a route selected by refuge staff using existing roads and covering as much potential habitat as possible.

Investigate and research methods of habitat management favoring proliferation of Chironomids in the moist-soil rotation scheme (shorebird phase). Drawdowns among moist-soil units should be staggered and overlapped and continue slowly to provide mud-flat habitat throughout the entire migration period, mid-July to November.

Develop a moist-soil habitat rotation scheme which provides fall shorebird habitat on at least 25 percent of the acreage being rotated.

Install tilt pipes for precise water control in all impoundments used for shorebird management.

Keep records of habitat conditions, including water levels (weekly). Record dates that mudflats are exposed.

Develop forest management plans that provide preferred woodcock habitat that include: Diurnal cover and foraging habitat (i.e., thickets and shrub areas with high vertical stem density in the understory and wet soil). These habitats can be created in existing forest stands through patch or group thinning and patch clearcuts that also benefit other high priority bird species; and nocturnal habitat (wet agricultural fields (not fall disked) and wet "old field" or grassland habitats with exposed soil and patchy cover 1 to 3 feet in height created by cool fall burns). The 275-acre field at Coldwater River refuge should be maintained as an old field by strip disking and burning portions on a 3-year rotation.

Take advantage of rights-of-way and other permanent forest openings to create woodcock habitat.

Inventory suitable woodcock wintering habitat on the refuges. Conduct evening flight counts, nighttime counts, and flush counts to assess woodcock presence/absence and relative abundance on the refuge at least twice monthly from mid-November to mid-March. Night-lighting in the fields is another option preferred by some experienced in woodcock surveys to determine use.

Utilize hunter surveys and flush counts using dogs (pointers) to assess presence/absence and relative densities of woodcock.

Preserve all "cane" habitat areas on the refuge and recognize the need to maintain scrub/shrub wetlands/uplands preferred by this species.

Determine the feasibility of developing woodcock habitat demonstration sites to serve as educational opportunities for public and private land managers, realizing that habitat management for woodcock is similar to management for other priority species.

Objective1-7: Forest Birds
Within two years of the plan's approval, survey forest breeding birds with point counts tied to spatially discrete, georeferenced, habitat-specific locations to assess the preferred habitat, presence/absence, and relative abundance of all forest breeding species

Discussion: No comprehensive survey of forest birds, breeding or migratory, has been completed on the Complex. As such, there is no information on what areas and habitats are most widely used.

Despite being highly fragmented, the productive hardwood forests of the Mississippi Delta play an important role in providing migration and breeding habitat for forest breeding birds. By increasing block size and improving timber stand structure, there is potential for this habitat to play a much larger role for this wide range of non-game birds. As it has with setting waterfowl habitat objectives, the LMRVJV has undertaken a coordinated effort to identify Bird Conservation Areas (BCA's) throughout the LMRV for restoration of forest blocks that support sustainable breeding populations of area-sensitive, high priority forest breeding bird species. There are seven BCA's in the Complex work area with established forest block size objectives. Selective reforestation through private land programs or expansion of existing refuges would contribute toward forest block objectives.

Bird population data are very limited for many of the refuges in Region 4. The Complex is no exception. Bird population data are critical for establishing baseline conditions that can later be used to assess management actions and compare future habitat conditions. Forest breeding birds should be surveyed with point counts using the protocol in Hamel et al., (1996).

In terms of achieving population objectives for forest landbirds, an average of 6-9 pairs of Swainson's warblers (drier end of the spectrum) and 11-19 pairs of prothonotary warblers (wetter end of the spectrum) per 100 acres within optimal habitat could be considered as indicators of healthy neotropical migratory bird populations overall. Spot-map protocols could provide these data. Monitoring nest success would provide better evidence of population health.

Overall future desired condition of mature wetland forests would be to emphasize: (1) increasing stand structural diversity by favoring retention of largest trees (removing surrounding potentially competing trees), (2) opening up stands to allow light to reach the ground in support of better understory structure, and (3) group selection-sized openings to further structural complexity and support regeneration of shade-intolerant tree species (oaks) where needed. (Refer to "General Recommendations for Hardwood Forest Management to Improve Wildlife Habitat in the LMRV.")

Priority species include the following: Extremely High - Swainson's warbler (breeding - nest in dense understory, forages on open moist ground), swallow-tailed kite (breeding - nest in superemergent trees, possibly cypress), cerulean warbler (breeding - nest and forage in canopy of sawtimber trees); High - prothonotary warbler (breeding - cavity nester, usually in trees over open water), red-headed woodpecker (breeding - cavity nester), northern parula (breeding - canopy, usually with Spanish moss), Kentucky warbler (breeding - nest in patches of dense ground cover), yellow-billed Cuckoo (breeding - midstory and canopy), wood thrush (breeding - midstory, forage on moist ground), American woodcock (forages on open moist ground but under very dense understory cover), black duck (wintering - open water); Moderate - wood duck (breeding - cavity nesting over or near open water), Acadian flycatcher (breeding - open midstory), eastern wood-pewee (breeding - open canopy), Carolina chickadee (breeding - cavity nester), Mississippi kite (breeding - nest in trees along edges in open country), Baltimore oriole (breeding - scattered hardwoods in open country), ruby-throated hummingbird (breeding - woody vegetation in moist habitats, usually near tubular flowers), blue-gray gnatcatcher (breeding - mature and moist hardwood forests), hooded warbler (breeding - dense understory), bald eagle (breeding - nests in superemergent trees large enough to support massive nests), rusty blackbird (wintering - winter roost in canopy, forages on the ground); Local or Regional Interest - yellow-throated warbler (breeding - canopy, usually with Spanish moss), American redstart (breeding - hardwood forests, usually near water), yellow-throated vireo (breeding - open canopy), summer tanager (breeding - open canopy), pileated woodpecker and ivory-billed woodpecker (breeding - mature and extensive forest, with dead trees for nesting).

Strategies:

Over the life of the CCP, increase existing acreage of mature forested habitats and increase the vertical structural diversity of reforested sites to significantly improve habitat conditions for forest breeding birds, with emphasis on priority species to meet the objectives established by Partners-in-Flight and the LMRVJV [see Table 7].

Collect baseline bird population data and monitor bird population responses to habitat restoration and management using, at a minimum, point counts (with 30 or more points per refuge) that will provide data for both canopy and understory species. All habitat types should be sampled proportionately, according to their presence on the refuge. All data will be reported to the LMVJV office.

Conduct annual surveys using the established protocol.

Ensure that georeferenced (GPS) habitat data are collected and documented on all point locations. All data should be translated into a GIS format for analysis and distribution.

Generate a GIS layer that displays georeferenced survey points by habitat types and associated structure and species distribution and occurrence.

Conduct point count surveys once per year during mid to late May.

Conduct the point counts in the same sequence from one year to the next (i.e., same direction, and sequence of points within a morning and among mornings), with the same observer, if possible.

Compare productivity of breeding birds in mature forest adjacent to "hard" agricultural edges and adjacent to "soft" moist-soil, scrub/shrub or reforested edges.

Begin more involved protocols after collecting five years of baseline data. These protocols should address not only species occurrences, but also their relative rates of reproductive success and/or post-fledging survival in response to management protocols.

Use a combination of private lands, land acquisition, and on-refuge work to reforest some strategic tracts, increasing the forest block size of BCA's and providing the greatest benefits to priority forest breeding birds. The LMRVJV has developed a model and maps that show priority reforestation sites that will provide the greatest benefits for forest breeding birds. The long-term objective is to meet the forest core objectives for each of the BCA's in the Complex work area.

Objective 1-8: Scrub/Shrub Birds
Maintain existing early successional habitats along buffer strips and within two years after the plan's approval convert up to 10 percent of acquired agricultural lands throughout the Complex to scrub/shrub, supporting priority scrub/shrub breeding species.

Discussion: The extensive edge habitat and likely elevated numbers of nest predators and brown-headed cowbirds may work against having a healthy and complete forest breeding bird community until reforestation efforts are well-advanced. Scrub/shrub associated species are another group of vulnerable species within the southeast. These species are generally considered a lower priority than mature forest species within the LMRV, but possibly some species will benefit temporarily during the early years of reforestation, especially white-eyed vireo, painted bunting, and orchard oriole (only one record for Bell's vireo from the area - Tunica County, but areas on and around the refuge should be searched for the presence of this species). However, good opportunities for overall effective bird conservation through the establishment and maintenance of scrub/shrub sites throughout Complex, including edges and small blocks within existing refuges and many of the Farm Service Agency tracts. Many of these tracts are generally isolated from larger forest blocks.

Scrub/shrub species apparently are able to withstand cowbird and depredation problems better within smaller blocks of habitat (i.e., 50-100 acres, possibly as small as 25-acre patches) than mature forest priority species, many of which require thousands of contiguously forested acres. With better information, the project leader and staff may want to consider targeting certain sites for this habitat phase. Sites selected for long-term maintenance of scrub/shrub will require periodic disturbances. One option for minimizing the frequency of disturbance (to set back succession) necessary to maintain scrub/shrub habitat would be to plant areas with native fruit-producing, shrub species such as plum, swamp dogwood, devil's-walking-stick, deciduous holly, and various species of hawthorn.

Habitat for these species should increase on existing reforested areas during the next five years. Each of these fields should be monitored for use by these species. This could be accomplished by conducting a series of point counts (if the habitat patch allows for several points to be established).

Priority species include the following: High - painted bunting (breeding - dense thickets of shrubs, saplings, or second-growth trees), white-eyed vireo (breeding - dense, and usually moist thickets), Bell's vireo (breeding - streamside thickets or upland scrub oaks), orchard oriole (breeding - scattered hardwood trees in open country); Moderate - yellow-breasted chat (breeding - dense cover of shrubs or saplings), northern bobwhite (breeding - ground-nester), field sparrow (breeding?, winter).

Strategies:

Test restoration of scrub/shrub habitats using 500 acres of converted agricultural land in patches of 20 to 100 acres at 5 to 20 locations. In the long term (15 year planning horizon), monitor bird response and if not getting breeding priority species (see below) or if maintenance of scrub/shrub habitats is too costly, then these areas should be reforested - either through replanting in trees or through natural succession.

Maintain scrub/shrub habitat and structure (vegetation no more than 20 ft. high), through species planted, disking, chemicals, or burning to set back succession.

Monitor bird population presence and responses to habitat restoration using direct counts and point counts focusing on breeding painted buntings, white-eyed vireos, and orchard orioles.

Establish line transects through scrub/shrub habitats to monitor transient songbird occurrence and stop-over activities. Transects should be surveyed a minimum of weekly (or at least bi-weekly) during both spring and fall migrations. It is recommended that coverage of two routes on consecutive mornings, once each week, from the last week of March to the last week of May, and again from late August (early July if possible) to the end of October be surveyed.

Reevaluate newly acquired/protected lands for the value of maintaining the scrub/shrub habitats vs. reforesting these areas to contribute to the creation of interior forest habitats.

Objective 1-9: Grassland Birds
Maintain existing acres of grasslands and within five years of the plan's approval convert up to 10 percent of acquired agricultural lands throughout the Complex to grasslands to support priority grassland bird species. Conduct baseline information surveys and continue to monitor bird responses to management and habitat alterations.

Discussion: The emphasis on "grassland" habitat conditions used by high priority species on the Complex is likely restricted to forest restoration sites actually more often dominated by "brushy" annuals. Priority grassland species are mostly found at the Complex during migration and winter, but a few species may breed in small numbers. Recently planted reforestation sites should constitute the primary habitats on the refuge. However, higher sites with sandy soils (i.e., poorer quality sites) dominated by broomsedge (*Andropogon spp.*) should be maintained in particular for wintering LeConte's sparrows. Priority grassland species include sparrows (principally LeConte's, but also grasshopper and possibly lark), sedge wren, bobolink, and raptors (most notably bald eagle, northern harrier, short-eared owl, and loggerhead shrike).

No specific population objectives have been established for these species at this time within the LMRV, but survey and monitoring protocols (i.e., transects and area searches) can be used for tracking peak movements on and off of the refuges and to document responses to habitat management.

Priority species include the following: High - Henslow's sparrow (wintering), sedge wren (wintering), short-eared owl (wintering), LeConte's sparrow (wintering); Moderate - dickcissel (breeding - herbaceous cover where vegetation is at least 2 feet [0.6 m] high), northern bobwhite (breeding - ground-nester), loggerhead shrike (breeding - tree or shrub nesting, forages on ground), field sparrow (breeding - scattered saplings, shrubs, and tall herbaceous cover; wintering - dense cover of herbs, particular tall composites), northern harrier (wintering), grasshopper sparrow (wintering), field sparrow (breeding?, winter).

Strategies:

Create and maintain open grassland habitat for selected bird species. The most likely candidate areas are the 275-acre field at Coldwater River refuge and Farm Service Agency tracts with unsuccessful reforestation to date.

Determine the location of "hotspots" (e.g., poorer quality sites with sandy soils) and promote the development of grassy-herbaceous ground cover, in particular, broomsedge.

Determine the extent and evaluate the use of grasslands and associated bird communities using point count and transect (e.g., project prairie bird) protocols focusing on breeding and wintering species. Conduct 3-6 surveys per season with at least one or two within each of the following periods: (1) 15 November-31 December, (2) 1 January-15 February, and (3) 16 February-10 March.

Maintain grassland habitat through burning, disking, chemicals, and select plantings.

Delay mowing and burning of levees and fields from March through mid-August.

Establish at least one transect of 100 m in each discrete patch of grassland habitat and use project prairie bird protocol to count wintering bird populations (as other areas are located/added, add new transects). If these habitats do not receive the bird response or become unmanageable, consideration must be given to allowing these areas, which were probably forested under natural conditions, to return to a forest condition. Refuge priorities to maintain grassland habitat must be weighed against other habitat and population management priorities to most effectively meeting the refuge purposes with limited staff and equipment.

Objective 1-10: Raptors
Within two years of the plan's approval, determine the extent and evaluate the use of refuge habitats by raptors at a Complex-wide scale.

Discussion: The northern harrier and all other raptors, as well as the loggerhead shrike, are best surveyed along an established route (i.e., roadside survey). Conducting surveys at least twice per month from mid-September to the end of March is recommended for non-breeding populations, including transients (and may include some early breeding for some species). The refuge staff should also participate in the National Midwinter Bald Eagle Count and report the data to the Raptor Research and Technical Assistance Center in Boise, Idaho.

Priority species include the following: Extremely High - swallow-tailed kite (migration, breeding - nest in superemergent trees, possibly cypress), Moderate - Mississippi kite (breeding - nest in trees along edges in open country), loggerhead shrike (breeding - nest in tree or shrub, forages on ground, wintering), northern harrier (wintering), bald eagle (wintering, nesting possible - nests in superemergent trees large enough to support massive nests).

Strategies:

Provide perching and nesting structures where necessary to enhance populations.

Implement a network of roadside surveys for wintering and breeding raptors, focusing on priority species. Alternate direction from one survey to the next.

Establish a migration hawk-watch station at a prominent site(s) on the refuge(s) to survey for migrating raptors.

Conduct transient bird surveys at least twice per month from mid-September to the end of March.

Conduct annual National Midwinter Bald Eagle count and report the data to the Raptor Research and Technical Assistance Center in Boise, Idaho.

GOAL 2 – Implement a program of science-based stewardship of the fish and wildlife resources associated with the North Mississippi National Wildlife Refuges Complex.

Background: The mission of the National Wildlife Refuge System is:

"To administer a national network of lands and waters for the conservation, management, and where appropriate, restoration of the fish, wildlife and plant resources and their habitats within the United States for the benefit of present and future generations of Americans."

While the Service and Refuge System's priority is the protection of federal trust species (migratory birds, threatened and endangered species, interjurisdictional fish, and marine mammals) this mission clearly states that these refuges also should provide for other wildlife, such as resident species. In other words, by acquiring refuge lands, we also assume responsibility for managing the resident wildlife that also may be dependent on these refuge resources. However, this management must never be to the exclusion or detriment of the purpose for which the refuge was established.

A variety of wildlife species indigenous to the LMRV inhabit the Complex. Some of the more notable wildlife are those easily seen by the general public (e.g., white-tailed deer, wild turkey, and cottontail rabbits). Many of these species are also available to the public for hunting opportunities, which elevates their importance to the public and land managers with hunting programs. However, Service policy requires us to maintain the "biological integrity, diversity, and environmental health of the National Wildlife Refuge System" (*Federal Register*, January 16, 2001). If we are to truly understand the biodiversity and environmental health of these lands, we must gather baseline information on all wildlife and their habitats to document their existence, monitor trends, and understand the impacts of refuge programs.

The following objectives are intended to provide the biological foundation to pursue the purpose and maximize the wildlife values of the Complex. Depending upon the availability of funds and personnel, Complex managers should attempt to fulfill these objectives within 15 years. Periodic reviews of the progress made toward accomplishment of these objectives and possible modifications should be conducted as advances are made in scientific knowledge affecting the management of fish and wildlife resources. The Complex plays a key role in a number of national, regional, and system-wide conservation plans that are referenced in this report. Fulfillment of the following objectives and strategies will contribute significantly to those plans.

Objective 2-1: Game Species
For the duration of the plan, manage game populations to maximize quality hunting opportunities while maintaining habitat for federal trust resources.

Discussion: Most resident game species are habitat generalists while the desired migratory bird community tends to gravitate toward habitat specialization. Three of five key game species (e.g., deer, rabbit, and quail) tend toward early habit successional stages, one (e.g., tree squirrels - both fox and gray) tends toward later habitat successional stages, and one (e.g., wild turkey) needs important components of both early and later successional stages.

The majority of early successional habitat on the Complex is a by-product of other management actions. The early successional habitats occurring on the Complex seem to be a function of one of three things: farming (USFWS or co-op; comprising a very small percentage [<5 percent] of total land area), reforestation efforts (currently available early successional habitat will be lost in less than 5 years), or flooding regimes (natural or man-made). The Complex currently maintains approximately 600 acres of fallow fields. These fields are mowed periodically to prevent invasion by wood plants.

Wildlife game studies have found that as little as 3-5 percent of a land base managed in early successional openings can yield appreciable population gains. This is demonstrably true for white-tailed deer, northern bobwhite, and wild turkey. It is also true for migratory species such as American woodcock, as well as herptile and invertebrate populations. Whether the openings occur as a result of small clearcuts, roadways, pipelines, tornadoes, or bulldozers, is of little importance. The important point is to maintain these critical feeding and reproductive areas – especially in the Complex where the emphasis is on contiguous blocks of bottomland hardwood forests. In fact, for resident wildlife game species, it would be difficult to overstate the importance of managed early successional areas in the Complex. Scarcity of areas important for brood-rearing or "bugging" for ground-nesting birds assures these patch openings will be used in far greater proportion to their availability. Mature, open, bottomland hardwood forests are biological deserts for most resident wildlife game species for nine months of every year if judged on food availability, brood-rearing, and nesting cover, although with good forest management this can be remedied. Focusing grassland and shrub management for birds on smaller blocks of land, such as Farm Service Agency properties, may be a practical alternative, depending on the surrounding habitat.

Hard mast production is highly variable in the south compared to the midwest. Southern hard mast crops may fail two out of every five years. Heavy hard mast crops occur generally every 4-6 years. To avoid constant fluxes in resident wildlife game populations due to hard mast crop variability, there must be openings somewhere in order to meet critical nesting, brood-rearing, "bugging", and browse habitat needs for ground nesting birds and white-tailed deer. With planning, these openings can be accomplished without sacrificing habitat requirements for desired avian species, such as neotropical migratory birds.

Managed early successional openings for resident and migratory wildlife game species do not mean agricultural co-op farming. Neither does it mean a clearcut allowed to regenerate naturally. It does mean an intended permanent opening allowed to regenerate in strips of natural vegetation up to 3 years, or openings that may be planted in an annual or perennial legume requiring a minimum of maintenance, while benefiting ground nesting resident game birds and white-tailed deer. These areas will be clear at ground level and will enhance invertebrate production. They may be strips within a field or may be an entire field. Openings should remain between 1-5 acres. By maintaining pH at or near 7.0 for optimum seed germination, combined with fall mowing or light fall disking, these openings should require only a single planting lasting for 5-7 years. However, in the interest of good forest management and the reduction of fragmentation, these openings should be along road shoulders, fire breaks, and other necessary and existing openings.

Strategies:

General

By 2007, develop and implement a Biological Inventory and Monitoring Plan. This plan will include key indicator resident wildlife species. Integrate population objectives for resident species into the refuge's habitat management plans.

Encourage research, inventory, and monitoring activities on the Complex, when compatible with the refuge purpose and management.

Manage lands to maintain representative flora and fauna characteristic of the LMRV, and serve as a repository of fauna and flora native to the LMRV and the Complex, when compatible with refuge purposes and management.

Identify and maintain 3-4 percent of Complex landbase in a variety of early successional areas in ecotonal sites as critical nesting and brood-rearing sites for resident wildlife reproduction.

Identify, maintain, and enhance areas/species of soft mast production to help mitigate effects of drought and lack of hard mast availability during the year.

Maintain annual survey indices (e.g., call counts, spotlight surveys, brood surveys) and harvest/visitor use records for resident wildlife game species.

Burn (wherever possible), strip disk (on the thirds principle) or herbicide (spot treat as needed) old fields to set back natural plant succession, and increase nesting and brood rearing habitat in larger areas not reforested in oak seedlings. Lightly disk fire lanes surrounding forested stands to encourage growth of legumes, attract insects, and create a mosaic of bare ground and vegetation that provides feeding and brood-rearing cover.

White-tailed deer

Maintain a stable deer population through a program of either-sex hunting. Aim for removal of approximately one-third to one-half of the herd annually with a 1:1 harvest ratio of the sexes.

Conduct herd health checks every 5-7 years and monitor habitat conditions to determine the health and population of deer on the Complex.

Construct deer grazing exclosures (10' x 10' or larger) throughout habitat types and in closed areas (where deer become concentrated) to help gauge herd densities and impacts to refuge vegetative communities and migratory bird management programs.

Evaluate deer populations and adjust hunting programs as needed. Be prepared to increase the length of deer season, the use of rifles, the doe harvest, or all the above as the deer population increases.

Upland game birds

Refrain from mowing levees, powerline/pipeline rights-of-way, and roadsides until August 1. These are the only reproduction areas for resident ground nesting birds (especially as seedlings in reforestation areas increase in age). Peak reproductive effort barring a flood year will have occurred prior to August, even for second and third re-nesting efforts. Areas of high vehicular use should be mowed prior to May 1 to make them less attractive to birds attempting to nest. These practices will also minimize brown-headed cowbird habitat.

Plant and maintain understory species such as dogwood, wild cherry, grapes, and berries. All of these are important in the wild turkey's year-round diet. These species benefit a variety of both wildlife and migratory birds and should be protected wherever they appear during cutting and thinning operations.

Leave field borders or 20-ft. buffer strips around large fields. This small field loss can result in 20-25 percent gains in reproductive effort. Reduce back to bare soil every third year.

Do not use chemicals on the buffer strips and use chemicals minimally within fields. Some chemicals have direct toxic impacts on quail, particularly chicks, and chemicals have indirect impacts by reducing the insect populations that quail depend on for food.

Within fields maintained for quail habitat, maintain 15-20 percent woody cover, 10-15 percent fallow areas, 15-20 percent grassy areas, and 40-60 percent row crop. Woody cover should be available every 200 yards.

Monitor population responses to quail management practices and hunting programs.

Develop partnerships with Mississippi Department of Wildlife, Fisheries and Parks and interested non-governmental organizations to assist in upland game bird management.

Objective 2-2: Non-Game Species
Within 10 years of the plan's approval, reestablish historical hydrological and habitat regimes to increase refuge biodiversity to the maximum extent feasible. Biannually monitor non-game species response to restoration activities.

Discussion: Historically, the extent and duration of seasonal flooding from the Mississippi River fluctuated annually, recharging the LMRV's aquatic systems and creating a rich diversity of dynamic habitats that supported a vast array of fish and wildlife resources. Instead of natural hydrology, large-scale man-made hydrological alterations have changed the spatial and temporal patterns of flooding throughout the entire LMRV. In addition, these alterations have reduced both the extent and duration of annual seasonal flooding (with the conspicuous exception of most of Coldwater River refuge). The loss of this annual flooding regime has had a huge impact on the forested wetlands and their associated wetland-dependent species.

In view of these profound hydrologic changes, it is very difficult – if not impossible – to fully simulate or reconstruct the structure and functions of a natural wetland. Restoration of wetland functions is especially difficult since wetlands depend on a dynamic interface of hydrologic regimes to maintain water, vegetation, and animal complexes and processes. Attempts to restore the hydrological regime in the LMRV and on the Complex include greentree reservoirs and water control devices that serve to manage and create moist-soil units.

Reptiles and amphibians are significant components of the LMRV. They are abundant on the Complex and are functionally important in most freshwater and terrestrial habitats. Many species of herpetofauna are wide-ranging and may serve as key indicator species in evaluating the environmental health of an ecosystem. Knowledge of which species occur on the North Mississippi National Wildlife Refuges Complex is fundamental to an understanding of the biological diversity of the area.

Identifying and conserving breeding sites for amphibians, especially for salamander species, are critical. The habitat type is variable according to species, but one type, which is easily overlooked in management, is ephemeral pools. Depressions that hold water for less than a year may be found in almost any area, but additional factors such as vegetation characteristics, water quality, and historic use determine whether a given species may use them for breeding sites. Many salamanders are philopatric, returning as adults to breed in the site where they hatched and developed. If breeding sites are active, this is an indication that suitable habitat exists or has recently existed nearby to support adult populations.

Manipulating habitats for other species opens the possibility of inadvertently eliminating breeding sites. This would be highly disruptive and possibly devastating to the local population, especially in the case of salamanders, which are less mobile than frogs and reptiles and more apt to be impacted by loss of a breeding site. In the interest of diversity and of managing for all native species, breeding sites should be identified and conserved, especially for species which are not common.

Currently, the refuge staff is conducting calling frog surveys to monitor refuge frog populations, as well as beginning an overall inventory of amphibians and reptiles on the three traditional refuge properties. This information will be incorporated into a GIS-based database. The calling frog survey data will be submitted to a national database (the North American Amphibian Monitoring Program).

In terms of monitoring populations, clearly not everything can be done (or even the majority of items) without additional personnel and financial support. However, the highest priority needs may be identified and then a determination made as to which protocols can be accomplished immediately, which can be done with additional volunteers or slight adjustments to present staff work schedules, requiring additional resources.

Although the majority of acreage in the Complex has been in the National Wildlife Refuge System for over 10 years, very little is known regarding the species which exist on this acreage. In order to fully inventory the species occurring on the complex, it will be necessary to obtain additional staff (Biologist, Biological Technician, etc.) and develop partnerships with local universities and museums.

Most properties managed by the Complex are located in the Mississippi Delta. Additional attention needs to be directed to the few properties located in the hills' portion of the state. There are likely to be species on these properties that are absent from the sites on the Delta.

Strategies:

General

By 2007, develop and implement a Biological Inventory and Monitoring Plan (also mentioned under previous objective). This plan will include key indicator resident wildlife species, including non-game animals.

Encourage research, inventory, and monitoring activities on the Complex, when compatible with the refuge purpose and management.

Manage lands to maintain representative flora and fauna characteristic of the Delta region of the LMAV, and serve as a repository of flora and fauna native to the LMAV and the Complex, when compatible with refuge purpose and management.

Work with partners (e.g., state museum and universities) to conduct formal censuses on refuge properties, including Farm Service Agency lands.

By 2007, develop and maintain a GIS database for recording wildlife sightings on refuge properties.

Conduct timber stand improvement to help develop a thicker understory/midstory component of saplings, seedlings, etc., conducive to non-game bird groups and woodcock.

Non-game birds

See previous sections under Goal 1.

Reptiles and amphibians

By 2008, conduct amphibian and reptile inventories to establish baseline information on species occurrence and habitat utilization.

Locate and map (using GIS) reptile and amphibian breeding sites and identify species of use.

Conserve breeding sites by maintaining the current vegetation component and water regime. Establish buffer zones, if necessary, to protect from pesticide or silt contamination.

Conduct annual counts of egg masses to determine use of sites by salamanders and frog species.

Conduct a calling frog survey, at least three times annually, according to the North American Amphibian Monitoring Program protocols.

Establish standardized reporting methods for incidental sightings to include: species, date, property, specific location, and habitat type, as minimum information, and size, sex, and age data as additional information where possible.

Objective 2-3: Fishes
For the duration of the plan, continue to enhance spawning habitats and improve water quality at Coldwater River, Dahomey and Tallahatchie refuges to maintain healthy, sustainable fish populations.

Discussion: There is evidence that Tippo Bayou, the most notable aquatic resource on Tallahatchie refuge, is being used as a staging area for spawning by paddlefish. Spawning, however, has not been documented on the refuge to date.

For all three refuges in the Complex, very little is known regarding non-game fish occurrence. Coldwater River refuge experiences flooding on an annual basis with water backing up from the Tallahatchie River and the Panola-Quitman Floodway. Dahomey refuge is transected by numerous drainage ditches and bayous. In addition to Tippo Bayou, Tallahatchie refuge has numerous oxbows and sloughs that are disconnected from any flowing waters. All three of these refuges should host a diverse assortment of minnows and rough fish.

Strategies:

Support efforts of Private John Allen National Fish Hatchery to restore warm and cool water species of concern in the Central Gulf Coast and Lower Mississippi Valley Ecosystems.

Provide assistance when requested by the Private John Allen National Fish Hatchery.

Conduct fish inventories to establish baseline information on species occurrence and habitat utilization.

Work with Private John Allen National Fish Hatchery or other interested groups to determine the extent of use of Tippo Bayou by paddlefish.

GOAL 3 – Protect and restore habitat for federal and state threatened and endangered species found in the Lower Mississippi River Ecosystem.

Background: Recovery and protection of threatened and endangered plants and animals is an important responsibility delegated to the Service and its national wildlife refuges. Several federal threatened and endangered species are thought to use, or could use, North Mississippi National Wildlife Refuges Complex lands, including the bald eagle, wood stork, Louisiana black bear, and the least tern. In addition, the federally listed endangered pondberry potentially exists on the refuge. It has been found on a Service easement in Bolivar County. Its presence on Dahomey refuge in Bolivar County has not yet been verified; however, an ecological assessment concludes that suitable habitats for pondberry do exist and that its presence there is very likely.

As do many states, the State of Mississippi keeps a continually updated list of sensitive plants and animals that are threatened, endangered, or of concern in Mississippi itself. The Mississippi Natural Heritage Inventory, maintained by the Mississippi Museum of Natural History, uses a ranking system developed by The Nature Conservancy, under which each listed species is assigned two ranks, one representing its range-wide or global status, and the other representing its status in the state. With regard to animals, Bolivar County has fifteen listed species, Grenada has six species, Quitman has one species, and Tallahatchie has five species. The species represent a wide range of taxa, including birds, mollusks, turtles, fish, and crustaceans. With regard to plants, Bolivar County has nine listed species, Grenada has forty-two species, Quitman five species, and Tallahatchie County has twelve species. A number of these species undoubtedly occur on the Complex refuges and Farm Service Agency properties.

Objective 3-1: Inventory
By 2009, inventory the distribution and habitat use of all threatened and endangered species on the Complex and contribute to their recovery.

Discussion: In that the three listed bird species (bald eagle, wood stork, least tern) above are occasional visitors to the Complex and the one plant species has not actually been discovered to date (although it is strongly suspected to occur), the most appropriate actions staff can take at this time are to inventory and monitor occurrences of threatened and endangered species. Likewise with state-listed species, no systematic inventories have been taken.

Strategies:

Support the efforts of Private John Allen National Fish Hatchery to restore populations of paddlefish, alligator gar, pallid sturgeon, and native walleye within the Central Gulf and Mississippi Alluvial Valley Ecosystems.

Support the efforts of the Jackson Field Office to restore populations of Louisiana and American black bear to the Mississippi delta.

By 2007, prepare a Biological Inventory and Monitoring Plan for the Complex, to include protocols for monitoring threatened and endangered species.

Monitor and maintain records of sightings of all threatened and endangered species on the Complex including location and habitat type.

Implement vertebrate and invertebrate species inventories on the Complex to identify the presence, population status, and distribution of threatened and endangered species.

Enhance, restore, protect, and manage imperiled species habitat using available conservation tools, including habitat management on existing land (federal, state and private), conservation easements, partnership agreements, conservation agreements, and land acquisition from willing sellers.

Monitor the population status of species of special concern and candidate species on the Complex.

Objective 3-2: Habitat development and management for black bears
By 2015, ensure that the Forest Management Plan is compatible with habitat management for black bears.

Discussion: Special consideration should be given to population monitoring and habitat management for any black bears on the Complex. Due to the lack of substantial blocks of forested habitats in the upper Mississippi River Delta, reforestation of bottomland hardwood forests could provide connecting corridors from the river riparian area to much of the Complex. This would provide additional habitats for an expanding population of bears. Efforts with regards to bears should focus on forest management and education.

Habitat management to benefit bears generally focuses on maintaining suitable den sites, ensuring availability of preferred food resources, and maintaining or creating adequate travel and dispersal corridors. Timber species, size classes, cavities, openings, corridors, food sources, etc., are important considerations for all phases of forest management. However, most forest management practices for resident fish and wildlife populations will generally benefit bears. Identification of properties that could provide wooded corridors between the Mississippi River riparian areas and the Complex should be given a priority.

Whether bears move naturally into the area or are reintroduced, public education is vital. This may come in the form of school programs, landowner workshops, posted signs, pamphlets, town meetings, etc. The Complex should have Service personnel trained in bear relocation techniques. Also, protocol to deal with potential human/bear conflicts should be established. Complex personnel are also encouraged to work with state bear restoration groups and others to accomplish this goal.

Strategies:

Forest Management

Provide a diverse mix of hard and soft mast producing species to provide year-round food and cover.

Protect existing den trees and create den areas by leaving felled treetops for ground nesting cover on areas of higher elevation.

Utilize uneven age stand management and limit clearcut areas.

Monitor and maintain records of bear sightings, bear sign (scat, prints, clawed trees), and potential den trees (>36" dbh, especially if cypress, tupelo or oak and containing a cavity, or any large tree with claw marks), including exact location and habitat type. Records should also be reported to the Mississippi Department of Wildlife, Fisheries and Parks state bear biologist.

Establish forested corridors connecting areas of the Complex with other forested lands and the riparian lands along the Mississippi River through the Partners for Fish and Wildlife Program and the formation of other partnerships.

Education

Provide staff training to promote bear awareness and education in the vicinity of the Complex.

Provide staff training on bear relocation and human/bear issues.

GOAL 4 – Maintain and/or restore ecological systems within the Mississippi Alluvial Valley and Central Gulf Ecosystems, which mimic historical conditions.

Background: Habitat management will be used to maintain and, where appropriate and practical, restore elements of ecological integrity, while providing benefits to a wide range of resident, migratory, and threatened and endangered species. The refuge's habitat management procedures, including activities ranging from no intervention to intensive manipulation of soils, water, topography, and vegetation, would be consistent with the Service's Refuge Manual.

Objective 4-1: Moist Soil
Manage a minimum of 6,689 acres of shallow impounded wetlands (see Table 15) on the 3 traditional refuges for optimum production of moist-soil plants, invertebrates, or hard mast for a variety of wetland-dependent migratory birds while meeting the objectives established for dabbling ducks by the LMRVJV.

Discussion: Moist-soil management refers to management of land to provide moist-soil conditions during the growing season to promote the natural production of beneficial plants. Seeds produced by these plants often attract and concentrate waterfowl and other wetland wildlife species. The decomposing vegetative parts of moist-soil plants also provide substrate for invertebrates, which are critical food for many wetland wildlife and fish. Although small grain crops provide high energy for migrating waterfowl, these artificial foods do not provide the same nutrients found in these natural foods. The loss of wetlands in the surrounding areas has made these artificial wetlands essential to the health and survival of wetland-dependent wildlife species.

It is imperative to only manage those acres which can be managed well. Poorly managed moist-soil units provide greatly reduced benefits to waterfowl and shorebirds and may develop into thick willow stands or cultivate invasive and pest plants.

Strategies:

Install depth gauges on all impoundments.

Maintain early successional moist-soil plant communities and control undesirable plants by mechanical disking, herbicides, water level manipulation, or rotating agricultural crops periodically (considering the magnitude of the moist-soil objective, every effort needs to be made in terms of strategies to keep the designated acreage in moist-soil habitat).

Control perennials and other emergents, maintain deep water levels, greater than 3 feet, while providing loafing and feeding areas for waterfowl and waterbirds, and habitat for fish and developing populations of invertebrates, including crawfish.

Provide shallow water depths in late spring and early summer to concentrate prey for long-legged waders such as wood storks (state listed), little blue herons, and white ibis (both declining).

Begin final drawdown of water levels in mid-summer to expose mud-flats for southbound shorebirds.

Actively solicit and logistically support research by universities, U.S. Geological Survey, or other research entities to conduct applied investigations to answer management questions and enhance capabilities to provide for target species.

Work closely with Wildlife Habitat and Management and LMRVJV biologists to develop and implement a system to record water levels, habitat manipulations, plant coverage, and migratory bird response in all appropriate impoundments and use adaptive management procedures to improve results.

Work toward complete water control on all shallow impoundments managed for waterfowl.

Develop a protocol for managing moist-soil areas with only partial water control, using 400 pounds per acre as a minimum production rate. If the minimum cannot be achieved, consider planting millet or converting to row crops.

Develop a step-down management plan for all impounded water, including moist-soil, field impoundments, permanent water, and greentree reservoirs, incorporating all listed strategies.

Develop a GIS database of all water management units that includes floodable acreage, water control structures, soil types, vegetation transects, flood chronologies, and manipulations.

Conduct and keep records of in-depth plant surveys at least twice annually in all moist-soil management units.

Objective 4-2: Forest Management
Manage existing forest areas according to the existing forest management plan for the Complex. Reforest additional acquisitions where appropriate.

Discussion: About 80 percent of the forest lands in the LMRV has been cleared and converted to other land uses, leaving only remnant forested tracts. Fish and wildlife resources have been similarly affected, leaving remnant populations that must be managed to meet the refuge purpose and to achieve the maximum potential. To date, the forest resources have had a minimum of inventory work conducted. A stand inventory and GIS mapping database must be established. A Forest Habitat Management Plan has recently been completed. Some of the most unique forested habitat remaining in the Delta is forested ridges. Because of the importance of the remaining forests to the wildlife resources on the refuge and conservation priorities set forth in various plans, the forest resources should be managed to mimic old growth forests and increase vertical vegetative structure.

Several species of waterfowl heavily utilize flooded forested habitat in winter for resting and foraging for acorns, other fruits, various seeds, and invertebrates. Wood ducks seek these habitats almost exclusive of other habitats. Mallards, gadwall, and wigeon all utilize flooded forested habitat as one of the complex of preferred habitats.

These areas are vital to waterfowl for pair bonding, loafing, sanctuary, thermal cover, and feeding. It is important to manage these areas to provide all of these elements. These areas can be enhanced for waterfowl utilization by making them more accessible. Ducks like openings in the woods to allow them easy access. Small groups of trees (3-5) that dominate canopy coverage can be removed to provide the opening that ducks prefer for landing. Care should be taken in the timing, frequency, and duration of flooding.

Flooding in winter should mimic or enhance natural flood conditions. Typically, flooding should occur only during the dormant period for deciduous hardwoods common in each impoundment. Flooding should never occur before the dormant period starts in late fall (mid-November to late-December) and only rarely after green-up in the spring. Flooding dates and duration should be varied annually and in some years should not be flooded. Fredrickson's Greentree Reservoir Management Handbook (Fredrickson and Batema 1993) should be consulted for management guidance.

Strategies:

Follow the recently developed Forest Habitat Management Plan, including its wildlife and tree species to be favored, reforestation methods, prescription-writing methods, timber marking and thinning procedures, harvest policy, and record-keeping procedures.

Complete a forest inventory and a GIS mapping database of the refuge forests. Utilize database information to schedule stand treatments and project manpower and other resource needs. The inventory may be a light baseline inventory of approximately 1 percent using the compartmental breakdown of like habitats noted in the Dahomey refuge assessment. A more intense cruise will be needed prior to prescription writing.

Take advantage of carbon sequestration dollars to complete remaining reforestation activities (new plantings and re-plantings).

Prioritize reforestation efforts to enhance or create: (1) landscape linkages for wide-ranging species such as black bear, and (2) a critical forested habitat mass to benefit forest interior birds and other species needing larger blocks of habitat.

Manage for a natural representation of tree species and densities in reforestation efforts, with reasonable attempts made at mimicking natural spacing (i.e., avoid "planted rows").

Direct reforestation efforts to produce a merchantable forest that is desirable to commercial loggers to help implement forest management practices in the future.

Consider increasing species diversity at time of establishment. Plant a greater percentage of hard mast species in areas where light-seeded species are less than 1/4 mile away, allowing those species to reseed naturally.

Develop and implement management guidelines and practices for existing hardwood plantations using the attached "General Recommendations for Hardwood Forest Management to Improve Wildlife Habitat in the Lower Mississippi River Valley."

Develop treatments to improve species diversity and habitat value of plantations. Pursue a general forest management strategy to provide the most natural species representation and structure to benefit the widest array of site-appropriate species and forest management options.

Consider the feasibility of spot planting specially grown containerized trees (e.g., root pruned or other) to help ensure a hard mast component within a reasonable period of time, especially on Farm Service Agency properties.

Flood greentree reservoirs only during the dormant period - never flood before dormancy and rarely after green-up. Flooding dates and duration should be varied annually and in some years should not be flooded.

Inventory and monitor tree vigor and diversity, including regeneration of red oaks. Modify flood management to achieve forest and wildlife management objectives.

Continue to establish firelanes around reforestation areas until crown closure lowers the level of fuels resulting from herbaceous plants in the understory.

Hire a forester even though the forested land base is currently fairly small. Areas such as Dahomey refuge will not receive the attention they deserve until a position is created for someone who can devote a considerable amount of time to caring for the forest. Additionally, hire a technician to assist in management activities, such as cruising timber, marking, and monitoring.

Survey refuges for any potential endangered species (e.g., pondberry) that may influence timber management decisions.

Objective 4-3: Invasive and Pest Management
For the duration of the plan, inventory, monitor, and control, where possible, invasive plant and animal populations to minimize or eliminate negative effects on native flora and fauna.

Discussion: A pest is any terrestrial or aquatic plant or animal which interferes or threatens to interfere at an unacceptable level with the attainment of refuge objectives or which poses a threat to human health. Currently there are several species of plants and wildlife occurring on the Complex that have achieved this status as a "pest."

Many invasive moist-soil plant species are difficult to control without intensive herbicide use. Soil disturbances and water level fluctuations necessary for migratory shorebird and waterfowl management often encourage germination of those invasive species present in the natural seed bank. Eradication of undesirable species is often impossible and unnecessary to achieve. Some of these plants, such as coffeeweed (*Sesbania spp.*) and willow (*Salix spp.*), offer desirable vertical structure when occurring in low densities in southern moist-soil impoundments. Other aggressive plant species, such as trumpet creeper, morning glory, and redvine, offer little food value or cover and are extremely difficult to control once established except with approved herbicide treatments.

Similarly, wildlife pests, some native, some non-native, are often difficult to control and impossible to eradicate. The nutria is an introduced species that can rapidly attain high population levels. Nutria feed largely on aquatic plants, typically uprooting the plant as it feeds. At high densities, nutria can rapidly remove a large proportion of the wetland vegetation. Additionally, nutria burrow into earthen levees and can cause them to leak or blow out. Currently, the Walker Tract of Tallahatchie refuge and Coldwater River refuge support high densities of nutria. Nutria occur throughout the Delta and have been detected infrequently on Dahomey refuge and the main tract of Tallahatchie refuge.

The beaver is a native species with both advantages and disadvantages. Situated along major watercourses, the Complex will continue to hold and attract beaver. Periodic and persistent dam removal should occur as needed where dams impede desired water flow necessary for shorebird and waterfowl management or cause damage to bottomland hardwood forests and reforestation sites.

The Complex should be extremely concerned with the presence of wild hogs. In addition to a hog's ability as an omnivore to eat virtually anything, studies have shown that an adult wild hog will consume 160 pounds of hard mast during a single winter. Where hard mast is present, as much as 84 percent of a hog's diet will consist of acorns. In areas like the Complex where the major habitat type is bottomland hardwoods and its associated hard mast production, feral hogs will be efficient competitors with native wildlife, including deer, turkey, quail, squirrels and waterfowl, for available hard mast resources. Competition for food resources is only one part of a feral hog problem. In addition to being a host of various diseases, such as swine brucellosis, feral hogs cause enormous structural damage to levees and roadways by rooting large holes while feeding on grasses, roots, and stems. The feral hog population on the Complex should be curtailed by any means possible; such control is both practical and attainable.

Other native species such as striped skunks, raccoons, and double-crested cormorants can occasionally reach such high population densities that they interfere with Complex objectives and may require control.

Strategies:

By 2008, develop GIS inventory and monitoring of problem areas for plants, as well as areas in the natural seed bank that are producing beneficial wildlife plants that meet refuge objectives. Inventory, monitor, and control populations of wildlife that have become pests.

To control willows, cut and flood, dry and apply Roundup, or hack and squirt using herbicides. Disk every 3 years to set back succession.

In problem impoundments, use Rodeo to kill unwanted vegetation prior to manipulating water levels. Thus, desirable moist-soil plants can thrive. Disking and mowing may also be advantageous in certain scenarios. Consider using cooperative farming in problem impoundments when staff is unavailable to help set back succession.

By 2008, establish standardized method of reporting problem areas where plants/animals are discovered.

Track hog movements as it tends to establish movement patterns. Use baiting in the summer to attract individual feral hogs to a trap. Use "repeater traps" to increase the number of hogs captured in a single trap. Take advantage of naturally occurring funnels leading into fields used by feral hogs to set traps.

Increase hunter harvest of feral hogs through education and additional hunting opportunities.

Use traps and rifles to reduce nutria populations. Focus efforts in late winter and early spring when the young are most vulnerable and the adults appear less wary.

Utilize GS-7 biological technician to implement trapping program of identified pest species (e.g., beaver, nutria, hogs) on the Complex.

Develop management guidelines (contracts, special use permits, and special conditions) to administer a trapping program consistent with sound biology, Service guidelines, refuge purposes, and the conservation of ecosystem functions.

Set protocol in dealing with different species. Some species can be managed with mechanical disturbance or simply adjusting the timing of the initiation and rate of drawdown. If necessary, use herbicides to control aggressive plant species, ensuring that label directions are followed. (Monitor areas that are sprayed to ensure that non-target organisms are not impacted. Discontinue use of herbicide if negative impact is detected.) If beaver are not impacting a roadway, water control structure, or other critical juncture, they should be left alone.

Establish and prioritize units that most need protection from invasive plant or animal pest species presence.

Identify and take advantage of naturally occurring beneficial plant stands or beaver "ponds" that can be drawn down and seeded in late summer then reflooded by beavers for waterfowl use.

Develop a Complex-wide Integrated Pest Management Plan by 2006.

Install effective beaver guards or water diversion structures on all water control structures that are perpetually disabled by beaver dams.

GOAL 5 – Increase the land base of the Complex and contribute to the protection and restoration of fish and wildlife resources found within Northern Mississippi.

Background: The authorized acquisition boundaries of Coldwater River, Dahomey and Tallahatchie refuges allow for considerable expansion in the size of individual refuges within the Complex. This expansion will take place over the long term, and will emphasize those tracts that have the greatest potential to enhance the ecological integrity of the protected land base.

Objective 5-1: Land Acquisition
Continue to acquire the remaining 31,573 acres of land within the current refuge acquisition boundaries, with special emphasis on those areas that would (1) improve access, (2) contribute to national and regional objectives, (3) reduce impacts to refuge resources, or (4) provide additional wildlife-dependent recreational opportunities.

Discussion: The Complex has acquired approximately one third of the lands within its current acquisition boundaries. Certain critical inholdings are still needed to meet habitat and public use objectives. These include foraging and sanctuary habitats for waterfowl and Bird Conservation Area forest block objectives, as well as providing access to visitors, reducing off-refuge impacts, and protecting unique habitats, with opportunities to expand and establish manageable units. The lands within and surrounding Dahomey refuge are part of interior forest objectives established by the LMRVJV in support of the Partners-in-Flight Plan for the LMRV.

Strategies:

Highest acquisition priority should be placed on acquiring inholdings and other tracts that will significantly improve management opportunities to meet objectives established by various national and regional plans.

By 2006, develop an outreach program that provides information on land acquisition and easement programs, for the benefit of landowners within the boundary expansion areas.

Develop partnerships with conservation organizations such as The Nature Conservancy, The Trust for Public Land, and The Conservation Fund to support land acquisition needs.

Focus land acquisition efforts on properties adjacent to existing refuge lands within the Bird Conservation Areas.

Objective 5-2: Private Lands
Provide assistance to private landowners within the 26-county Complex work area. This assistance will be directed towards restoring habitats for wintering waterfowl and forested wetlands to achieve objectives of national and regional plans for the LMRV and Central Gulf Ecosystems.

Discussion: Service authorities for involvement with private landowners in developing and carrying out habitat improvement projects are found in the National Wildlife Refuge System Improvement Act of 1997 and the policy documents for the Partners for Fish and Wildlife Program (PFW). Additional authorities reside within the Fish and Wildlife Act and the Fish and Wildlife Coordination Act.

Much of the land in the vicinity of the Complex is privately owned. These privately owned lands play an important role in the restoration and reestablishment of native habitats needed to support the diverse fish and wildlife resource for which this geographic area was historically known. Existing or potential habitat on private lands is essential for achieving the goals and objectives of national and regional plans such as the North American Waterfowl Management Plan, Partners-in-Flight, Mississippi River Alluvial Valley Bird Conservation Plan, and Strategic Fisheries Plan.

The Service has several existing programs that are directed to providing technical assistance and funding for priority habitat projects on private lands. The Service's primary project delivery mechanism for habitat projects on private lands is the PFW Program. Additional funding and technical assistance support for private lands is also available through several other Service funded programs, including the Challenge Cost-Share Program, the Mississippi Partners for Wildlife Program, Migratory Birds Program, and several grant programs within the Threatened and Endangered Species Program.

Under the PFW Program, landowners may receive up to $25,000 for on-the-ground project implementation. PFW projects typically receive a minimum 50 percent in-kind cost share and require a minimum 10-year commitment from the landowner. Typically, landowner agreements are for more than 20 years. Since the PFW Program was initiated in 1988, approximately 87,000 acres of bottomland hardwood forest wetlands have been planted, and over 20,000 acres of other habitat projects have been completed within the LMRV. The PFW Program provides base funding for one full-time private lands biologist stationed at the Complex.

The Mississippi Partners for Wildlife Program is funded separately from the PFW Program, receiving funding primarily through the Service's Refuge Challenge Cost-Share (CCS) Program. The CCS Program also requires at least a 50 percent cost-share from other partners. In Mississippi, this partnership involves the private landowners, Ducks Unlimited, Delta Wildlife, Mississippi Fish and Wildlife Foundation, and the Mississippi Department of Wildlife, Fisheries and Parks. Approximately $40,000 in Service funds are made available each fiscal year through this partnership agreement. These funds are used to provide water-control structures to private landowners to flood harvested cropland during the fall/winter (November 15-February 28). This partnership provides significant benefits for wintering waterfowl, other migratory birds, and water quality.

The Farm Bill conservation programs, available through the USDA under the 2002 Farm Bill, provide significant opportunities for the development and implementation of habitat improvement projects on private lands. These programs include the Wetland Reserve Program (WRP), the Conservation Reserve Program, the Wildlife Habitat Incentives Program, and the Environmental Quality Incentives Program. Many millions of dollars are available to eligible private landowners for habitat conservation under these programs. For example, under the WRP, administered by the Natural Resources Conservation Service, over 100,000 acres of permanent and 30-year easements, directed to restore natural wetlands and native vegetation, have been implemented in Mississippi since 1990.

Strategies:

Develop a 5-year Strategic Plan for developing and carrying out habitat improvement projects within defined habitat focus areas on private lands within the Complex work area. The plan should focus restoration and other efforts on priority reforestation sites established by coordinated planning efforts like the LMRVJV, rather than simply an opportunistic approach to project selection.

Develop and carry out an Annual Work Plan for addressing priority private lands issues identified under the 5-year plan and other appropriate sources.

Target private lands within Bird Conservation Areas for projects through the Partners for Fish and Wildlife (PFW) program.

Expand the PFW/private lands program at the Complex to more effectively involve other interested partners, such as the Mississippi Department of Wildlife, Fisheries and Parks, NRCS, Delta Wildlife, Ducks Unlimited, and the Mississippi Fish and Wildlife Foundation, in program development, policy, and implementation.

To the extent possible, leverage Service project funds and technical assistance with private landowners and other partners (e.g., Mississippi Department of Wildlife, Fisheries and Parks, Ducks Unlimited, Mississippi Fish and Wildlife Foundation, etc.).

Integrate Service private lands programs and initiatives with existing USDA conservation programs under the 2002 Farm Bill. Ensure that all Service projects on private lands are coordinated with the appropriate district conservationist with NRCS in order to maximize technical assistance and access to all appropriate conservation programs and opportunities.

Ensure that the PFW biologist assigned to the Complex is fully utilized in developing and carrying out authorized activities under approved Service strategic plans and activities defined under the PFW and other private lands initiatives.

Objective 5-3: Focus Areas
Use conservation tools such as conservation easements, partnership agreements, and technical assistance to protect, restore, and manage the highest priority habitats within this area (see Figure 8).

Discussion: The work area for the Complex includes 28 counties in northern Mississippi. Within this work area are two "focus areas." Each focus area is a contiguous block made up of refuge lands, Bird Conservation Zones, other public lands, and private lands. The objective for these "Partners for Conservation" focus areas will be to work with partners (state, federal, and non-governmental organizations) and private landowners to focus available resources to (1) help achieve the objectives of national and regional plans; (2) develop corridors for wildlife; (3) create habitat for waterfowl, wintering and breeding; (4) reduce off-refuge impacts to refuge resources; (5) provide better public access to refuge lands; and (6) restore critical interior forest habitat for trust species needing large blocks of interior bottomland hardwood forests. By concentrating efforts within these focus areas, the program is likely to provide more wildlife benefits than if the effort were spread throughout the Complex work area.

The focus areas are primarily cleared agricultural lands interspersed with small remnants of bottomland hardwoods, seasonally flooded and permanent wetlands, and cypress brakes. Alluvial floodplains, hydric soils, and old river scars characterize this area. Although now a landscape of cotton, corn, soybeans, rice, and catfish ponds, this area was once a rich network of bottomland hardwood wetlands interspersed with natural openings that supported an immense variety of forest interior birds and other fish and wildlife.

As with any plan or recovery project, by concentrating resources and partnership efforts, a more structured program can be created that will encourage future endeavors to be "focused" on lands that will have the greatest impact on national and regional recovery and management plans for imperiled federal trust species and their habitats. The three refuges in the Complex are identified in separate Bird Conservation Zones (BCZ), in an effort to provide maximum benefits for neotropical migratory birds. The "Partners for Conservation" focus areas will link several BCZ's and provide increased opportunities for partnership efforts. These areas include: 1) Dahomey refuge BCZ, the Whittington BCZ along the east side of the Mississippi River, and lands linking the two areas, and 2) the Malmaison BCZ surrounding Tallahatchie refuge, the O'Keefe BCZ surrounding Coldwater River refuge, the Coldwater Creek BCZ to the north of Coldwater River refuge, and lands linking these three BCZs.

Strategies:

Conduct further analysis of habitats and land ownership within the focus areas to serve as a basis for building partnerships with landowners desiring to improve wildlife habitat on their lands.

By 2008, develop a "Partners for Conservation" outreach program that explains the concept and objectives of this focused partnership, private lands effort.

Maintain a list of landowners within the "Partners for Conservation" focus area to provide information on opportunities to participate in future conservation programs in their area.

All future boundary expansion proposals will be within these focus areas.

Within one year of the plan's approval, develop a mailing list of potential partners, including state, federal, and conservation organizations.

Figure 8. North Mississippi National Wildlife Refuges Complex focus areas

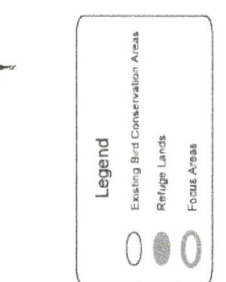

Continue to monitor contaminants concentrations in fish, wildlife, and waterbodies of the refuges while reducing siltation.

Discussion: The Fish and Wildlife Service contracted with North Carolina State University to conduct the Lower Mississippi River Ecosystem Study, which investigated chemical contamination at 26 national wildlife refuges in the LMRV. The field sampling for the study spanned a 6-year period and involved sampling water, sediment, and fish at the refuges. Dahomey and Tallahatchie refuges were included in the study. Sixty-four water samples, ten fish samples, and fourteen sediment samples were collected from the refuges and analyzed for organochlorine pesticides, mercury, and current use pesticides. The benthic fish species collected included common carp, channel catfish, and smallmouth buffalo, and the predator fish species included largemouth bass, white crappie, and spotted gar.

Results of the analyses of the samples indicate that contaminant problems exist at both refuges. Concentrations of DDTM were above the predator protection level of 1.0 ppm in benthic fish species, and those concentrations are high enough to issue a limit consumption advisory for benthic fish. The Mississippi Department of Environmental Quality will issue a limit fish consumption advisory when DDTM concentrations in fish reach 1.0 ppm. Toxaphene concentrations were above the predator protection level of 0.1 ppm in benthic and predator fish. Toxaphene concentrations were high enough to issue a limit fish consumption advisory for both benthic and predatory fish. Fish consumption advisories are issued when toxaphene reaches a concentration of 0.4 ppm in fish. DDTM concentrations were above concern levels in sediment samples. Concentrations of current use pesticides, DDTM, and toxaphene exceeded the U.S. Environmental Protection Agency's chronic water quality criteria in water samples.

Field inspections have been completed on the stream and lakes. It is suspected that concentrations of suspended solids, nutrients, and turbidity are elevated most of the year in the waterbodies, and that there are extended periods when dissolved oxygen levels are at or near zero. In addition, water temperatures in the streams probably rise above 95 degrees Fahrenheit during the summer months.

Many of the fertilizers and pesticides leave fields attached to soil particles and it appears that sheet erosion on agricultural land in the watershed is the cause of the contaminants/water quality problems common throughout the Lower Mississippi Valley. It is also the primary source of the contaminant problems at the refuge.

Beginning in 2001, malformed frog surveys have been conducted annually on Dahomey and Tallahatchie refuges. Surveys have shown that as much as 17 percent of the metamorphs collected had some type of deformity. The normal rate of deformity is about 3 percent or less. This finding indicates that something may be adversely affecting amphibians on the refuge. Some possible causes of the high rate of deformities include pesticides, metals, bacteria, viruses, ultraviolet radiation from thinning of the ozone layer, and elevated nutrients.

Coldwater River refuge is composed of abandoned catfish ponds and former agricultural fields. During normal rainfall, drainage from the adjacent agricultural lands flows east to the Tallahatchie River, and does not flow onto the refuge lands. However, highly turbid, contaminated flood waters from the Tallahatchie River appear to back onto the refuge where the water slows, allowing larger soil particles to drop out of suspension and colloidal particles are adsorbed onto leaves, trees, and woody debris. When the flood waters reach the abandoned catfish ponds, most of the contaminated soil has fallen out in the surrounding forested land. As a result, it is not likely that serious contaminant/water quality problems occur on the refuge. Even though serious contaminant/water quality problems are not expected, investigations should be conducted to determine contaminant levels in water, sediment, fish, and aquatic oriented wildlife.

Also at Coldwater River refuge, large growths of filamentous algae can occur during the late spring and summer months on the catfish ponds. These large algae growths likely deplete the oxygen in the ponds when they begin to die. The large algal blooms are likely caused by nutrients originating from the surrounding agricultural land. These nutrients reach the abandoned catfish ponds because they are water soluble and would not fall out of suspension. These ponds typically receive water from the surrounding drainage ditches that is backed into the ponds during the late fall and winter. Spraying the algae with herbicides or adding super-phosphate would help control the algae.

Strategies:

Reduce sheet erosion within the watershed.

Determine if DDTM and toxaphene are elevated in aquatic-oriented wildlife species, including wood ducks, raccoons, and fish eating birds and mammals.

At a minimum of once every five years, monitor contaminants concentrations in fish and wildlife species of the refuges.

On a bimonthly basis, determine concentrations of nutrients, suspended solids, fecal coliform bacteria, and dissolved oxygen on lakes and streams.

Implement BMPs (drop inlet structures, reforestation, vegetative field borders, etc.) on agricultural land with high sediment yields by using the Service's Private Lands Program, the Natural Resources Conservation Service's Wetland Reserve and Conservation Reserve Programs, and the Mississippi Soil and Water Conservation Commission's Clean Lake Program.

Collect fish samples every three to five years and have the samples analyzed for organochlorine pesticides.

Write contaminants study proposals and submit to the Lower Mississippi River Ecosystem Team, the Washington Office, and outside sources for funding.

Continue to monitor breeding pools to determine extent and severity of malformations in frogs. Obtain funding to conduct contaminant investigations on the areas at Dahomey refuge that contained frogs with a high rate of deformity. Monitor areas receiving runoff from herbicides applied to manage invasive species on the refuge to ensure that refuge management activities are not adversely affecting non-target organisms.

Reduce large, filamentous algal blooms in the catfish ponds through application of herbicides at the appropriate time.

GOAL 6 – Identify and protect cultural resources on the Complex in accordance with federal and state historic preservation laws and regulations.

Objective 6-1: Cultural Resources
By 2010, identify, evaluate the importance of, and seek the appropriate protective designation of cultural resources throughout the Complex, in accordance with existing legal requirements,

regulations, and professional standards. Where significant cultural resources exist, provide public outreach opportunities where appropriate.

Background: The Complex follows standard National Historic Preservation Act Section 106 procedures to protect the public's interest in preserving its cultural/historic legacy that may potentially occur on the Complex. Whenever construction work is undertaken that involves any excavation with heavy earth-moving equipment like tractors, graders and bulldozers, such as for the development of moist-soil units, the Complex contracts with a qualified archaeologist/cultural resources expert to conduct an archaeological survey of the subject property. The results of this survey are submitted to the RHPO as well as the SHPO, which in Mississippi is an official within the Historic Preservation Division of the Mississippi Department of Archives and History. The SHPO reviews the surveys and determines whether cultural resources will be impacted, that is, whether any properties listed in or eligible for listing in the National Register of Historic Places (NRHP) will be affected. If cultural resources are actually encountered during construction activities, the Complex is to notify the SHPO immediately. To date, no properties on the Complex have been determined to be eligible for the NRHP.

Strategies:

By 2010, conduct a Phase I archaeological survey of the non-flooded areas of the refuges, by qualified personnel, as a necessary first step in cultural resources management.

Conduct a Phase II investigation if archaeological resources are identified during the Phase I survey. In this, the eligibility of identified resources for listing on the NRHP is evaluated prior to any disturbance.

Conduct a Phase III data recovery if resources identified in Phases I and II are determined to be eligible. This will recover data and mitigate adverse effects of any undertaking.

By 2009, prepare a Cultural Resources Management Plan (CRMP) for the Complex.

Follow procedures outlined in CRMP for consultation with RHPO, SHPO, and potentially interested American Indian tribes.

Follow procedures detailed in CRMP for inadvertent discoveries of human remains.

Ensure archaeological and cultural values are described, identified, and taken into consideration prior to implementing undertakings.

Develop a step-down plan for surveying lands to identify archaeological resources and for developing a preservation program.

GOAL 7 – Increase the public understanding, use, and enjoyment of the natural resources of the Complex, consistent with the principle that wildlife comes first on national wildlife refuges.

Background: The National Wildlife Refuge System Administration Act, as amended by the National Wildlife Refuge System Improvement Act of 1997, states that compatible wildlife-dependent recreational uses are the priority public uses of the National Wildlife Refuge System (hunting, fishing, wildlife observation, wildlife photography, and environmental education and interpretation) and will receive enhanced consideration over other general public uses. Other uses will be permitted only when it is determined that they are legally mandated, provide benefits to the Service, occur due to special circumstances, or facilitate one of the priority wildlife-dependent recreational uses. See 605 FW 1, General Guidance, and 603 FW 1, Appropriate Refuge Uses. Where conflicts do not exist with the refuge purpose (e.g., migratory bird management, where applicable), refuge properties should be open for priority, wildlife-dependent public uses of the refuges as listed in the National Wildlife Refuge Improvement Act of 1997.

Objective 7-1: Visitor Services Plan
By 2009, develop a Visitor Services Plan.

Discussion: Through comprehensive conservation plans and visitor services plans, goals are set, measurable objectives are determined, strategies identified, and evaluation criteria established for all visitor services. Careful planning provides the visiting public with opportunities to enjoy and appreciate fish, wildlife, plants, and other resources. As a result, the visiting public will develop an understanding and will build an appreciation of each individual's role in the environment today and into the future.

Currently there is not a Visitor Services Plan for the Complex.

Strategies:

By 2009, develop a Visitor Services Plan that reflects current legislation, director's orders, initiatives, policy, and the mission of the Complex, the Refuge System and the Service. The plan should also address the current and future visitor services and recreation needs of refuge visitors.

When funding becomes available, hire one public use staff person for the Complex.

Objective 7-2: Visitor Centers
By 2014, explore the feasibility of building visitor centers on Highway 82 at the Povall Farm Service Agency Tract and jointly with the Private John Allen National Fish Hatchery.

Discussion: At the present time, the Complex does not have a visitor center. It is proposed to add 2 in the next 15 years that would be located to attract visitors in different parts of the Complex. The Service should consider cooperating with the Private John Allen National Fish Hatchery in planning, constructing, and operating a visitor center that would serve both the hatchery and the Complex.

Strategies:

Work with the Service to develop visitor centers with architecture that is resource-efficient and energy-conserving, and/or reflective of local or regional cultural and historic themes.

Complex management and outreach personnel should work closely with exhibit designers to develop exhibits based on appropriate themes for the Complex.

One or both visitor centers should have a small theater that could project slide shows or wildlife-oriented documentary films.

By 2009, develop an introductory audio-visual program to welcome and orient visitors to the Complex.

Develop a cadre of volunteers who could assist with staff of the visitor centers.

<u>Objective 7-3: Visitor Contact/Administration Stations</u>
By 2014, develop Visitor Contact/Administration Stations at all 3 traditional refuges on the Complex.

Discussion: At present, the Complex has two visitor contact/administration stations, one at the Complex headquarters in Grenada, and one at Dahomey refuge. At both locations, visitors can obtain Complex brochures, maps, hunting and fishing regulations, and other Service information. They can also meet and speak with Complex staff. This objective would keep these two visitor contact stations and add two more at Coldwater River and Tallahatchie refuges. These stations would be in addition to the two proposed visitor centers mentioned above.

Strategies:

Obtain and place good signs for motorists on approach routes to visitor contact stations.

Work with Mississippi DOT to place road signs at nearby intersections of major routes.

Visitor contact stations should be well-stocked with adequate informational literature and staffed, if possible.

To serve the public after hours or when the visitor contact station is closed, install kiosks at all visitor contact stations with information and brochures about the Fish and Wildlife Service, Refuge System, and Complex.

<u>Objective 7-4: Hunting</u>
Expand current hunting program throughout the Complex and continue to provide a quality and safe outdoor experience.

Discussion: The National Wildlife Refuge System Improvement Act of 1997 recognizes hunting as one of the six priority public uses of the Refuge System. These uses, "where compatible with the Refuge System mission and purposes of the individual refuges," are considered "legitimate and appropriate public uses…through which the American public can develop an appreciation for fish and wildlife" and shall receive "priority consideration in refuge planning and management." The Act further states that, "In administering the Refuge System, the Secretary shall…provide increased opportunities for families to experience compatible wildlife-dependent recreation, particularly opportunities for parents and their children to safely engage in traditional outdoor activities, such as hunting and fishing...."

Dahomey and Tallahatchie refuges allow hunting for squirrel, rabbit, bobwhite quail, raccoon, deer, turkey (Dahomey only), waterfowl, snipe, woodcock, and feral hogs. In addition, there are youth hunts for deer, turkey (Dahomey only), waterfowl, and squirrel. Dates for small game, bow hunting (deer), and primitive weapon hunting (deer) approximate the state's seasons. Duck and goose hunting are allowed Wednesday/Saturday/ Sunday mornings during state seasons. During the conservation order, snow goose hunting is allowed seven days a week, one-half hour before sunrise to one-half hour after sunset. Unplugged shotguns and electronic calling devices are allowed and there are no bag or possession limits and no stamps needed. Special facilities are available for mobility impaired hunters. Each hunter must obtain from one of the Hunter Information Stations a user information card. There is a $12.50 permit required to hunt on Dahomey refuge, Tallahatchie refuge, and select Farm Service Agency tracts (small game only).

Strategies

Develop 1-2 panel kiosks at each check station and at the boat launch that state the Service and Refuge System missions along with refuge purposes. Consider the use of in-house graphics in the short-term.

Objective 7-5: Fishing
Work closely with Private John Allen National Fish Hatchery to expand current fishing opportunities over the next 10 years as outlined in the Biological Review.

Discussion: A 50-acre oxbow (Long Branch) on Tallahatchie refuge, as well as several Farm Service Agency tracts under refuge administration, has potential for aquatic resource management. Two tracts hold a total of ten ponds formerly used for catfish production. Three of these, a 40-acre pond at the Scott-90 tract, and two 20-acre ponds at the Henson-165 tract, would be managed for sport fishing. In addition to the Tallahatchie refuge oxbow lake, there are existing oxbows on the following tracts, each of which would require a water control structure, a boat ramp, and parking area: the Trainor-219 tract with a 10-acre oxbow of the Tallahatchie River; the Robertson-655 tract with 8-acre oxbow of the Yalobusha River; and the Lindsey-160 and Povall-180 tracts, each with a 10-acre oxbow of the Sunflower River. A 300-acre moist-soil unit on the Wilkins tract shows potential for incorporating crawfish production into the waterfowl management water regime and is addressed under "Crawfish Management."

If habitat alterations for sport-fishing were necessary and practical at any of these water bodies, recommendations outlined below would apply. Otherwise, the ponds would be surveyed and managed according to results of the survey.

At Coldwater River refuge, there are 25 old commercial catfish ponds located on the north boundary, which range from 9 to 20 acres in size. The Baton Rouge Fisheries Resource Office proposes that the four northernmost ponds (units A, B, I, J) be managed as a fishery. These units, totaling approximately 64 acres, are adjacent to wells for filling, each has a water control structure, and their location at the north boundary of the refuge may limit trespass into closed areas. The key to establishment and maintenance of a healthy sport fishery is habitat, which includes adequate water quality, spawning substrate, and depth. Harvest management is also important, especially if fishing pressure is heavy. Only bank fishing should be allowed.

At least 5 percent of each pond would be 8 feet deep with most of the remainder 4 to 5 feet deep. Banks should slope approximately 2.5:1 (4-foot depth 10 feet from bank) with very little depths shallower than 3 feet. Islands or bank fingers created from the excavated bottom substrates can serve as isolated fish spawning sites and shorebird/wading bird habitat. Additionally, at least six 10 ft. x 10 ft. pea-gravel spawning beds for "bream" would be constructed in each unit. Ideally, the gravel would be enclosed in a treated-wood frame, on a level substrate at least 3 feet deep and away from bank fisherman disturbance. If possible, one or two of these beds should be placed around isolated islands away from the bank in 2 to 3 feet of water.

Strategies:

Annually survey waterbodies to obtain status of fish populations and suitability of existing habitats to support sport fisheries.

By 2010, install water control structures on oxbows and as feasible add launch and parking facilities.

Rehabilitate those waterbodies requiring habitat enhancement measures as determined by the survey.

By 2009, establish a sport fishery by rehabilitating, stocking, and managing catfish ponds A, B, I, and J on Coldwater River refuge and in those waterbodies where stocking is necessary, follow the procedure outlined below.

Drain and rehabilitate each unit as per narrative.

Stock bluegill and redear sunfish (1000/acre at 65 -35 percent ratio), and channel catfish (100/acre) in the fall.

The following spring stock largemouth bass fingerlings at 100/acre.

Fertilize monthly or as necessary from March 15 to October 15 using powdered N-P-K with high phosphorous (@40 percent) to maintain an algal bloom (18-inch visibility) to support the fish population.

Initiate a 14-inch minimum length limit on bass when the season is opened for fishing, the second summer (2 1/2 years) after initial stocking. Restrict bass creel to three per person per day. State restrictions on other species should apply.

Open the area to fishing each year as per refuge waterfowl guidelines (March 15 - October 15).

By 2007, incorporate rice or moist-soil plant production with crawfish production to enhance aquatic resources for wildlife and public use on the Wilkins Farm Service Agency tract with a target yield of 100-500 pounds of crawfish per acre.

Incorporate crawfish life cycle requirements, which mimic rice/moist-soil plant production water regime (i.e., drain and plant May-June, inundate September-November) on the Wilkins Farm Service Agency tract. Where natural crawfish populations (red swamp) don't exist, stock adult crawfish at 10 pounds/acre on a one-time basis or a total of 500 pounds if the whole tract is to be managed for recreational crawfish harvesting.

By 2007, allow use by the public on the Wilkins Farm Service Agency tract from April 1 through May 30, with a 70-pound (two onion sacks or one 48-quart cooler) limit per vehicle per day.

Open the area to fishing each year as per refuge waterfowl guidelines (March 15 - October 15).

Objective 7-6: Environmental Education
Within 3 years of the plan's approval, the Complex will receive five teacher-led class visits per year.

Discussion: Complex staff members have developed and delivered environmental education programs (EE) to local school and civic groups. Additionally, there are endangered species and wetlands kits available for teachers to use with their classes. In general, there is a high demand for EE programs and current staffing levels are insufficient to meet that demand.

Groups that are interested in partnering with the refuge to develop environmental education opportunities include Delta State University and the Audubon Society. There are four universities within a 1-hour drive of Grenada. Each of these universities has an annual conservation festival.

Each refuge staff person will assess his/her potential to work with schools in providing an appropriate level of environmental education. The Complex intends to support, if feasible, environmental education through the use of facilities, equipment, educational materials, teacher workshops, and study sites that are safe and conducive to learning.

Strategies:

Designate two events per year for staff to participate, such as field days and career days.

Develop a teacher packet for Hasserway Trail. This could be part of a pre-visit package sent from Corps of Engineers Grenada Lake Visitor Center (work with Regional Office EE coordinator to develop this packet).

If funding permits, hire full-time, seasonal, or temporary employee to do EE work, camps, develop kits/trunks (possibly a teacher in summer).

Develop an educational nature trail behind headquarters at Dahomey.

Partner with Delta State to do EE – seek funding from National Fish and Wildlife Foundation to do the traveling (bookmobile) part of these efforts.

Develop a volunteer EE staff.

Develop one teacher workshop per year to train teachers to do self-guided field studies.

Objective 7-7: Wildlife Interpretation
Within 5 years of the plan's approval, at least 75 percent of visitors will understand the Complex's contribution to protection and restoration of the Lower Mississippi Alluvial Valley.

Discussion: There is currently limited interpretation on the refuges. Through a partnership with Ducks Unlimited, an interpretive trail (Hasserway Trail) was developed at Grenada Lake Recreation Area. There are no interpretive kiosks at any of the offices. The Complex has opportunities to significantly expand interpretation and increase the awareness of the visiting public. Through this heightened awareness, the Complex hopes to inspire visitors to take positive actions supporting refuge goals and the Refuge System mission.

Strategies:

On Hasserway Trail, add directional signs at decision points on trail by 2006; arrange for or do trail maintenance.

By 2006, install interpretive kiosks at Grenada and Dahomey refuge headquarters.

By 2007, install an interpretive kiosk at Coldwater River refuge.

Interpretation should be organized by themes that will reinforce the most important messages to visitors; examples of themes include:
- deforestation and reforestation
- history of Farm Service Agency lands
- culture/history of the area

- bottomland hardwoods and the wildlife that depend on this habitat
- migratory birds (waterfowl, neotropical songbirds, shorebirds, etc.)
- Mississippi Delta
- Moist-soil management
- history of the names 'Dahomey' and 'Tallahatchie'

Objective 7-8: Wildlife Observation and Photography
Within 2 years of plan approval, develop one new trail at each refuge and one observation site/deck each at Coldwater River and Tallahatchie refuges.

Discussion: Viewing and photographing wildlife in natural or managed environments will foster a connection between visitors and natural resources. There are limited wildlife viewing opportunities on the Complex at present. Coldwater River refuge has the greatest potential for wildlife observation. The number and variety of shorebirds, wading birds, and waterfowl create a spectacular sight. The proximity of this refuge to Memphis, and to the Interstate highway, provides a potentially larger population base from which to attract visitors. The Audubon Society is proposing to develop a Great River Road Birding Trail in the vicinity of Dahomey refuge.

There are two photo-blinds at Tallahatchie refuge which could be incorporated into hiking trails.

Strategies:

By 2006, develop walking trail around portion of impoundments at Coldwater River refuge and partner with Ducks Unlimited to develop an observation deck in conjunction with the walking trail.

By 2006, partner with Mississippi DOT to develop an observation site on Highway 8 (possibly at the area south of Highway 8 just before the boat launch).

By 2006, develop a trail on Tallahatchie refuge in the area that is down the gravel road on the south side of Highway 8 just past the boat launch road.

By 2006, develop a trail at Dahomey refuge next to inholding on Highway 446.

Assist with the development of the Audubon Society's Great River Road Birding Trail.

Ensure there is a trail site that is accessible for a school bus and has bus parking and turn-around.

GOAL 8: Provide personnel, funding, and facilities needed to ensure that the goals and objectives identified in this comprehensive conservation plan can be achieved.

Background: The administrative functions associated with a refuge include a wide array of activities that are critical to the mission of the Refuge System and the purpose of each refuge. These functions include staffing, training, budgeting, planning, refuge access, law enforcement, facilities, community relations, partnering, and maintenance. Refuges must have appropriate staff, facilities, equipment, and funding in order to accomplish their overall goals and objectives.

Objective 8-1: Facilities
By 2014, develop 25 percent more office space and maintenance facilities both at the Complex headquarters and at each refuge to enable the expansion of refuge programs and ensure safe and efficient operations – consistent with Service and federal standards – and commensurate with the expansion of the refuge land base.

Discussion: Office space is needed at each of the three refuges if programs are going to expand at any level. Current strategies include additional positions to meet the goals and objectives identified in this plan. Facilities vary by station. A newly completed facility at Dahomey refuge contains a small maintenance shop and limited office space. Currently, there are no facilities at either Coldwater River or Tallahatchie refuges.

Strategies:

Build additional office space and maintenance facilities at each of the refuges as they continue to expand to their respective acquisition boundaries.

Incorporate office space into proposed visitor centers.

Utilize existing structures, if suitable, on acquired lands for either maintenance or equipment storage.

Objective 8-2: Personnel
By 2019, obtain additional staff (18 FTE's) and resources needed as funding allows to accomplish the comprehensive management programs as outlined in this document commensurate with the expansion of the refuge land base.

Discussion: Many of the proposed strategies cannot be implemented without the addition of personnel. For example, the maintenance of early successional habitat is labor intensive, the objectives for which must be modified in accordance with availability of personnel. Some work, such as bird count surveys, may be taken on by volunteers or interns. Slight adjustments to present staff work schedules can be considered, although this, too, requires additional resources.

If the refuge is to make a serious impact on meeting migratory bird objectives and other important biological management objectives, there is a need to add two or three biologists, a forester, and three or four biological/forestry technicians/equipment operators to the current staff. This level of staffing would be expected to provide biological data and management needed to meet many of the "all bird" planning objectives coordinated by the LMRVJV. Highest priority would be to add a refuge biologist and biotech/equipment operator to focus work on the catfish ponds and other priority habitat management and population monitoring work at Coldwater River refuge.

Following the biological review, the Complex filled an existing FTE with a biologist. However, although this added a biologist to the staff, it did not increase the overall number of FTE's for the Complex.

Strategies:

Hire the personnel indicated above for the purpose of optimizing refuge management activities.

Implement a Complex-wide program that ensures equal consideration is given to all stations within the Complex when funding and other resources become available.

Have quarterly budget meetings with all refuge managers to ensure highest priority projects and maintenance backlogs are identified and ranked across the Complex.

Once funding is allocated, give each refuge manager overseeing a sub-headquarters responsibility for managing his/her station budget based on identified priorities and planning budget exercises, ensuring each refuge's needs are being met.

Provide continuing education and training opportunities to all staff to ensure a highly competent and motivated team.

Provide safe and efficient equipment and vehicles to perform needed refuge operations and maintenance.

Provide training to refuge staff on computer-based systems needed to ensure all refuge data is stored in a manageable, retrievable database that can be used for analysis and data sharing.

By 2008, hire a public use specialist/volunteer coordinator if funding allows.

Objective 8-3: Law Enforcement
Improve Complex law enforcement program with 1.5 additional FTE's and partnerships.

Discussion: The National Wildlife Refuge System consists of more than 540 refuges and 37 wetland management districts. The Refuge System manages over 95 million acres, in every state and several territories. Visitation is increasing at an annual average of 6.6 percent. Between 2.3 and 2.4 million additional visitors will be serviced by refuge officers over the next several years.

Protecting the natural resources of the Complex and ensuring the safety of refuge visitors are fundamental responsibilities of the Refuge System. Currently, the Complex law enforcement program consists of one full-time officer and two collateral duty officers. During periods of high public use, such as hunting seasons, the majority of collateral duty officers' time is spent conducting law enforcement activities, which, many times, is at the sacrifice of other equally crucial functions.

This plan recommends a substantial increase in public use facilities offered to the visiting public over the next 15 years. As a result of this increase, there will certainly be a substantial increase in visitation. If we are to continue offering a very safe place for visitors to enjoy the outdoors, additional full-time law enforcement officers are necessary.

Strategies:

Increase law enforcement personnel from current level to a minimum of 2 FTE's if funding allows.

Provide up-to-date training and equipment to law enforcement officers.

Develop Memoranda of Understanding with state and local law enforcement agencies to facilitate cooperation and assistance in law enforcement activities.

Provide education and outreach programs in the local community as part of a preventive law enforcement effort.

Provide assistance to Service Special Agents and Mississippi Department of Wildlife, Fisheries and Parks conservation officers for off-refuge activities as needed.

Objective 8-4: Friends Group, Volunteers, Partners, and Intern Programs
Provide a highly visible and dynamic volunteer and intern workforce and establish one or more Friends Groups to assist and support all aspects of Complex operations, including environmental education, wildlife interpretation, habitat improvement, visitor facilities maintenance, funding needs, etc.

Discussion: Volunteers and refuge support groups fortify refuge staffs with their gift of time, skills, and energy and are integral to the future of the National Wildlife Refuge System. Refuge staff will initiate and nurture relationships with volunteers and refuge support groups, and continually support, monitor, and evaluate these groups with the goal of fortifying important refuge activities. The National Wildlife Refuge System Volunteer and Community Partnership Enhancement Act of 1998 (P.L. 105-242) strengthens the Refuge System's role in developing effective partnerships with various community groups. Whether through volunteers, refuge support groups, or other important partnerships in the community, refuge personnel should seek to make the refuge an integral part of the community, giving rise to a stronger Refuge System. Currently, Dahomey refuge is developing a friends group.

The Complex has acquired three FEMA trailers to be used as possible housing for volunteers. At present there is minimal use of volunteers. The complex does have a Youth Conservation Corps crew in the summer.

Strategies:

Continue to look for opportunities to partner with (on-going):
- local universities and colleges
- Ducks Unlimited
- local high school and elementary school system
- Audubon Society
- U. S. Department of Agriculture/Natural Resources Conservation Service
- Farm Services Administration
- Chambers of Commerce
- The Natural Conservancy and other land trusts

Utilize pad and trailer at Dahomey refuge and headquarters to encourage participation by individuals needing living space and by those with trailers needing parking space.

Develop camper pad at Coldwater River for RV campers for bird walks, security, and maintenance.

By 2008, hire a public use specialist/volunteer coordinator for the Complex.

V. Plan Implementation

This comprehensive conservation plan outlines an ambitious course of action for the management of the North Mississippi National Wildlife Refuges Complex over the coming 15 years. The ability to enhance wildlife habitats on the Complex, while expanding the area of those habitats within the acquisition boundary of each refuge, will require a significant commitment of staff and funding from Congress and the Service. Likewise, expanding the relatively limited public use facilities now available on the three refuges will take increased resources. Consequently, the Complex will continually need appropriate operational and maintenance funding to implement the objectives in this plan.

FUNDING

In the preceding chapters, this plan has outlined a vision for the Complex and included the management goals, objectives, and strategies needed to realize the vision. The current level of refuge funding will not move the Complex beyond a slow deterioration of the current habitat and public use condition. Pre-plan staff levels do not allow adequate interactions with the public for education, interpretation, information, safety, or enforcement purposes. In addition, habitat management objectives and strategies are not achievable with the current staffing. The rate at which each refuge achieves its full potential of contributing locally, regionally, and nationally important wildlife outputs will depend on the resources provided for those purposes. Increased staffing and funding on each refuge unit will result in long-lasting protection, maintenance, and enhancements to Delta forest, wetland, and moist-soil habitats and public use facilities and programs.

The following provides a brief description of the highest priority refuge projects (Tier 1), as chosen by the Complex staff and listed in the Refuge Operating Needs System (RONS). A full listing of unfunded refuge projects and operational needs can be found in Appendix C.

REFUGE OPERATING NEEDS – TIER 1 (HIGHEST PRIORITY)

Dahomey National Wildlife Refuge – Provide for a full-time law enforcement officer
Objective 8-3
Estimated cost: $123,000
Provide for a full-time law enforcement officer at Dahomey refuge, the largest remaining tract of bottomland hardwoods in the northern Mississippi Delta. Dahomey refuge boasts a large hunting program and a growing "non-consumptive use" constituency. There is not currently a full-time law enforcement officer stationed at Dahomey refuge to protect visitors or wildlife and their habitats. Being located near Delta State University, the refuge gets extensive use by researchers, students, and school groups. This project will permit a law enforcement presence and also facilitate data collection during the long and varied hunting seasons, helping to make better informed habitat and public use management decisions. Project benefits will include a decrease in poaching and theft, and a higher degree of public safety and enjoyment on the refuge.

North Mississippi National Wildlife Refuges Complex – Inventory and monitor bottomland hardwood forests
Objective 4-2
Estimated cost: $108,000
The Complex administers three national wildlife refuges and numerous Farm Service Agency lands that encompass approximately 32,000 acres in northwest Mississippi. Approximately 12,000 acres of this land consist of mature bottomland hardwood forest habitat. About 13,000 acres consist of lands that have either been recently reforested or will be reforested in the next 2-3 years. None of the mature forest lands has been completely inventoried and their overall conditions (e.g., health, diversity, age class structure, amount of regeneration, etc.) have not been documented or evaluated. A monitoring program will be implemented for all areas that have been recently reforested in order to evaluate their general conditions over time. Information gained will then be used to implement appropriate management practices within all forested areas for the enhancement of wildlife resources.

Coldwater River National Wildlife Refuge – Provide for a maintenance worker
Objectives 4-1 & 8-2
Estimated cost: $125,000
Provide for a maintenance worker at Coldwater River refuge, so existing facilities and resources can be managed and maintained. Coldwater River refuge contains moist-soil units, service-owned roads, and bridges. A maintenance worker is needed to maintain service-owned roads for the benefit of visitor and employee health and safety, and to conduct critical habitat management efforts.

Coldwater River National Wildlife Refuge – Provide for a GS-12 Refuge Manager
Objective 8-2
Estimated cost: $152,000
Provide a GS-12 Refuge Manager at Coldwater River refuge. This is a new refuge and a Refuge Manager meets staffing requirements. A Refuge Manager is needed to provide for adequate administration of all the refuge functions and operations. This project would provide for adequate administration of this refuge and fulfill public use needs that are currently not being met.

Dahomey National Wildlife Refuge – Provide for a maintenance worker
Objectives 4-1, 4-2 & 8-2
Estimated cost: $125,000
Provide for a maintenance worker at Dahomey refuge, so existing facilities and resources can be managed and maintained. This refuge does not have any maintenance personnel to maintain existing facilities, equipment, and other resources. Therefore, necessary habitat management and maintenance activities are not being implemented, and investments in facilities and habitat management projects are being lost. Dahomey refuge, the largest remaining tract of bottomland hardwoods in the northern Mississippi Delta region, contains moist-soil units, greentree reservoirs, service-owned roads, cooperatively farmed lands, visitor information stations, heavy and light duty equipment, and a headquarters facility. This project will provide a maintenance worker, so essential management and maintenance activities can be implemented and refuge-owned roads can be maintained in a manner that is safe for public use.

Tallahatchie National Wildlife Refuge – Provide for a full-time law enforcement officer
Objective 8-3
Estimated cost: $123,000
The 4,000-acre Tallahatchie refuge is experiencing poaching and theft year-round. This project will provide a full-time law enforcement officer, a need that remains unmet, to better ensure visitor safety and to better protect refuge wildlife and their habitats. An estimated 65,000 migratory waterfowl are documented annually on this refuge that issues 1,600 public use permits each year. Myriad other wildlife, from deer and turkey to otter and bobcat, use this new refuge that is undergoing extensive forest restoration. Resource protection and public safety are suffering without a strong law enforcement presence.

Dahomey National Wildlife Refuge – Create moist-soil units
Objective 4-1
Estimated cost: $157,000
Create moist-soil units on Dahomey refuge for the primary benefit of resident and migratory water birds, restoring 1,000 acres of wetland habitat. This project will also provide for the establishment of greentree reservoirs within existing forest habitat. Channelization and drainage activities implemented prior to refuge ownership have changed natural water patterns in these wetland areas. This project will include the installation of needed water control structures and other water management features to return the area to more natural conditions, benefiting not only water birds, but numerous wetland-associated wildlife species. Located in the ecologically and culturally unique Mississippi Delta, Dahomey refuge is the largest remaining tract of bottomland hardwoods in the northern Delta.

Tallahatchie National Wildlife Refuge – Provide for a secretary/clerk
Objective 8-3
Estimated cost: $118,000
Project will provide for a secretary/clerk on Tallahatchie refuge, a station without any on-site administrative support. This position is necessary to provide essential administrative assistance for permit sales, clerical functions, and basic visitor services that are critical for effective refuge operations. The refuge issues 1,600 hunting permits annually, and without a secretary, the administrative requirements necessary for effective operations of the refuge cannot be met unless the refuge manager refocuses his/her energies. This diminishes the effectiveness of habitat management and other public use management programs. Public needs are presently not being fulfilled due to the lack of necessary administrative support.

North Mississippi National Wildlife Refuges Complex – Provide for wildlife biologist to develop and implement CCP
All objectives
Estimated cost: $139,000
Initiate planning for the entire North Mississippi National Wildlife Refuges Complex by providing for a wildlife biologist who will lead the development of, and help implement, an effective management direction for three national wildlife refuges and more than 100 Farm Service Agency lands that total over 30,000 acres. The entire refuge complex does not and has not ever had a biologist to lead inventorying, monitoring, or research or help with long-range planning to most effectively realize potential benefits for wildlife and the visiting public.

Dahomey National Wildlife Refuge – Provide for a secretary/clerk
Objectives 7-4 & 8-2
Estimated cost: $118,000
Project will provide for a secretary/clerk on Dahomey refuge, a station without any on-site administrative support. This position is necessary to provide essential administrative assistance for permit sales, clerical functions, and basic visitor services that are critical for effective refuge operations. The refuge sells approximately 1,000 hunting permits annually, and without a secretary, the administrative requirements necessary for effective operations of the refuge cannot be met unless the refuge manager refocuses his/her energies. This diminishes the effectiveness of habitat management and other public use management programs. Public needs are presently not being fulfilled due to the lack of necessary administrative support.

Tallahatchie National Wildlife Refuge – Provide for a maintenance worker
Objectives 4-1 & 8-2
Estimated cost: $125,000
Tallahatchie refuge, boasting active public hunting and forest restoration programs, does not have a maintenance worker to properly maintain public facilities or help effectively manage refuge habitats to benefit a host of wildlife species. This project will provide a maintenance worker at this unstaffed refuge. Maintenance of existing roads and facilities is necessary to meet public expectations for a safe, enjoyable refuge visit.

North Mississippi National Wildlife Refuges Complex – Provide for a full-time secretary/clerk
Objective 8-2
Estimated cost: $110,000
Provide a full-time secretary/clerk to meet the requirements of the refuge fee program, contracting requirements, and other budget and administration duties/policies. Due to the large volume of work at this three-refuge, 30,000-acre, 100+ Farm Service Agency-tract complex, a second administrative person is needed to meet minimum Service compliance and enable effective operation of purchasing, budget tracking, property management, filing/typing, public inquiry response, and personnel actions. We cannot presently provide the quality and quantity of services expected by the public for the many refuge programs.

Dahomey National Wildlife Refuge – Provide for a biologist for critical habitat and wildlife surveys
Multiple objectives under Goals 1, 2 & 4
Estimated cost: $139,000
A newer national wildlife refuge that was never provided startup funding or staffing, Dahomey refuge is the largest remaining tract of bottomland hardwoods in the northern Mississippi Delta. This project will provide for a biologist to obtain and evaluate critical habitat and wildlife surveys. This refuge does not have a biologist, and biological information necessary to help make the most informed management decisions is not being obtained. Partnership potential to conduct inventorying and monitoring is great, with the refuge receiving extensive use by researchers, students, and school groups and being located near Delta State University.

Tallahatchie National Wildlife Refuge – Provide for a biological technician
Multiple objectives under Goals 1 & 2 and Objective 4-2
Estimated cost: $97,000
Provide a biological technician to monitor habitats and habitat restoration activities on Tallahatchie refuge, a newer national wildlife refuge that was never provided startup funding or staffing. This unstaffed refuge is a research site for the Mississippi Forestry Division and a "mitigation bank" for the Mississippi Department of Transportation. Tallahatchie refuge could serve as an outstanding example of bottomland hardwood forest restoration, yet does not have biological staff to obtain, interpret, and share critical habitat and wildlife survey data. Without any biological staff, information necessary to help make the most informed management decisions is not being obtained.

North Mississippi National Wildlife Refuges Complex – Provide for a public outreach specialist
Objective 7-1
Estimated cost: $72,000
Provide a public outreach specialist to create a quality public outreach program for the three-refuge, 30,000-acre, 100+ Farm Service Agency-tract North Mississippi National Wildlife Refuges Complex. This Complex hosts some of the largest tracts of remaining bottomland hardwood forest left in the ecologically and culturally unique Mississippi Delta region. Currently, the Complex has no outreach personnel or staff to establish close partnerships with many potential community support groups, school groups, and other wildlife-oriented organizations, which can provide tremendous volunteer assistance and issues advocacy support. This position will also lead all efforts related to exhibits, news releases, festivals, newsletter, brochures, and public inquiries.

Dahomey National Wildlife Refuge – Provide for an assistant refuge manager
Multiple objectives under all goals and Objective 8-2
Estimated cost: $107,000
Provide an assistant refuge manager to oversee field operations and help direct overall management programs at Dahomey refuge. Because the refuge is understaffed, there is a 1,000-acre cooperative farming program that does not receive adequate supervision to properly maximize the program's great potential benefit to wildlife. This project would provide the needed staff to also assist with other refuge activities, such as public hunting, outreach, education, and the implementation of this plan.

Dahomey National Wildlife Refuge – Provide a forester to manage Dahomey refuge's hardwood forests.
Objective 4-2
Estimated cost: $139,000
Provide a forester to more effectively manage Dahomey refuge, the largest tract of bottomland hardwood forest in the northern Mississippi Delta. Important to a wide variety of wildlife species, the refuge has tremendous potential for forest restoration and management through the planting of trees, appropriate thinning of the existing stand, and the proper management of water levels. However, there is only a refuge manager and an equipment operator stationed at this 9,600-acre refuge, and many parts of the forests are dying due to lack of care. This project will enable forest resources of this refuge to be managed to their fullest potential to provide the fish and wildlife values and recreational benefits expected by the public.

Dahomey National Wildife Refuge – Provide a refuge manager
Multiple objectives under all goals and Objective 8-2
Estimated cost: $152,000
Provide a refuge manager at Dahomey refuge to ensure effective habitat management and provide appropriate wildlife-oriented recreation expected by the public. This 10,000-acre refuge, the largest tract of bottomland hardwood forest in the northern Mississippi Delta, was established in 1992 and has only recently been staffed by a refuge operations specialist and biological technician. A refuge manager is needed on this popular refuge to provide adequate leadership and administration for all the required management programs, including the care of 40 outlying properties. Being located near Delta State University and having a strong constituency of area residents, potential refuge improvement projects abound, but are not being met due to lack of attention.

Tallahatchie National Wildlife Refuge – Provide for a wildlife biologist
Multiple objectives under Goals 1 & 2 and Objective 4-2
Estimated cost: $139,000
Provide a wildlife biologist to conduct critical wildlife surveys and manage habitat development projects on Tallahatchie refuge. The refuge, Mississippi Department of Transportation, and private partners, such as Ducks Unlimited, have invested hundreds of thousands of dollars in facilities and habitat improvement. This unstaffed refuge is a research site for the Mississippi Forestry Division and a "mitigation bank," having thousands of acres recently reforested. However, this newer refuge was neither initially staffed nor funded. This project will enable important restoration work to be continued and critical habitat and wildlife surveys to be conducted.

Tallahatchie National Wildlife Refuge – Provide for a refuge operations specialist/assistant refuge manager
Objective 1-1
Estimated cost: $139,000
Provide a refuge operations specialist/assistant refuge manager to manage existing refuge farm lands for the continuing benefit of wintering migratory waterfowl and other wildlife species. Approximately 65,000 ducks and geese utilize the refuge annually on 3,000 acres that are presently being farmed through private partners. However, due to lack of staffing at this unstaffed refuge, the farmers are not adequately supervised to ensure maximum program benefit and policy compliance. This position will also ensure more effective operations of other habitat management programs, as well as maintenance and public use programs.

Tallahatchie National Wildlife Refuge – Provide for a refuge manager
Multiple objectives under all goals and Objective 8-2
Estimated cost: $152,000
Tallahatchie refuge, which encompasses 4,199 acres and boasts progressive partnerships with the Mississippi Division of Forestry, the Mississippi Department of Transportation, and private partners in a large forest restoration program, contains numerous roads, levees, water control structures, and wetland impoundments. The refuge also has a large contingent of hunters, anglers, and other outdoor enthusiasts who regularly visit the area. Despite all of this, this newer refuge has never been staffed. Maintenance, public use coordination, habitat management, and other management activities that are essential for effective refuge operations are not being adequately implemented, due primarily to lack of staffing. This project will provide for a refuge manager to lead, coordinate, and enhance the overall effectiveness of refuge management programs.

Appendix C contains a full list of unfunded refuge projects and operational needs on the Complex (RONS). This information will be updated annually along with the Maintenance Management System (MMS). These two databases are used to track and manage refuge operations and maintenance budgeting each year. These changes will focus on "means" adjustments, while major changes to the desired future condition will be documented in future revisions to this plan. Some adjustments to the means of getting to the defined future conditions may also occur when step-down plans, such as Visitor Services and Forest Management Plans, are prepared and a greater level of detail is developed.

FUTURE STAFFING REQUIREMENTS

Implementing the vision set forth in this plan will require changes in the organizational structure of the Complex and each of the refuges. Existing staff will direct their time and energy in new directions and new staff members will be added to assist these efforts. Many of the Tier 1 RONS items above involved obtaining new staff to carry out expanded responsibilities. The following table (Table 16) and organizational chart identifies the additional positions and future structure of the Complex. A total of 18.0 FTEs would be needed to fully implement this plan.

Table 16. Additional staff identified to implement the Comprehensive Conservation Plan for the North Mississippi National Wildlife Refuges Complex

Position	Full-time Equivalent (FTEs)	Station Assigned
Refuge Manager	3.0	Coldwater River (1), Dahomey (1), Tallahatchie (1)
Assistant Refuge Mgr.	1.0	Dahomey (1)
Asst. Refuge Mgr./ Refuge Ops. Spec.	1.0	Tallahatchie (1)
Law Enforcement Officer	2.0	Dahomey (1), Tallahatchie (1)
Forester	1.0	Dahomey (1)
Public Outreach Spec.	1.0	Complex (1)
Maintenance Worker	3.0	Coldwater River (1), Dahomey (1), Tallahatchie (1)
Wildlife Biologist	3.0	Complex HQ(1), Dahomey (1), Tallahatchie (1)
Biological Technician	1.0	Tallahatchie (1)
Secretary/Clerk	3.0	Complex HQ (1), Dahomey (1), Tallahatchie (1)
TOTAL FTEs	19.0	Complex HQ (3), Coldwater River (2), Dahomey (7), Tallahatchie (7)

Figure 9 is shows a staffing chart for the Complex at present and Figure 10 shows the proposed staffing chart, which includes the above positions.

Figure 9. North Mississippi National Wildlife Refuges Complex current staffing chart

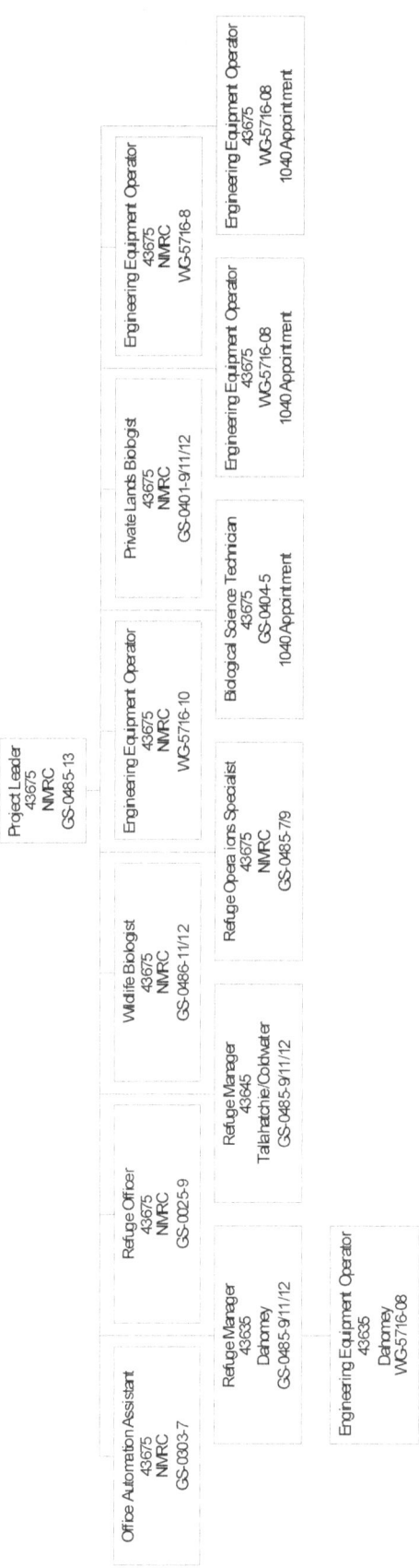

Figure 10. North Mississippi National Wildlife Refuges Complex proposed staffing chart

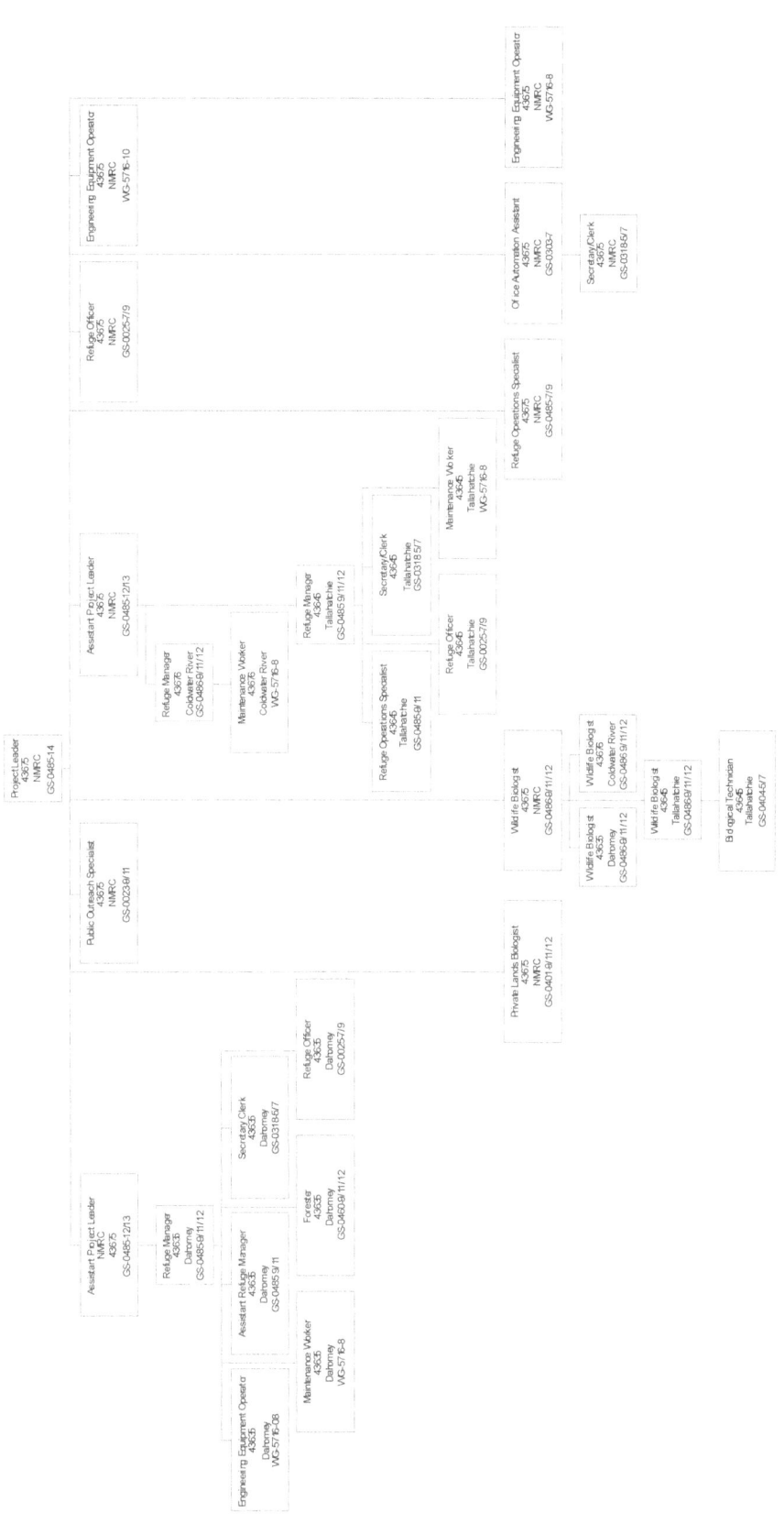

STEP-DOWN MANAGEMENT PLANS

Several step-down management plans describe specific actions that support the accomplishment of refuge objectives. The management plans identified in Table 17 will be reviewed and revised as necessary to achieve the results anticipated in this comprehensive conservation plan.

Table 17. Step-down Management Plans

Plan	Date Completed	Anticipated Revision
Forest Habitat Management Plan	2002	2012
Biological Inventory/Monitoring Plan	2005	2015
Integrated Pest Management Plan	2006	2016
Strategic Plan for Private Lands	2005	2010
Cultural Resources Management Plan	2007	2016
Visitor Services Plan	2007	2016
Hunt Plan	1992/97	2005
Habitat Management Plan	2004	2014

PARTNERSHIP OPPORTUNITIES

Partnerships are an essential element for the successful accomplishment of Complex goals, objectives, and strategies. Indeed, the Complex cooperates with a number of organizations and individuals at present, including other agencies like the USDA Natural Resources Conservation Service, the Army Corps of Engineers, and the Mississippi Department of Wildlife, Fisheries and Parks; the Chamber of Commerce in Grenada; non-profit conservation groups like the Audubon Society and Ducks Unlimited; broad conservation initiatives like the Lower Mississippi Valley Joint Venture Area and Partners-In-Flight; and last but not least, many private individuals.
The objectives outlined in this plan need the support and the partnerships of federal, state, and local agencies, non-governmental organizations, and private citizens. This broad-based approach to managing fish and wildlife resources extends beyond social and political boundaries and requires a foundation of support from many. The Complex will continue to seek creative partnership opportunities to achieve its vision for the future.

Many national wildlife refuges have partner non-profit organizations, often called Friends groups, which serve as advocates for the refuge. These associations have the ability to reach out to the community for support and assistance for refuge projects and conservation issues. Due to the relative newness of each refuge in the Complex, no Friends groups have yet formed to support Coldwater River or Tallahatchie refuges, although the "Friends of Dahomey NWR, Inc.," group was recently established. The refuge staff welcomes the assistance of a Friends group or association and encourages supportive local citizens to form such a group or to join the existing group.

MONITORING AND EVALUATION

The direction set forth in this plan, plus specifically identified strategies and projects, will be monitored throughout the life of the plan. On a periodic basis, the Service will assemble a station review team whose purpose will be to visit the North Mississippi National Wildlife Refuges Complex and evaluate current Complex and refuge activities in light of this plan. The team will review all aspects of Complex and refuge management, including direction, accomplishments and funding. The goals and objectives presented in this plan will provide the baseline from which this field station will be evaluated.

PLAN REVIEW AND REVISION

The comprehensive conservation plan for the North Mississippi National Wildlife Refuges Complex is meant to provide guidance to Complex and refuge managers and staff over the next 10-15 years. However, the plan is also a dynamic and flexible document and several of the strategies contained herein are subject to such things as drought, floods, windstorms, and other uncontrollable events. Likewise, many of the strategies are dependent upon Service funding for staff and projects. Because of all these factors, the recommendations in the plan will be reviewed periodically and, if necessary, revised to meet new circumstances.

Appendix A: List of Preparers

North Mississippi National Wildlife Refuges Complex
Comprehensive Conservation Plan

Robert Barkley, Refuge Manager, North Mississippi National Wildlife Refuges Complex

Mike Dawson, Natural Resource Planner, Fish and Wildlife Service

Alejandro Galvan, Refuge Manager, Dahomey National Wildlife Refuge

Stephen Gard, Project Leader, North Mississippi National Wildlife Refuges Complex

Chuck Hayes, Private Lands Biologist, North Mississippi National Wildlife Refuges Complex

Kimberly Hayes, Refuge Operations Specialist, North Mississippi National Wildlife Refuges Complex

Leon Kolankiewicz, Project Manager, Mangi Environmental Group

Becky Rosamond, Wildlife Biologist, North Mississippi National Wildlife Refuges Complex

Appendix B: Glossary

Alternative | A set of objectives and strategies needed to achieve refuge goals and the desired future condition.

Biological Diversity | The variety of life and its processes, including living organisms, the genetic differences among them, and the communities and ecosystems in which they occur.

Compatible Use | An allowed use that will not materially interfere with, or detract from, the purposes for which the unit was established (Service Manual 602 FW 1.4).

Compatibility Determination | A compatibility determination is required for a wildlife-dependant recreational use or any other public use of a refuge. A compatible use is one which, in the sound professional judgment of the Refuge Manager, will not materially interfere with or detract from fulfillment of the Refuge System Mission or refuge purpose(s).

Comprehensive Conservation Plan | A document that describes the desired future conditions of the refuge, and specifies management actions to achieve refuge goals and the mission of the National Wildlife Refuge System.

Community | A distinct assemblage of plants that develops on sites characterized by particular climates and soils, and the species and populations of wild animals that depend on the plants for food, cover. and/or nesting.

Ecosystem | A dynamic and interrelated complex of plant and animal communities and their associated non-living environment.

Ecosystem Approach | A strategy or plan to protect and restore the natural function, structure, and species composition of an ecosystem, recognizing that all components are interrelated.

Ecosystem Management | Management of an ecosystem that includes all ecological, social, and economic components that make up the whole of the system.

Ecotone | Edge or transition zone between two or more adjacent but different plant communities, ecosystems, or biomes.

Endangered | Any species of plant or animal defined through the Endangered Species Act as being in danger of extinction throughout all or a significant portion of its range.

Endangered

Species (State)	A plant or animal species imperiled in the state because of rarity or because of some factor(s) making it vulnerable to extirpation.
Environmental Assessment (EA)	A systematic analysis to determine if proposed actions would result in a significant effect on the quality of the environment.
Extirpation	The localized extinction of a species that is no longer found in a locality or country, but still exists elsewhere in the world.
Goals	Descriptive statements of desired future conditions.
Issue	Any unsettled matter that requires a management decision. For example, a resource management problem, concern, a threat to natural resources, a conflict in uses, or in the presence of an undesirable resource condition.
National Wildlife Refuge System	All lands, waters, and interests therein administered by the Fish and Wildlife Service as wildlife refuges, wildlife ranges, wildlife management areas, waterfowl production areas, and other areas for the protection and conservation of fish, wildlife, and plant resources.
Non-consumptive, Wildlife-oriented Recreation	Photographing or observing plants, fish, and other wildlife.
Objectives	Actions to be accomplished to achieve a desired outcome or goal. Objectives are more specific, and generally more measurable, than goals.
Preferred Alternative	The Service's selected alternative identified in the Draft Comprehensive Conservation Plan.
Scoping	A process for determining the scope of issues to be addressed by a comprehensive conservation plan and for identifying the significant issues. Involved in the scoping process are federal, state and local agencies; private organizations; and individuals.
Species	A distinctive kind of plant or animal having distinguishable characteristics, and that can interbreed and produce young. In taxonomy, a category of biological classification that refers to one or more populations of similar organisms that can reproduce with each other but is reproductively isolated from – that is, incapable of interbreeding with – all other kinds of organisms.
Strategies	A general approach or specific actions to achieve objectives.

Wildlife-dependent Recreational Use	A use of refuge that involves hunting, fishing, wildlife observation, wildlife photography, and environmental education and interpretation, as identified in the National Wildlife Refuge System Improvement Act of 1997.
Threatened Species (Federal)	Plant or animal species likely to become endangered species throughout all of or a significant portion of their range within the foreseeable future. A plant or animal identified and defined in accordance with the 1973 Endangered Species Act.
Vegetation	Plants in general, or the sum total of the plant life in an area.
Vegetation Type	A category of land based on potential or existing dominant plant species of a particular area.
Visitor Center	A permanently staffed building offering exhibits and interpretive information to the visiting public. Some visitor centers are co-located with refuge offices, others include additional facilities, such as classrooms or wildlife viewing areas.
Visitor Contact Station	Compared to a visitor center, a contact station is a smaller facility, which may not be permanently staffed.
Watershed	The entire land area that collects and drains water into a stream or stream system.
Wetland	Areas such as lakes, marshes, bogs, and streams that are inundated by surface or ground water for a long enough period of time each year to support, and that do support under natural conditions, plants and animals that require saturated or seasonally saturated soils.
Wildlife Diversity	A measure of the number of wildlife species in an area and their relative abundance.

Appendix C: Priority Complex Operational and Maintenance Needs

Refuge Operating Needs System (RONS)
Tier 1 Project Description List

Priority	Project Number	$000	Refuge	Project Description
10	96014	123	Dahomey	Provide for a full-time law enforcement officer at Dahomey refuge, the largest remaining tract of bottomland hardwoods in the northern Mississippi Delta. A full-time law enforcement officer is not stationed at Dahomey to protect visitors or wildlife and their habitats on this refuge with a large hunting program and a growing "non-consumptive" constituency. Being located near Delta State University, the refuge receives extensive use by researchers, students, and school groups. This project will permit a law enforcement presence and also facilitate data collection during the long and varied hunting seasons, helping to make better informed habitat and public use management decisions. Project benefits will include a decrease in poaching and theft, and higher degree of public safety and enjoyment on the refuge.
12	00033	108	North Mississippi Refuges Complex	North Mississippi National Wildlife Refuges Complex administers three national wildlife refuges and numerous Farm Service Agency lands that encompass approximately 32,000 acres in northwest Mississippi. Approximately 12,000 acres of this land consist of mature bottomland hardwood forest habitat. About 13,000 acres consist of lands that have either been recently reforested or will be reforested in the next 2-3 years. None of the mature forest lands have been completely inventoried and the overall conditions (e.g., health, diversity, age class structure, and amount of regeneration) have not been documented or evaluated. A monitoring program will be implemented for all areas that have been recently reforested in order to evaluate their general conditions over time. Information gained will then be used to implement appropriate management practices within all forested areas for the enhancement of wildlife resources.

Priority	Project Number	$000	Refuge	Project Description
27	00013	125	Coldwater River	Provide for a maintenance worker at Coldwater River refuge so existing facilities and resources can be managed and maintained. Coldwater River refuge contains moist-soil units, service-owned roads, cooperative farmed lands, and bridges. A maintenance worker is needed to maintain service-owned roads, facilities, and equipment for the benefit of visitor and employee health and safety, and to conduct critical habitat management efforts.
36	00012	152	Coldwater River	Provide a GS-12 Refuge Manager at Coldwater River refuge. This is a new refuge and a Refuge Manager meets staffing requirements. A Refuge Manager is needed to provide for adequate administration of all the refuge functions and operations. This project would provide for adequate administration of this refuge and fulfill public use needs that are currently not being met.
109	98002	125	Dahomey	Provide for a maintenance worker at Dahomey refuge so existing facilities and resources can be managed and maintained. This refuge does not have any maintenance personnel to maintain existing facilities, equipment, and other resources. Therefore, necessary habitat management and maintenance activities are not being implemented, and investments in facilities and habitat management projects are being lost. Dahomey refuge, the largest remaining tract of bottomland hardwoods in the northern Mississippi Delta region, contains moist-soil units, greentree reservoirs, service-owned roads, cooperatively farmed lands, visitor information stations, heavy and light duty equipment, and a headquarters facility. This project will provide for a maintenance worker, so that essential management and maintenance activities can be implemented and refuge-owned roads can be maintained in a manner that is safe for public use.

Priority	Project Number	$000	Refuge	Project Description
110	96015	123	Tallahatchie	The 4,000-acre Tallahatchie refuge is experiencing poaching and theft year-round. This project will provide a full-time law enforcement officer, a need that remains unmet, to better ensure visitor safety and to better protect refuge wildlife and their habitats. An estimated 65,000 migratory waterfowl are documented annually on this refuge that issues 1,600 public use permits each year. Myriad other wildlife, from deer and turkey to otter and bobcat, use this new refuge that is undergoing extensive forest restoration. Resource protection and public safety are suffering without a strong law enforcement presence.
219	96002	157	Dahomey	Create moist-soil units on Dahomey refuge for the primary benefit of resident and migratory water birds, restoring 1,000 acres of wetland habitat. This project will also provide for the establishment of greentree reservoirs within existing forest habitat. Channelization and drainage activities implemented prior to refuge ownership have changed natural water patterns in these wetland areas. Project will include the installation of needed water control structures and other water management features to return the area to more natural conditions, benefiting not only water birds, but numerous wetland-associated wildlife species. Located in the ecologically and culturally unique Mississippi Delta, Dahomey refuge is the largest remaining tract of bottomland hardwoods in the northern Delta.
220	00028	118	Tallahatchie	Project will provide for a secretary/clerk on Tallahatchie refuge, a station without any on-site administrative support. This position is necessary to provide essential administrative assistance for permit sales, clerical functions, and basic visitor services that are critical for effective refuge operations. The refuge issues 1,600 hunting permits annually, and without a secretary, the administrative requirements necessary for effective operations of the refuge cannot be met unless the refuge manager refocuses his/her energies. This diminishes the effectiveness of habitat management and other public use management programs. Public needs are presently not being fulfilled due to the lack of necessary administrative support.

Priority	Project Number	$000	Refuge	Project Description
221	97001	139	North Mississippi Refuges Complex	Initiate comprehensive conservation planning for the entire North Mississippi National Wildlife Refuges Complex by providing for a wildlife biologist who will lead the development of, and help implement, an effective management direction for three national wildlife refuges and more than 100 Farm Service Agency lands that total over 30,000 acres. The entire refuge complex does not and has not had a biologist to lead inventorying, monitoring, or research, or assist with long-range planning to most effectively realize potential benefits for wildlife and the visiting public.
320	98028	118	Dahomey	Project will provide for a secretary/clerk on Dahomey refuge, a station without any on-site administrative support. This position is necessary to provide essential administrative assistance for permit sales, clerical functions, and basic visitor services that are critical for effective refuge operations. The refuge sells approximately 1,000 hunting permits annually, and without a secretary, the administrative requirements necessary for effective operations of the refuge cannot be met unless the refuge manager refocuses his/her energies. This diminishes the effectiveness of habitat management and other public use management programs. Public needs are presently not being fulfilled due to the lack of necessary administrative support.
321	96011	125	Tallahatchie	Tallahatchie refuge, boasting active public hunting and forest restoration programs, does not have a maintenance worker to properly maintain public facilities or help effectively manage refuge habitats to benefit a host of wildlife species. This project will provide a maintenance worker at this unstaffed refuge. Maintenance of existing roads and facilities is necessary to meet public expectations for a safe, enjoyable refuge visit.

Priority	Project Number	$000	Refuge	Project Description
322	96010	110	North Mississippi Refuges Complex	Provide a full-time secretary/clerk to meet the requirements of the refuge fee program, contracting requirements, and other budget and administration duties/policies. Due to the large volume of work at this 3-refuge, 17,000-acre, 100+ tract complex, a second administrative person is needed to meet minimum Service compliance and enable effective operation of purchasing, budget tracking, property management, filing/typing, public inquiry response, and personnel actions. The Complex cannot presently provide the quality and quantity of services expected by the public for the many refuge programs.
403	96001	139	Dahomey	A newer national wildlife refuge that was never provided startup funding or staffing, Dahomey refuge is the largest remaining tract of bottomland hardwoods in the northern Mississippi Delta. This project will provide for a biologist to obtain and evaluate critical habitat and wildlife surveys. This refuge does not have a biologist, and biological information necessary to help make the most informed management decisions is not being obtained. Partnership potential to conduct inventorying and monitoring is great, with the refuge receiving extensive use by researchers, students, and school groups and being located near Delta State University.
404	98001	97	Tallahatchie	Provide a biological technician to monitor habitats and habitat restoration activities on Tallahatchie refuge, a newer national wildlife refuge that was never provided startup funding or staffing. This unstaffed refuge is a research site for the Mississippi Forestry Division and a "mitigation bank" for the Mississippi Department of Transportation. Tallahatchie refuge could serves as an outstanding example of bottomland hardwood forest restoration, yet does not have biological staff to obtain, interpret, and share critical habitat and wildlife survey data. Without any biological staff, information necessary to help make the most informed management decisions is not being obtained.

Priority	Project Number	$000	Refuge	Project Description
405	96008	72	North Mississippi Refuges Complex	Provide a public outreach specialist to create a quality public outreach program for the 3-refuge, 17,000-acre, 100+ tract-North Mississippi National Wildlife Refuges Complex containing some of the largest tracts of remaining bottomland hardwood forests left in the ecologically and culturally unique Mississippi Delta region. Currently, the Complex does not have any outreach personnel or the necessary staff to establish close partnerships with many potential community support groups, school groups, and other wildlife-oriented organizations that can provide tremendous volunteer assistance and issues advocacy support. This position will also lead all efforts related to exhibits, news releases, festivals, newsletter, brochures, and public inquiries.
491	96004	107	Dahomey	Provide an assistant refuge manager to oversee field operations and help direct overall management programs at Dahomey refuge. Because the refuge is understaffed, there is a 1,000-acre cooperative farming program that does not receive adequate supervision to properly maximize the program's great potential benefit to wildlife. This project would provide the needed staff to also assist with other refuge activities, such as public hunting, outreach, education, and the forthcoming, extensive comprehensive conservation planning process.
492	96005	139	Dahomey	Provide a forester to more effectively manage the largest tract of bottomland hardwood forest in the northern Mississippi Delta, Dahomey refuge. Important to a wide variety of wildlife species, the refuge has tremendous potential for forest restoration through the planting of trees, appropriate thinning of the existing stand, and the proper management of water levels. However, there is only a refuge manager and a biological science technician stationed at this 9,600-acre refuge, and many parts of the forests are dying due to lack of care. This project will enable forest resources of this refuge to be managed to their fullest potential to provide the fish and wildlife values and recreational benefits expected by the public.

Priority	Project Number	$000	Refuge	Project Description
493	96007	152	Dahomey	Provide a refuge manager at Dahomey refuge to ensure effective habitat management and provide appropriate wildlife-oriented recreation expected by the public. This 10,000-acre refuge, the largest tract of bottomland hardwood forest in the northern Mississippi Delta, was established in 1992 and has only recently been staffed by a refuge operations specialist and biological technician. A refuge manager on this popular refuge is needed to provide for adequate leadership and administration of all the required management programs, including the care of 40 outlying properties in addition to the core 10,000-acre refuge. Being located near Delta State University and having a strong constituency of area residents, potential refuge improvement projects abound but are not being met due to lack of attention.
494	96013	139	Tallahatchie	Provide a wildlife biologist to conduct critical wildlife surveys and manage habitat development projects on Tallahatchie refuge. The refuge, Mississippi Department of Transportation, and private partners, such as Ducks Unlimited, have invested hundreds of thousands of dollars in facilities and habitat improvement. This unstaffed refuge is a research site for the Mississippi Forestry Division and a "mitigation bank," having thousands of acres either reforested or planned for reforestation. However, this newer refuge was never initially staffed or funded. This project will enable important restoration work to be continued and critical habitat and wildlife surveys to be conducted.
495	96012	139	Tallahatchie	Provide a refuge operations specialist/assistant refuge manager to manage existing refuge farm lands for the continuing benefit of wintering migratory waterfowl and other wildlife species. Approximately 65,000 ducks and geese utilize the refuge annually on 3,000 acres that are presently being farmed through private partners. However, due to lack of staffing at this unstaffed refuge, the farmers are not adequately supervised to ensure maximum program benefit and policy compliance. This position will also ensure more effective operations of other habitat management programs, as well as maintenance and public use programs.

Priority	Project Number	$000	Refuge	Project Description
496	98026	152	Tallahatchie	Tallahatchie refuge, which encompasses 8,000 acres and boasts progressive partnerships with the Mississippi Division of Forestry, Mississippi Department of Transportation, and private partners in a large forest restoration program, contains numerous roads, levees, water control structures, and wetland impoundments. The refuge also has a large contingent of hunters, anglers, and other outdoor enthusiasts who regularly visit the area. Despite all of this, this newer refuge has never been staffed. Maintenance, public use coordination, habitat management, and other management activities that are essential for effective refuge operations are not being adequately implemented, due primarily to lack of staffing. This project will provide for a refuge manager to lead, coordinate, and enhance the overall effectiveness of refuge management programs.

Refuge Operating Needs System

Project Number	Org Code	Refuge	Project Title	Cost Estimate (Thousands)	Station Rank	Region Rank
98010	43635	Dahomey	Acquire a transport truck and trailer for hauling heavy equipment at Dahomey refuge	$190K	11	999
98018	43635	Dahomey	Acquire a low-boy transport for transporting heavy equipment.	$150K	12	999
98008	43635	Dahomey	Acquire excavator trackhoe for the management and maintenance of wetland habitats.	$150K	13	999
98006	43635	Dahomey	Acquire a large bulldozer for the management and maintenance of wetland impoundments.	$160K	14	999
98011	43635	Dahomey	Acquire a backhoe for wetland enhancement and development.	$90K	015	999
98004	43635	Dahomey	Acquire a road grader for the maintenance of Service roads.	$150K	17	999
98020	43635	Dahomey	High pressure wash facility	$30K	18	999
98003	43635	Dahomey	Acquire two ATV's	$20K	19	999
98013	43635	Dahomey	Acquire fuel storage tanks	$50K	20	999
00035	43675	North Mississippi Refuges Complex	Establishment of an environmental education program	$35K	1	54
98023	43675	North Mississippi Refuges Complex	Conduct aerial waterfowl surveys	$25K	2	166
98025	43675	North Mississippi Refuges Compex	Improve bottomland hardwood management capabilities.	$140K	3	999
98030	43675	North Mississippi Refuges Complex	Improve transportation capabilities of fire dozer and plow.	$150K	4	999

Project Number	Org Code	Refuge	Project Title	Cost Estimate (Thousands)	Station Rank	Region Rank
96003	43675	North Mississippi Refuges Complex	Provide a forestry technician to implement bottomland hardwood forest restoration.	$124K	5	999
96009	43675	North Mississippi Refuges Complex	Improve wildfire suppression capabilities.	$50K	6	999
98027	43675	North Mississippi Refuges Complex	Improve wetland management and road maintenance capabilities.	$20K	8	999
02001	43675	North Mississippi Refuges Complex	Improve Safety, Environmental Compliance, and Asset Management (Assistant Manager - Facilities)	$134K	999	118
98024	43645	Tallahatchie	Provide a bush-hog mower to facilitate mission critical activities of refuge management and public use.	$20K	2	204
00034	43645	Tallahatchie	Provide a two-ton truck and transport needed to transport equipment to sites occurring on and off refuge.	$150K	3	999
98019	43645	Tallahatchie	Provide an excavator for wetland management purposes.	$150K	4	999
98017	43645	Tallahatchie	Provide a D4 bull dozer.	$95K	5	999
98016	43645	Tallahatchie	Provide a bulldozer, essential for achievement of mission critical goals on 8000 refuge acres.	$150K	7	999
98022	43645	Tallahatchie	Provide enough ATVs to fulfill mission critical duties	$25K	8	999
00030	43645	Tallahatchie	Create moist-oil units for the benefit of resident and migratory water birds.	$150K	9	999

Appendix D: Compatibility Determinations

Introduction

The Fish and Wildlife Service reviewed several uses for compatibility during the comprehensive conservation planning process for the North Mississippi National Wildlife Refuges Complex. Descriptions and anticipated impacts of each of these uses are addressed separately by refuge. The Refuge Name through the National Wildlife Refuge System Mission sections, as well as the Approval of Compatibility Determination section, apply to each described use, however, for brevity, are only listed once for each refuge. If one of these uses is considered outside of the Comprehensive Conservation Plan for the North Mississippi National Wildlife Refuges Complex, then those sections become part of that compatibility determination.

Refuge Name: Coldwater River National Wildlife Refuge

Uses: Several uses were evaluated to determine their compatibility with the Refuge System and mission and purposes of the refuge: 1) environmental education and interpretation; 2) recreational fishing; 3) hunting; 4) off-road vehicles; 5) resource research studies; and 6) wildlife observation and photography.

Location: Tallahatchie and Quitman Counties, Mississippi

Establishing and Acquisition Authority: Fish and Wildlife Act of 1956

Refuge Purposes: "…for the development, advancement, management, conservation, and protection of fish and wildlife resources…" 16 U.S.C. § 742f(a)(4) "…for the benefit of the United States Fish and Wildlife Service, in performing its activities and services. Such acceptance may be subject to the terms of any restrictive or affirmative covenant, or condition of servitude…" 16 U.S.C. § 742f(b)(1) (Fish and Wildlife Act of 1956)

National Wildlife Refuge System Mission: The mission of the National Wildlife Refuge System is "to administer a national network of lands and waters for the conservation, management, and where appropriate, restoration of the fish, wildlife, and plant resources and their habitats within the United States for the benefit of present and future generations of Americans."

Description of Use: *Environmental Education and Interpretation*

Environmental education and interpretation would consist primarily of teacher workshops, visitor education, teaching students, and interpretation.

Those activities seek to increase the public's knowledge and understanding of wildlife and contribute to the conservation of such wildlife. Activities would include traditional environmental education such as teacher or staff-led on-site field trips, off-site programs in classrooms, nature study, such as teacher and student workshops, and interpretation of wildlife resources on the refuge. Environmental education and interpretation have been identified in the National Wildlife Refuge System Improvement Act of 1997 as priority public uses provided they are compatible with the purpose for which the refuge was established.

Environmental education and interpretation could occur in the core area of Coldwater River refuge, an area of approximately 2,000 contiguous acres located approximately 4 miles south of Crowder, Mississippi; the "Warwick Tract," an approximately 300-acre tract bordering the Corps levee on the south beginning approximately ¼ miles south of the Paducah Wells Road and continuing south for approximately 2 miles to the County bridge across Black Bayou; and the "Schiele Tract," a 40-acre tract approximately 3 miles south of Crowder boarding the east side of the county line road.

These are year-round activities, conducted on an as requested basis. Although the activities do not require special use permits, they are most often closely coordinated with the refuge manager.

The refuge will serve as an outdoor classroom for a variety of audiences with an interest in wildlife conservation and management. Typically, teachers, students, and other groups will learn from hands-on demonstrations, projects, and activities delivered by refuge staff. Activities will be conducted on-site utilizing existing refuge facilities. Group size will typically be limited to ensure effective presentation of desired materials, which may be specifically tailored to meet the educational needs of the group.

Environmental education and interpretation are utilized to encourage understanding in citizens of all ages to develop land ethics, foster public support, increase visibility, and improve the image of the Service.

Availability of Resources: Funding for these activities is borne by annual operation and maintenance funds, which support activities involving the public, such as outdoor recreation, wildlife photography, and refuge hunting and fishing programs. The cost of operating and maintaining the present environmental education and interpretation program would be approximately $6,000 annually within the annual North Mississippi National Wildlife Refuges Complex budget of approximately $750,000. Therefore, the program is in compliance with specific funding requirements of the Refuge Recreation Act.

Special equipment, facilities, or improvements necessary to support the use: $1,000

Maintenance costs: $4,000

Monitoring costs: $1,000

Offsetting revenues: None

Anticipated Impacts of the Use:

Short-term impacts:

The use of on-site, hands-on, action-oriented activities by groups of teachers/students to accomplish environmental education objectives may impose a low-level impact on those sites used for these activities. Impacts may include trampling of vegetation and temporary disturbance to wildlife species in the immediate vicinity during the activities. Since most activities would take place on existing roads, trails and at other facilities, impacts would be minimal.

Long-term impacts:

Current utilization of these uses is incidental to overall refuge programs and no long-term adverse impacts have been experienced. Long-term beneficial impacts include the furthering of the refuge mission through the education of the general public.

Cumulative impacts:

No adverse cumulative impacts are anticipated.

Public Review and Comment: The period of public review and comment began on September 9, 2004, and ended on October 21, 2004. The following methods were used to solicit public review and comment:

> Posted notice at refuge headquarters
> Public notice in newspapers with wide local distribution
> Public meeting(s)

This compatibility determination was part of the Draft North Mississippi National Wildlife Refuges Complex Comprehensive Conservation Plan and Environmental Assessment, which was announced in the *Federal Register* and made available for public comment for 30 days.

Determination (check one below):

> __X__Compatible with the following stipulations

> _____Not Compatible

Stipulations Necessary to Ensure Compatibility: On-site activities should be held where minimal impact would occur. Evaluations of sites and programs should be conducted periodically to assess if objectives are being met and that natural resources are not being degraded. If evidence of unacceptable adverse impacts begins to appear, it may be necessary to change the location of the outdoor activities.

Justification: Environmental education and interpretation are used to encourage understanding in citizens of all ages in order to act responsibly in protecting a healthy ecosystem. They are tools to use in building land ethic, developing political support, and decreasing wildlife violations. They constitute one method of increasing visibility in the community and improving the image of the Service.
Environmental education at the refuge is incidental to other programs since there is no full-time staff to conduct these activities. However, the program is important and provides visitors with an awareness of refuge-specific issues, such as wetland ecology, migratory bird management, and issues relating to the entire Refuge System. Environmental education and interpretation activities are expected to increase while ensuring compatibility with the purpose for which the refuge was established.

At the present time, however, public entry to include visitors involved in environmental education and interpretation is not permitted on the core area of Coldwater River refuge, or on the Schiele Tract, except by special use permit. Environmental education and interpretation are permitted on the Warwick Tract.

The core area of the refuge is intensively managed for migratory waterfowl, shorebirds, and wading birds. Management efforts are successful with large numbers of migratory waterfowl using the refuge from October to March. Extensive shorebird use of the refuge occurs in March and April and again from July through October. Large numbers of wading birds use the refuge for foraging and roosting beginning in May and lasting through September. Experience has shown that birds using the refuge are very susceptible to disturbance.

The core area of the refuge and the Warwick Tract experience extensive flooding annually from January through April or May. The only improved road on the core area of the refuge extends for 1.5 miles and is normally under water and impassable from January to May. Periods of intensive rainfall frequently result in this road becoming impassable numerous times during the June to December timeframe. Except for this 1.5-mile road, there are no additional roads, either improved or unimproved, on the core area of the refuge. Due to the flooding regime and prohibitive construction costs, no additional roads are envisioned. There are no roads, either improved or unimproved, on the Warwick or Schiele Tracts.

Depending on flooding conditions, groups interested in environmental education and interpretation activities can view the refuge from the public roads along the north side of the Warwick Tract, the west side of the Schiele Tract, and along both the east and west sides of the core area. The public road along the east side of the core area, and along the north side of the Warwick Tract, offers excellent viewing opportunities.

Areas which are closed to all public entry are clearly marked with appropriate signs.

NEPA Compliance for Refuge Use Description: *Place an X in appropriate space.*

_____Categorical Exclusion without Environmental Action Statement
_____Categorical Exclusion and Environmental Action Statement
___X___Environmental Assessment and Finding of No Significant Impact
_____Environmental Impact Statement and Record of Decision

Mandatory 10- or 15-Year Re-evaluation Date: September 2020

Description of Use: *Recreational Fishing*

Fishing was a traditional recreational use of Coldwater River refuge prior to its inclusion in the National Wildlife Refuge System and continues to be a recreational pursuit with the public. The refuge provides additional public fishing opportunities in an area that is lacking sufficient amounts of fishing open to the public. Fish populations currently support a sustainable harvest under a regulated fishing program.

Fishing, a wildlife-dependent recreational pursuit, has been identified in the National Wildlife Refuge System Improvement Act of 1997 as a priority public use provided it is compatible with the purpose for which the refuge was established.

Fishing is permitted in the borrow pits at the foot of the Army Corps of Engineers' Panola Quitman Floodway Levee beginning at the southeast corner of the refuge and continuing north along the Corps levee for approximately ¾-mile. Fishing is also permitted on the Warwick Tract of Coldwater River refuge. The area open to fishing on the Warwick Tract consists of the borrow pits at the foot of the Corps levee beginning approximately ¼-mile south of Paducah Wells Road and continuing south for approximately 2 miles to the county bridge across Black Bayou.

The use is conducted year-round from sunrise to sunset. Fishing is conducted subject to regulations established by the Mississippi Department of Wildlife, Fisheries and Parks. Fishing is further restricted on the refuge by regulations, which prohibit commercial fishing on the refuge, prohibit the use of certain fishing methods, and prohibit access after dark. The purchase of an annual hunting and fishing permit is required in order to fish on the refuge.

This use is being proposed to provide fishable waters to the public in an area where public fishing opportunities are limited and to utilize a sustainable natural resource.

Availability of Resources: Funding for the fishing program is borne by annual operation and maintenance funds, which support activities involving the public, such as recreation, interpretation, environmental education, and refuge hunting and fishing programs. The North Mississippi National Wildlife Refuges Complex spends approximately $8,000 of a budget of approximately $750,000 in direct support of the fishing program on the refuge. Therefore, the program is in compliance with specific funding requirements of the Refuge Recreation Act.

Special equipment, facilities, or improvements necessary to support the use: None

Maintenance costs: $5,000

Monitoring costs: $3,000

Offsetting revenues: $200

Anticipated Impacts of the Use:

Short-term impacts:

Minor impacts such as litter and gasoline contamination could occur but not at a level that would cause great concern.

Long-term impacts:

Since the number of persons fishing on the refuge is small and the activity occurs primarily during high-water periods in the spring, no long-term impacts are expected.

Cumulative impacts:

No cumulative impacts are known to occur.

Public Review and Comment: The period of public review and comment began on September 9, 2004 and ended on October 21, 2004. The following methods were used to solicit public review and comment:

Posted notice at refuge headquarters
Public notice in newspapers with wide local distribution
Public meeting(s)

This compatibility determination was part of the Draft North Mississippi National Wildlife Refuges Complex Comprehensive Conservation Plan and Environmental Assessment, which was announced in the *Federal Register* and made available for public comment for 30 days.

Determination (check one below):

   __X__Compatible with the following stipulations

   _____Not Compatible

Stipulations Necessary to Ensure Compatibility: Commercial fishing and possession or use of jugs, seines, nets, hand-grab baskets, or any other similar devices are prohibited. Persons are prohibited from accessing the refuge after dark.

Justification: While the number of participants is limited, fishing has been an important activity of the refuge resulting in only very temporary disturbance to refuge habitats and wildlife populations, and has caused no noticeable impact on the abundance of species sought or other wildlife affected by angler disturbance. Current regulations limit the impacts to trust species and provide a safe and rewarding experience for the refuge visitor.

The areas of Coldwater River refuge closed to all public entry are clearly marked with appropriate signs.

NEPA Compliance for Refuge Use Description: *Place an X in appropriate space.*

_____Categorical Exclusion without Environmental Action Statement
_____Categorical Exclusion and Environmental Action Statement
__X__Environmental Assessment and Finding of No Significant Impact
_____Environmental Impact Statement and Record of Decision

Mandatory 10- or 15-Year Re-evaluation Date: September 2020

Description of Use: *Hunting*

Hunting consists of small game, large game, and migratory game birds. Hunting activities are permitted with a valid refuge hunt permit and appropriate state licenses.

The refuge hunt program is an excellent wildlife management and public relations tool, which provides quality recreational opportunities for the public while regulating specific animal populations at desired levels. The refuge hunt plan was developed to ensure that associated public recreation and wildlife management objectives are met in a responsible and consistent manner.

Hunting, a wildlife-dependent recreational pursuit, has been identified in the National Wildlife Refuge System Improvement Act of 1997 as a priority public use provided it is compatible with the purpose for which the refuge was established.

Hunting could occur in the core area of Coldwater River refuge, an area of approximately 2,000 contiguous acres located approximately 4 miles south of Crowder, Mississippi; the "Warwick Tract," an approximately 300-acre area bordering the Corps levee on the south beginning approximately ¼-mile south of the Paducah Wells Road and continuing south for approximately 2 miles to the County bridge across Black Bayou; and the "Schiele Tract," a 40-acre tract approximately 3 miles south of Crowder bordering the east side of the county line road.

All hunting seasons are established annually through coordination with the Mississippi Department of Wildlife, Fisheries and Parks.

A. Squirrel season and bag limits coincide with State season and regulations except that the season is closed during the general gun deer hunts.

B. Raccoon season dates are January 1 to February 28. Bag limits per State regulations.

C. Rabbit season dates and bag limits coincide with State season and regulations except that the season is closed during general gun deer hunts.

D. Quail season dates and bag limits coincide with State season and regulations except that the season is closed during general gun deer hunts.

E. Deer season dates and bag limits for archery and primitive weapons coincide with State seasons and regulations. The general gun deer hunt is 5 days in mid-December. State bag limits and regulations apply.

F. Migratory game bird hunting (ducks, mergansers, coots, and geese) is allowed during specified State season on Wednesdays, Saturdays, and Sundays, 30 minutes before sunrise until noon. After duck, merganser, and coot season closes, light geese may be hunted daily during the period and time defined in the Conservation Order.

G. Turkey season is normally held during the entire month of April with bag limits that coincide with State regulations.

H. Season dates and bag limits for youth hunts for squirrel, deer with general gun, and turkey are set within State seasons and regulations.

I. Feral hogs can be taken with no bag limit during any open refuge season with weapons legal for that hunt.

Public hunting opportunities in the northwest delta portion of the Yazoo Basin are limited with Service-managed refuges and State-managed wildlife management areas representing virtually all the public lands open to hunting. Private lands offer hunting opportunities only to those willing and able to purchase hunting rights through long-term leases or private ownership. The demand for public hunting areas in this portion of Mississippi is increasing as the area shifts toward a more urbanized society, and refuges are expected to meet an increasing part of this demand.

Availability of Resources: Funding for the hunting program is borne by annual operation and maintenance funds, which supports activities involving the public, such as fishing, wildlife observation, wildlife photography, and environmental education and interpretation. The cost of operating and maintaining the present small game, big game, turkey, and migratory waterfowl seasons would be approximately $15,000 annually within the annual North Mississippi National

Wildlife Refuges Complex budget of approximately $750,000. Therefore, the program is in compliance with specific funding requirements of the Refuge Recreation Act.

Special equipment, facilities, or improvements necessary to support the use: $5,000

Administration costs: $4,000

Law enforcement costs: $3,500

Outreach, education, and monitoring costs: $1,500

Signs, brochures, and maintenance costs: $1,000

Offsetting revenues: $250

The refuge is a participant in the Recreational Fee Demonstration Project, which currently returns 80 percent of fees generated from recreational activities back to the refuge. The offsetting revenues are from the sale of hunting and fishing permits.

Anticipated Impacts of the Use:

Short-term impacts:

National wildlife refuges administered by the North Mississippi National Wildlife Refuges Complex have been open to hunting since 1992, with no documented disturbance to refuge habitats and no noticeable impact on the abundance of species hunted or other associated wildlife. While managed hunting opportunities may result in localized disruption of individual animals' daily routines, no noticeable effect on populations has been noticed or documented. Restrictions within the hunting program, notably the closure of small game hunting during the general gun deer hunt, the requirement that all hunters, except those hunting turkey or waterfowl, wear fluorescent orange-colored material above the waistline, and the prohibition of hunting or shooting across any open field from ground level have been implemented due to safety concerns. These restrictions will be closely monitored for effectiveness.

Long-term impacts:

To date, there is no indication of adverse biological impacts associated with the Complex's hunting program. Should, however, it become necessary, the refuge has the latitude to adjust hunting seasons and bag limits annually, or even close the refuge entirely if safety or other concerns merit such actions. This latitude, coupled with monitoring of wildlife populations and habitat conditions by the Service and the Department of Wildlife, Fisheries and Parks, will ensure that long-term negative impacts to either wildlife populations and/or habitats on the refuge are unlikely.

Should hunting pressure increase on the refuge, alternatives, such as quota hunts, a reduction in the number of days of hunting, or restrictions on that part of the refuge open to hunting, can be utilized to limit impacts.

Cumulative impacts:

The timing and duration of the refuge's hunting program does not coincide with most other uses of the refuge and would not result in cumulative impacts to refuge resources.

Public Review and Comment: The period of public review and comment began on September 9, 2004 and ended on October 21, 2004. The following methods were used to solicit public review and comment:

> Posted notice at refuge headquarters
> Public notice in newspapers with wide local distribution
> Public meeting(s)

This compatibility determination was part of the Draft North Mississippi National Wildlife Refuges Complex Comprehensive Conservation Plan and Environmental Assessment, which was announced in the *Federal Register* and made available for public comment for 30 days.

Determination (check one below):

> __X__Compatible with the following stipulations

> _____Not Compatible

Stipulations Necessary to Ensure Compatibility: At the present time, public entry to include hunters is not permitted on the core area of Coldwater River refuge or on the Schiele Tract. Migratory game bird hunting (ducks, mergansers, coots, and geese) is allowed on the Warwick Tract during the specified State season on Wednesdays, Saturdays, and Sundays, 30 minutes before sunrise until noon. After duck, merganser, and coot season closes, light geese may be hunted daily during the period and time defined in the Conservation Order.

Hunting seasons and bag limits are established annually as agreed upon during the annual hunt coordination with State personnel. These generally fall within the State framework. The refuge can, and has, established more restrictive seasons and bag limits to prevent over-harvest of individual species or disturbance to trust species. All hunters are required to purchase and possess a refuge hunting permit while participating in refuge hunts. This permit, which augments the State hunting regulations, explains not only the general hunt regulations but the refuge-specific regulations, as well. Law enforcement patrols are frequently conducted throughout the hunting season to ensure compliance with refuge laws and regulations. The refuge has included a Refuge Operating Needs System (RONS) project for a fulltime officer to ensure compatibility long term.

Justification: The core area of the refuge is intensively managed for migratory waterfowl, shorebirds, and wading birds. Management efforts are successful with large numbers of migratory waterfowl using the refuge from October to March. Extensive shorebird use of the core area occurs in March and April and again from July through October. Large numbers of wading birds use the refuge for foraging and roosting beginning in May and lasting through September. Experience has shown that birds using the refuge are very susceptible to excessive disturbance.

From January to May, the core area of the refuge and the Warwick Tract experience extensive flooding on an annual basis. When flooding of these areas begins, resident wildlife species congregate on small areas of high ground, which makes them vulnerable to excessive harvest. Also, during periods of high water, the only access road to the core area floods, halting all vehicular traffic.

Since establishment of the core area of Coldwater River refuge, all the property surrounding the refuge for many miles in any direction has been acquired or leased for hunting migratory waterfowl. The core area thus represents the only "safe harbor" waterfowl habitat in a large geographical area. Without this "safe harbor" habitat, waterfowl in large numbers would not be present for extended periods of time in the general area of the refuge.

The Schiele Tract comprises 40 acres and with no way to regulate numbers, hunting on this small area would represent a safety issue.

The recently acquired Warwick Tract is a long and narrow ownership consisting primarily of a series of borrow pits on one side and the Panola Quitman Floodway on the other side. Flooding is frequent, oftentimes with long duration. Due to scouring associated with out-of-bank flooding and the associated sediment deposition, habitat improvements consisting of levees, water control structures, and moist-soil areas are not practicable. Natural habitat does exist--the degree and value dependent on the impact of the last flood event. An elevated and well traveled public road on top of the Corps levee borders the Warwick Tract.

Those areas of Coldwater River refuge closed to all public entry are clearly marked with appropriate signs.

NEPA Compliance for Refuge Use Description: *Place an X in appropriate space.*

_____Categorical Exclusion without Environmental Action Statement
_____Categorical Exclusion and Environmental Action Statement
___X___Environmental Assessment and Finding of No Significant Impact
_____Environmental Impact Statement and Record of Decision

Mandatory 10- or 15-Year Re-evaluation Date: September 2020

Description of Use: *Off-Road Vehicles*

The proposed use is to allow off-road vehicles (e.g., 4-wheel all-terrain) on refuge lands.

Off-road vehicle use is not a priority public use; however, it can occur on the refuge provided it is compatible with the purpose for which the refuge was established.

The general public could participate in the use of off-road vehicles year-round from sunrise to sunset on Coldwater River refuge, an area of approximately 2,300 acres south of Crowder, Mississippi. Off-road vehicles may be used on unimproved dirt roads and fire breaks by visitors who possess a valid hunting and fishing permit, and who are gaining access to interior portions of the refuge for hunting and fishing opportunities.

The use of off-road vehicles is proposed in response to questions raised during the scoping process. These questions centered on opportunities to provide visitors who possess a valid hunting and fishing permit off-road vehicle access to internal areas of the refuge for the purpose of hunting and fishing.

Availability of Resources: Funding for this program would be borne by annual operation and maintenance funds, which support activities involving the public, such as wildlife photography, environmental education and interpretation, and refuge hunting and fishing programs. The North Mississippi National Wildlife Refuges Complex would spend approximately $25,000 of an annual budget of approximately $750,000 in direct support of this program on Coldwater River refuge.

Special equipment, facilities, or improvements necessary to support the use: $7,500

Maintenance costs: $10,000

Law enforcement costs: $5,000

Monitoring costs: $2,500

Offsetting revenues: $1,000

The refuge does not have the resources to administer this use. Currently, the North Mississippi National Wildlife Refuges Complex does not have law enforcement personnel to monitor this activity. The Complex has included a Refuge Operating Needs System (RONS) package for a full-time law enforcement officer for Coldwater River refuge. Additionally, this activity would require considerable operation and maintenance funds to maintain the existing unimproved dirt roads and firebreaks. It is expected that $1,000 of offsetting revenues would be generated by the sale of hunting and fishing permits to visitors who would not use the refuge unless they could also use off-road vehicles while accessing hunting and fishing areas.

Anticipated Impacts of the Use:

Short-term impacts:

Adverse impacts to unimproved roads and fire breaks by the repeated use of off-road vehicles are well documented, and disturbance to wildlife, plants, and their habitats would occur. Such use would be limited primarily to the hunting and fishing seasons, which also coincide with extended periods of heavy rainfall. As use continues, the unimproved roads and firebreaks, which would be used for access, become wallowed out and rainfall accumulates in the "wet" areas. Repeated use exacerbates this condition. Conflicts would occur between those hunters and anglers who use off-road vehicles and those who object to the disturbance and noise associated with the vehicles.

Long-term impacts:

Long-term impacts from the repeated use of off-road vehicles by the public would be compounded over time. Unimproved roads and fire breaks would continue to deteriorate and annual maintenance costs would increase. Additional damage to plants and habitats would be experienced as access for the heavy equipment required to maintain these access routes is developed. Conflicts between hunters who use off-road vehicles and those who object to the associated disturbance and noise would continue. Repeated disturbance to feeding and resting migratory waterfowl, shorebirds, and wading birds would result in a reduction of birds using the refuge.

Cumulative impacts:

No cumulative impacts are expected because other forms of public use are not permitted on the core area of the refuge or on the Schiele Tract. Conflicts would continue to occur between those hunters and anglers who use off-road vehicles and those who object to the disturbance and noise associated with the vehicles.

Public Review and Comment: The period of public review and comment began on September 9, 2004 and ended on October 21, 2004. The following methods were used to solicit public review and comment:

> Posted notice at refuge headquarters
> Public notice in newspapers with wide local distribution
> Public meeting(s)

This compatibility determination was part of the Draft North Mississippi National Wildlife Refuges Complex Comprehensive Conservation Plan and Environmental Assessment, which was announced in the *Federal Register* and made available for public comment for 30 days.

Determination (check one below):

> _____Compatible with the following stipulations

> __X__Not Compatible

Stipulations Necessary to Ensure Compatibility: None

Justification: At the present time, public entry to include off-road vehicle users is not permitted on the core area of Coldwater River refuge, an area of approximately 2,000 contiguous acres approximately 4 miles south of Crowder, Mississippi, or on the Schiele Tract, a 40-acre tract approximately 3 miles south of Crowder bordering the east side of the county line road. Migratory game bird hunting is permitted on the Warwick Tract, an approximately 300-acre area bordering the Corps levee on the south beginning approximately ¼-mile south of the Paducah Wells Road and continuing south for approximately 2 miles to the county bridge across Black Bayou. Fishing is also permitted in the borrow pits at the foot of the Corps of Engineers Panola Quitman Floodway Levee on the core area of the refuge and on the Warwick Tract. Access for fishing and migratory bird hunting is only available by use of the Army Corps of Engineers levee.

The core area of the refuge is intensively managed for migratory waterfowl, shorebirds, and wading birds. Management efforts are successful with large numbers of migratory waterfowl using the refuge from October to March. Extensive shorebird use of the core area occurs in March and April and again from July through October. Large numbers of wading birds use the refuge for foraging and roosting beginning in May and lasting through September. Experience has shown that birds using the refuge are very susceptible to disturbance.

From January to May, the core area of the refuge and the Warwick Track experience extensive flooding on an annual basis. These floodwaters inundate existing unimproved dirt roads and fire breaks on the core area and have prevented conversion of these unimproved roads to all-weather roads.

Due to the costs and the disturbance to migratory waterfowl, shorebirds, and wading birds, the Service does not anticipate construction of all-weather roads on the core area or permitting public access on the core area.

The previous owner of the Warwick Tract extensively developed the property for waterfowl hunting. A series of levees were constructed perpendicular to the Corps Levee and a levee was constructed along the top bank of the Panola Quitman Floodway. Off-road vehicle access was possible on these levees. However, out of bank flooding during the succeeding 2 years destroyed the levees on the tract. Currently, off-road vehicle access to the Warwick Tract is not possible and the Service has no plans to restore and maintain levees for this purpose.

The Schiele Tract is closed to public entry due to size and the lack of access. The Service has reforested the tract and does not anticipate construction of access roads. Use of off-road vehicles would result in extensive damage to the emerging forest.

NEPA Compliance for Refuge Use Description: *Place an X in appropriate space.*

_____Categorical Exclusion without Environmental Action Statement
_____Categorical Exclusion and Environmental Action Statement
___X___Environmental Assessment and Finding of No Significant Impact
_____Environmental Impact Statement and Record of Decision

Mandatory 10- or 15-Year Re-evaluation Date: _____**2015**_____

Description of Use: *Resource Research Studies*

This activity would allow university professors and their students, nongovernmental researchers, and governmental scientists access to Coldwater River refuge's natural environment to conduct both short- and long-term research projects and surveys. The outcome of this research would result in beneficial knowledge of our natural resources and improved methods to manage, monitor, and protect the refuge resources.

Resource research studies are not a priority public use within the Service, but do support the mission of the Service in gathering good scientific data to make management decisions.

These activities will be conducted throughout the refuge in a variety of habitats. Activities carried out during approved research projects and surveys may be limited to avoid unnecessary disturbance to refuge resources or ongoing management activities.

The activities will vary in scope and duration to satisfy the requirements of the research project or survey. Projects may involve everything from a limited one-time sampling or survey to long-term study plots.

Research projects and surveys will be conducted by universities, state and federal governmental representatives, and rarely by private individuals. The refuge will act solely in a supportive role, providing minimal assistance in most cases.

Furthering the knowledge of the impacts and benefits of management decisions, life histories of wildlife species utilizing the refuge, and interrelationships of habitats and wildlife occurring on the refuge are crucial to the effective management of the refuge. The refuge provides secure sites for long-term evaluation of management actions, population trends, and ecological functions within the bottomland hardwood ecosystems in northwest Mississippi.

Availability of Resources: Funding for this program would be borne by annual operation and maintenance funds, which support activities involving the public, such as general recreation, interpretation, environmental education, and refuge hunting and fishing programs. The North Mississippi National Wildlife Refuges Complex spends approximately $1,000 of an annual budget of approximately $750,000 in direct support of these programs on Coldwater River refuge. Therefore, the program is in compliance with specific funding requirements of the Refuge Recreation Act.

Special equipment, facilities or improvements necessary to support the use: None

Maintenance costs: None

Monitoring costs: $1,000

Offsetting revenues: None

Anticipated Impacts of the Use:

Short-term impacts:

There should be no significant adverse impacts from scientific research on the refuge. The knowledge gained from the research activities would provide information towards improving management techniques for trust resource species. Impacts, such as trampling vegetation, removal of small numbers of plants and/or animals, and temporary disturbance to wildlife could occur, but should not be significant. The small number of individual plants and animals that may be collected for further study would not have a significant effect on the refuge plant and animal populations, and would require management approval prior to collection.

Long-term impacts:

Long-term benefits associated with improved management techniques developed through research or from survey data would outweigh any negative impacts which may occur.

Cumulative impacts:

No adverse cumulative impacts are anticipated.

Public Review and Comment: The period of public review and comment began on September 9, 2004 and ended on October 21, 2004. The following methods were used to solicit public review and comment:

    Posted notice at refuge headquarters
    Public notice in newspapers with wide local distribution
    Public meeting(s)

This compatibility determination was part of the Draft North Mississippi National Wildlife Refuges Complex Comprehensive Conservation Plan and Environmental Assessment, which was announced in the *Federal Register* and made available for public comment for 30 days.

Determination (check one below):

　　　　X　Compatible with the following stipulations

　　　　＿＿＿Not Compatible

Stipulations Necessary to Ensure Compatibility: Each request for use of the refuge for research or surveys would be examined on its individual merit. Questions of who, what, when, where, and why would be asked to determine if the requested proposal contributes to the refuge purposes and could be best conducted on the refuge without significantly affecting the resources. If so, the researcher would be issued a special use permit that would clearly define allowed activities. Progress would be monitored and the researcher would be required to submit annual progress reports and copies of all publications derived from the research.

Justification: The benefits derived from sound research provide a better understanding of species and the environmental communities present on the refuge. Research projects would be designed to minimize impacts and disturbance.

Those areas of Coldwater River refuge closed to all public entry are clearly marked with appropriate signs.

NEPA Compliance for Refuge Use Description: *Place an X in appropriate space.*

　　　　＿＿＿Categorical Exclusion without Environmental Action Statement
　　　　＿＿＿Categorical Exclusion and Environmental Action Statement
　　　X　Environmental Assessment and Finding of No Significant Impact
　　　　＿＿＿Environmental Impact Statement and Record of Decision

Mandatory 10- or 15-Year Re-evaluation Date: September 2015

Description of Use: *Wildlife Observation and Wildlife Photography*

Wildlife observation and wildlife photography have been identified in the National Wildlife Refuge System Improvement Act of 1997 as priority wildlife-dependent recreational uses provided they are compatible with the purpose for which the refuge was established.

Wildlife photography, including other image-capturing activities such as videography, has occurred on the refuge. There are no photography blinds or platforms on the refuge and none are proposed at this time. However, opportunities exist for photography on the refuge. This compatibility determination applies to personal photography only. Commercial photography or videography, if allowed, would require a special use permit by the refuge with specific restrictions.

Wildlife observation and photography could occur in the core area of Coldwater River refuge, an area of approximately 2,000 contiguous acres located approximately 4 miles south of Crowder, Mississippi; the "Warwick Tract," an approximately 300-acre tract boarding the Corps levee on the south beginning approximately ¼-mile south of the Paducah Wells Road and continuing south for approximately 2 miles to the county bridge across Black Bayou; and the "Schiele Tract," a 40-acre tract approximately 3 miles south of Crowder boarding the east side of the county line road.

Wildlife observation and wildlife photography can be accomplished while driving or walking on refuge roads open to public vehicular traffic. Also, these priority public uses can be accomplished by boating on refuge waters or walking the unimproved roads and fire breaks.

The National Wildlife Refuge System Improvement Act of 1997 identifies wildlife observation and wildlife photography as priority public uses for national wildlife refuges, along with hunting, fishing, and environmental education and interpretation. As expressed priority uses of the Refuge System, these uses take precedence over other potential public uses in refuge planning and management. The Service strives to provide priority public uses when compatible with the purposes of the refuge and the mission of the National Wildlife Refuge System.

Availability of Resources: Funding for this program would be borne by annual operation and maintenance funds, which support activities involving the public, such as environmental education and interpretation, and refuge hunting and fishing programs. The cost of operating and maintaining the present wildlife observation and wildlife photography programs would be approximately $5,000 of the $750,000 annual budget of the North Mississippi National Wildlife Refuges Complex. Therefore, the program is in compliance with specific funding requirements of the Refuge Recreation Act.

Special equipment, facilities, or improvements necessary to support the use: $3,000

Maintenance costs: $1,000

Monitoring costs: $1,000

Offsetting revenues: None

Anticipated Impacts of the Use:

Short-term impacts:

The refuge provides habitat for resident and migratory wildlife. As a result of these activities, individual animals may be disturbed by human contact to varying degrees. Examples of potential disturbance include flushing of birds from feeding, resting, or nesting areas, and trampling of plants from observers and photographers wandering off designated roads in order to get closer to subjects. Disturbance to trust species are expected to be minimal. Short-term impacts to facilities, such as roads and trails, can be avoided by special closures due to unsafe conditions. The wildlife observation and photography programs have been designed to avoid or minimize impacts anticipated to refuge resources and visitors.

Long-term impacts:

The vast majority of the activities associated with this use would be during the fall and early winter. Due to the recovery time between periods of expected use, no long-term impacts are expected.

Cumulative impacts:

No cumulative adverse impacts are anticipated. However, programs can be modified in the future to mitigate unforeseen impacts.

Public Review and Comment: The period of public review and comment began on September 9, 2004, and ended on October 21, 2004. The following methods were used to solicit public review and comment:

Posted notice at refuge headquarters
Public notice in newspapers with wide local distribution
Public meeting(s)

Determination (check one below):

  X Compatible with the following stipulations

      Not Compatible

Stipulations Necessary to Ensure Compatibility: At the present time, public entry to include visitors involved in wildlife observation and wildlife photography is not permitted on the core area of Coldwater River refuge or on the Schiele Tract, except by special use permit. Wildlife observation and wildlife photography are permitted on the Warwick Tract.

Justification: The core area of the refuge is intensively managed for migratory waterfowl, shorebirds, and wading birds. Management efforts are successful with large numbers of migratory waterfowl using the refuge from October to March. Extensive shorebird use of the refuge occurs in March and April, and again from July through October. Large numbers of wading birds use the refuge for foraging and roosting beginning in May and lasting through September. Experience has shown that birds using the refuge are very susceptible to disturbance.

From January to April or May, the core area of the refuge and the Warwick Tract experience extensive flooding on an annual basis. The only improved road on the core area of the refuge extends for 1.5 miles and is normally under water and impassable from January to May. Periods of intensive rainfall frequently result in the road becoming impassable numerous times during the June to December timeframe. Except for this 1.5-mile road, there are no additional roads, either improved or unimproved, on the core area of the refuge. Due to the flooding regime and prohibitive construction costs, no additional roads are envisioned. There are no roads, either improved or unimproved, on the Warwick and Schiele Tracts.

Depending on flooding conditions, visitors can observe and photograph wildlife from public roads along the north side of the Warwick Tract, the west side of the Schiele Tract, and along both the east and west sides of the core area of the refuge. Excellent opportunities for observing wildlife exist by traveling the public road, located on top of the Corps levee, along the east side of the refuge's core area and along the north side of the Warwick Tract.

Those areas of Coldwater River refuge closed to all public entry are clearly marked with appropriate signs.

NEPA Compliance for Refuge Use Description: *Place an X in appropriate space.*

_____Categorical Exclusion without Environmental Action Statement
_____Categorical Exclusion and Environmental Action Statement
___X___Environmental Assessment and Finding of No Significant Impact
_____Environmental Impact Statement and Record of Decision

Mandatory 10- or 15-Year Re-evaluation Date: September 2020

Refuge Name: Dahomey National Wildlife Refuge

Uses: Several uses were evaluated to determine their compatibility with the Refuge System and mission and purposes of the refuge: 1) Bicycling; 2) Environmental Education and Interpretation; 3) Farming Program; 4) Fishing; 5) Hunting; 6) Off-Road Vehicles; 7) Resource Research Studies; and 8) Wildlife Observation and Photography.

Location: Bolivar County, Mississippi

Establishing and Acquisition Authorities: Migratory Bird Conservation Act, Refuge Recreation Act, Fish and Wildlife Act of 1956

Refuge Purposes: "...the conservation of the wetlands of the Nation in order to maintain the public benefits they provide and to help fulfill international obligations contained in various migratory bird treaties and conventions..." 16 U.S.C. § 3901(b) (Emergency Wetlands Resources Act of 1986)

"...for use as an inviolate sanctuary, or for any other management purpose, for migratory birds." 16 U.S.C. § 715d (Migratory Bird Conservation Act)

"...for the development, advancement, management, conservation, and protection of fish and wildlife resources..." 16 U.S.C. § 742f(a)(4)...for the benefit of the United States Fish and Wildlife Service, in performing its activities and services. Such acceptance may be subject to the terms of any restrictive or affirmative covenant, or condition of servitude..." 16 U.S.C. § 742f(b)(1) (Fish and wildlife Act of 1956)

National Wildlife Refuge System Mission: The mission of the National Wildlife Refuge System is "to administer a national network of lands and waters for the conservation, management, and where appropriate, restoration of the fish, wildlife, and plant resources and their habitats within the United States for the benefit of present and future generations of Americans."

Description of Use: *Bicycling*

The proposed public use is bicycling to facilitate travel for the priority public uses on Dahomey National Wildlife Refuge. Priority public uses as identified in the National Wildlife Refuge Improvement Act of 1997 include hunting, fishing, wildlife observation, wildlife photography, and environmental education and interpretation.

The general public could participate in the proposed public use on Dahomey National Wildlife Refuge, an area of approximately 9,600 acres southwest of Cleveland, Mississippi.

Bicycles may be used on designated motorized vehicle access roads. Additionally, bicycles may be used on unimproved dirt roads, fire breaks, and logging roads.

To promote safety, bicycling hours are sunrise to sunset. Additionally, during the deer gun-hunting season, bicycling will only be allowed to facilitate hunter access. Cyclists during the deer gun-hunting season would need to possess a valid hunting and fishing permit. During other refuge hunting seasons, bicycle travel for non-consumptive priority public uses is allowed.

Bicycling to facilitate non-consumptive priority public uses involves observing the natural landscape from a bicycle. Riders stop to observe associated animals and plant communities. The use mainly occurs in groups with an average group size of 2-4 riders. Regarding consumptive uses, anglers can access refuge lands for fishing by bicycle travel on designated roads and trails. Hunters can do the same to access game. To promote safety with other users, prevent conflicts, and promote a quality wildlife observation environment, group size is limited to 10 bicyclists. Groups of more than 10 should contact the refuge office for a special use permit prior to using the refuge. This will help protect refuge resources and ensure that larger groups do not conflict with concurrent public uses.

Bicycle travel on the refuge is conducted in accordance with the stipulations necessary to ensure compatibility. Travel is limited to designated roads and trails.

Bicycle travel on the refuge provides increased opportunity for public participation in priority public uses. It is an alternative method of travel to view the refuge's diverse biological assets and can be less physically demanding than pedestrian travel.

Availability of Resources: Funding for this program is borne by annual operation and maintenance funds which support activities involving the public such as recreation, interpretation, environmental education, and hunting and fishing programs. The North Mississippi National Wildlife Refuges Complex spends approximately $3,000 of an annual budget of approximately $750,000 in direct support of this program on Dahomey refuge. Therefore, the program is in compliance with specific funding provisions of the Refuge Recreation Act.

Special equipment, facilities, or improvements necessary to support the use: $1,000

Maintenance costs: $1,000

Monitoring costs: $1,000

Anticipated Impacts of the Use:

Short-term impacts:

Bicycle use can cause soil compaction, particularly when soils are wet, which can degrade plant communities. Soil compaction can diminish the soil porosity, aeration, and nutrient availability.

It is anticipated that bicycle use could alter drainage features of roads and trails through erosion and compaction. Tires may create trail incision causing increased water channeling and erosion during wet conditions. These problems will be minimized because routes designated for bicycle use are existing improved roads, logging trails, and fire breaks. Based on current level of use and condition of designated routes, changes to hydrology because of this use are likely to be insignificant.

Anticipated impacts of bicycle use on wildlife include temporal disturbances to species using habitat on the trail or directly adjacent to the trail. These disturbances are likely to be short-term and infrequent based on current level of use.

Disturbance to trust species are minimal due to the locations of the designated gravel roads and unimproved roads and fire breaks. Short-term impacts to facilities, such as roads and trails, can be avoided by special closures.

Long-term impacts:

No long-term impacts are anticipated.

Cumulative impacts:

No cumulative adverse impacts are anticipated. However, programs can be modified in the future to mitigate unforeseen impacts.

Public Review and Comment: The period of public review and comment began on September 9, 2004 and ended on October 21, 2004. The following methods were used to solicit public review and comment:

>   Posted notice at refuge headquarters
>   Public notice in newspapers with wide local distribution
>   Public meeting(s)

This compatibility determination was part of the Draft North Mississippi National Wildlife Refuges Complex Comprehensive Conservation Plan and Environmental Assessment, which was announced in the *Federal Register* and available for public comment for 30 days.

Determination (check one below):

>   __X__Compatible with the following stipulations

>   _____Not Compatible

Stipulations Necessary to Ensure Compatibility: A 160-acre tract located immediately behind and to the east of the refuge headquarters has been reserved for disabled hunters. Bicycle use in this area would not be permitted. Bicycling, except for hunting use, is not permitted during the deer gun-hunting season. Hunters are allowed to use bicycles but they must remain on designated roads and trails. Bicycle group size is limited to 10 bicyclists, to promote public safety, accommodate other users, and provide a positive wildlife viewing experience. Group size greater than 10 requires a special use permit issued by the refuge manager.

Justification: Bicycling has been determined to be compatible provided the above stipulations are implemented. Bicycle use, as identified in this Compatibility Determination, is not expected to materially interfere with or detract from the mission of the National Wildlife Refuge System or the purposes for which the refuge was established. The use of bicycles to facilitate the priority public use is a reasonable mode of access on designated roads and trails. Monitoring would be conducted to ensure that this use remains compatible. If significant impacts are found, corrective actions would be taken to protect refuge resources.

NEPA Compliance for Refuge Use Description: *Place an X in appropriate space.*

_____Categorical Exclusion without Environmental Action Statement
_____Categorical Exclusion and Environmental Action Statement
___X__Environmental Assessment and Finding of No Significant Impact
_____Environmental Impact Statement and Record of Decision

Mandatory 10- or 15-Year Re-evaluation Date: September 2015

Description of Use: *Environmental Education and Interpretation*

Environmental education and interpretation would consist primarily of teacher workshops, visitor education, teaching students, and interpretation.

Those activities seek to increase the public's knowledge and understanding of wildlife and contribute to the conservation of such wildlife. Activities would include traditional environmental education, such as teacher or staff-led on-site field trips, off-site programs in classrooms, nature study such as teacher and student workshops, and interpretation of the wildlife resources incorporated in support of facilities such as interpretive trails, kiosks, and the visitor contact stations.

Environmental education and interpretation have been identified in the National Wildlife Refuge System Improvement Act of 1997 as priority public uses provided they are compatible with the purpose for which the refuge was established.

The entire refuge has the potential to be utilized for environmental education and interpretation.

These uses are year-round activities, conducted on an as requested basis. Although the activities do not require a special use permit, they are most often closely coordinated with the refuge manager.

The refuge would serve as an outdoor classroom for a variety of audiences with an interest in wildlife conservation and management. Typically, teachers, students, and other groups would learn from hands-on demonstrations, projects, and activities delivered by refuge staff. Activities would be conducted on-site utilizing existing refuge facilities. Group size would typically be limited to ensure effective presentation of desired materials, which may be specifically tailored to meet the educational needs of the group.

Environmental education and interpretation are utilized to encourage understanding in citizens of all ages to develop land ethics, foster public support, increase visibility, and improve the image of the Service.

Availability of Resources: Funding for these activities is borne by annual operation and maintenance funds, which support activities involving the public, such as outdoor recreation, wildlife photography, and the conduct of refuge hunting and fishing programs. The North Mississippi National Wildlife Refuges Complex spends approximately $8,000 of an annual budget of approximately $750,000 in direct support of these programs on Dahomey refuge. Therefore, the program is in compliance with specific funding requirements of the Refuge Recreation Act.

Currently, environmental education and interpretation activities are conducted as time and resources permit. Expanding the refuge's volunteer program would provide for further development of these activities.

Facilities (including kiosks, interpretive signs and brochures, visitor contact stations): $2,000

On-site activities: $2,000

Maintenance costs: $2,000

Monitoring costs: $2,000

Offsetting revenues: None

Anticipated Impacts of the Use:

Short-term impacts:

The use of on-site, hands-on, action-oriented activities by groups of teachers/students to accomplish environmental education objectives may impose a low level impact on those sites used for these activities. Impacts may include trampling of vegetation and temporary disturbance to wildlife species in the immediate vicinity during the activities. Since most activities would take place on existing roads, trails, and at other facilities, impacts would be minimal.

Long-term impacts:

Current utilization of this use is incidental to overall refuge programs and no long-term adverse impacts have been experienced. Long-term beneficial impacts include the furthering of the refuge mission through the education of the general public.

Cumulative impacts:

No adverse cumulative impacts are anticipated.

Public Review and Comment: The period of public review and comment began on September 9, 2004 and ended on October 21, 2004. The following methods were used to solicit public review and comment:

> Posted notice at refuge headquarters
> Public notice in newspapers with wide local distribution
> Public meeting(s)

This compatibility determination was part of the Draft North Mississippi National Wildlife Refuges Complex Comprehensive Conservation Plan and Environmental Assessment, which was announced in the *Federal Register* and made available for public comment for 30 days.

Determination (check one below):

> __X__Compatible with the following stipulations

> _____Not Compatible

Stipulations Necessary to Ensure Compatibility: On-site activities should be held where minimal impact would occur. Evaluations of sites and programs should be conducted periodically to assess if objectives are being met and that the natural resources are not being degraded. If evidence of unacceptable adverse impacts begin to appear, it may be necessary to change the location of the outdoor activities.

Justification: Environmental education and interpretation are used to encourage understanding in citizens of all ages in order to act responsibly in protecting a healthy ecosystem. They are tools to use in building land ethic, developing political support, and decreasing wildlife violations. They constitute a method of increasing visibility in the community and improving the image of the Service.

Environmental education at the refuge is incidental to other programs since there is no full-time staff to conduct activities. However, the program is important and provides visitors with an awareness of refuge-specific issues such as wetland ecology, migratory bird management, and issues relating to the entire Refuge System. Environmental education and interpretation activities are expected to increase while ensuring compatibility with the purpose for which the refuge was established.

NEPA Compliance for Refuge Use Description: *Place an X in appropriate space.*

_____Categorical Exclusion without Environmental Action Statement
_____Categorical Exclusion and Environmental Action Statement
__X__Environmental Assessment and Finding of No Significant Impact
_____Environmental Impact Statement and Record of Decision

Mandatory 10- or 15-Year Re-evaluation Date: September 2020

Description of Use: *Farming Program*

Cooperative farming has been a management tool on Dahomey refuge since 1992. Primarily serving as a supplement to natural food resources, this program is designed to assist the refuge in meeting wintering waterfowl goals. Cooperative agreements with farmers are entered into annually prior to the planting season. These agreements describe the location and amount of acreage to be planted during the coming year. The agreement is then signed by the cooperative farmer and the Service representative (refuge manager). Shares are acreage based with a 75 percent cooperator's share and a 25 percent refuge share. The cooperator assumes responsibility for all associated costs for the crops raised. Modifications to the original contract may occur throughout the farming season with amendments agreed upon and signed by all parties involved. Currently, cooperative farming occurs on 531 acres.

In addition to providing winter food resources, this program may be utilized to maintain a newly acquired tract of land in an open condition until decisions are made concerning the tract's ultimate vegetative community.

Farming is used to complement natural food production on the refuge and assist in meeting the minimum waterfowl maintenance objectives as determined in cooperation with the Lower Mississippi Valley Joint Venture Office of the North American Waterfowl and Wetlands Plan. Providing wintering and migrating habitat can be achieved in part through a successful cropland program. By incorporating a system of impoundments with the cropland program, the waterfowl maintenance objectives can be more easily met. Preferred waterfowl crops include corn, milo, rice, millet, soybeans, and natural (moist-soil) foods. By planting crops such as rice and milo in the impoundment areas and using wells to flood the areas during the wintering season, food availability for waterfowl is enhanced.

Farming is not a priority public use within the Service.

Cooperative farming is confined to those agricultural fields acquired as part of the refuge that have not been reforested or maintained in other vegetative communities. Tracts acquired in the future that include agricultural fields may also be farmed prior to determining ultimate vegetative communities.

Cooperative farming agreements are entered into annually, usually prior to April 15th and extend until the end of the harvest season.

Cooperative farming is conducted through a cooperative agreement wherein the cooperator provides all materials, equipment, and labor to fulfill the requirements of the contract. Facilities such as roads, gates, and access points are maintained by the refuge staff.

This use is necessary to fulfill refuge obligations to provide for the wintering needs of migratory waterfowl. While agricultural lands are abundant off the refuge, they do not provide a secure habitat for wintering waterfowl.

Availability of Resources: The North Mississippi National Wildlife Refuges Complex currently spends approximately $3,600 of an annual budget of approximately $750,000 in the administration of the refuge cooperative farming program. In order for the refuge to conduct the farming program in-house, specialized equipment would have to be acquired and maintained. It is estimated that utilizing refuge staff and equipment would cost approximately $52,000 per year.

Special equipment, facilities, or improvements necessary to support the use: None

Maintenance of roads, gates, and access points for cooperative farmers: $2,600

Monitoring cooperative contracts and cooperator activities: $1,000

Offsetting revenues: None

Anticipated Impacts of the Use:

Short-term impacts:

Soil disturbance is likely to occur when the areas are disked during the spring planting season. These impacts are lessened by the implementation of no-till and conservation tillage farming methods. Buffer strips adjacent to water bodies and other sensitive areas help trap sediments and hold agricultural run-off.

The application of pesticides is controlled by the Service and only used after Pesticide Use Proposals submitted by the refuge manager are approved. Pesticide amounts, kind, and method of application are controlled by the Service. Impacts are unknown but would be short-term.

Monotypic stands of agricultural crop reduce the diversity and suitability of refuge lands for some species of migratory and resident wildlife species.

Long-term impacts:

None

Cumulative impacts:

The cumulative impacts should be minimal due to limits on the use and kinds of pesticides, no-till, and conservation tillage farming practices and the use of buffer strips adjacent to water bodies and other sensitive areas.

Public Review and Comment: The period of public review and comment began on September 9, 2004 and ended on October 21, 2004. The following methods were used to solicit public review and comment:

Posted notice at refuge headquarters
Public notice in newspapers with wide local distribution
Public meeting(s)

This compatibility determination was part of the Draft North Mississippi National Wildlife Refuges Complex Comprehensive Conservation Plan and Environmental Assessment, which was announced in the *Federal Register* and made available for public comment for 30 days.

Determination (check one below):

    __X__Compatible with the following stipulations

    _____Not Compatible

Stipulations Necessary to Ensure Compatibility: Cooperators must meet conditions outlined in a Cooperative Farming Agreement, which is a contractual agreement between the refuge and the local farmer. Additionally, cooperators must follow conditions outlined under integrated pest management and within the Service's Pesticide Use Proposal process. Cooperators are subject to dismissal for not meeting these conditions.

Justification: Section 6 RM 4.1 of the National Wildlife Refuge System Refuge Manual states, "Service policy is to use the most natural means available to meet wildlife objectives. In situations where objectives cannot be met through maintenance of natural ecosystems, the artificial and intensive method of cropland management may be employed. The acreage devoted to croplands will be that required to meet minimum habitat objectives." The specific objective is as follows:

Using food as an index to carrying capacity, to provide wintering waterfowl habitat for:

Ducks - 0.5 million duck-use days
Geese - 0.5 million duck-use days

Since establishment in 1992, the acreage of agricultural lands at Dahomey refuge has been reduced from 1,595 acres to 531 acres. Most of the 1,064 acres of former agricultural fields have been reforested. Complete water management through the use of wells is available on the remaining 531 acres of agricultural lands. Augmented with 200 acres of moist-soil areas, the existing agricultural lands fail to meet the food requirements for duck-use days as specified in the North American Waterfowl and Wetland Plan.

Although cropland management will be directed primarily to satisfy certain habitat and life requirements of wintering waterfowl, other bird and mammal species will also benefit. The production of crops is essential for waterfowl management to meet the primary objectives for which the refuge was established. Farming is an essential management tool for providing "hot" foods for migratory birds.

The annual Cooperative Farming Agreement addresses the management of the refuge farm fields. These fields are farmed by a cooperator under a contractual agreement with the refuge. Under this agreement, the refuge receives a 25 percent share of each cooperative farmer's allotment where one acre out of four is planted for waterfowl food production. For their share, 75 percent, the cooperative farmer plants rice, corn, soybeans, or milo.

NEPA Compliance for Refuge Use Description: *Place an X in appropriate space.*

_____Categorical Exclusion without Environmental Action Statement
_____Categorical Exclusion and Environmental Action Statement
___X__Environmental Assessment and Finding of No Significant Impact
_____Environmental Impact Statement and Record of Decision

Mandatory 10- or 15-Year Re-evaluation Date: September 2015

Description of Use: *Fishing*

Fishing was a traditional recreational use of Dahomey refuge prior to its inclusion to the National Wildlife Refuge System and continues to be a popular recreational pursuit. The refuge provides additional public fishing opportunities in an area that is lacking sufficient amounts of acreage open to the public. Currently, fish populations support a sustainable harvest under a regulated fishing program.

Fishing is limited to one natural lake, one lake constructed by the refuge, and one natural stream course. Catfish, bluegill, crappie, and largemouth bass comprise the most sought after fish species on the refuge. Happy Hollow Lake, an unnamed lake south of Sawmill Road, and the stream course north of this unnamed lake are the water bodies on the refuge that provide fishing opportunities.

Fishing, a wildlife-dependent recreational pursuit, has been identified in the National Wildlife Refuge System Improvement Act of 1997 as a priority public use provided it is compatible with the purpose for which the refuge was established.

The three described water bodies, comprising perhaps 12 acres, provide the only sustainable fisheries on the refuge.

Fishing occurs year-round from sunrise to sunset, and is conducted subject to regulations established by the Mississippi Department of Wildlife, Fisheries and Parks. Fishing is further restricted on the refuge by regulations, which prohibit commercial fishing on the refuge, which prohibit the use of certain fishing methods, and which prohibit access after dark. The purchase of an annual hunting and fishing permit is required to fish on the refuge.

Availability of Resources: Funding for the fishing program is borne by annual operation and maintenance funds, which support activities involving the public, such as recreation, interpretation, environmental education, and refuge hunting and fishing programs. The refuge spends approximately $8,000 of an annual North Mississippi National Wildlife Refuges Complex budget of approximately $750,000 in direct support of the fishing program on the refuge. Therefore, the program is in compliance with specific funding requirements of the Refuge Recreation Act.

Special equipment, facilities, or improvements necessary to support the use: None

Maintenance costs: $6,000

Monitoring costs: $2,000

Offsetting revenues: $200

Anticipated Impacts of the Use:

Short-term impacts:

Minor impacts, such as litter and gasoline contamination, could occur but not at a level that would cause great concern.

Long-term impacts:

Since the number of persons fishing on the refuge is small and the activity occurs primarily in the spring, no long-term impacts are expected.

Cumulative impacts:

No cumulative impacts are known to occur.

Public Review and Comment: The period of public review and comment began on September 9, 2004 and ended on October 21, 2004. The following methods were used to solicit public review and comment:

> Posted notice at refuge headquarters
> Public notice in newspapers with wide local distribution
> Public meeting(s)

This compatibility determination was part of the Draft North Mississippi National Wildlife Refuges Complex Comprehensive Conservation Plan and Environmental Assessment, which was announced in the *Federal Register* and made available for public comment for 30 days.

Determination (check one below):

> __X__ Compatible with the following stipulations

> _____ Not Compatible

Stipulations Necessary to Ensure Compatibility: Commercial fishing and possession or use of jugs, seines, nets, hand-grab baskets, or any other similar devices are prohibited. Persons are prohibited from accessing the refuge after dark.

Justification: While the number of participants is limited, fishing has been an important activity on the refuge resulting in only very temporary disturbance to refuge habitats and wildlife populations, and has caused no noticeable impact on the abundance of species sought or other wildlife affected by angler disturbance. Current regulations limit the impacts to trust species and provide a safe and rewarding experience for the refuge visitor.

NEPA Compliance for Refuge Use Description: *Place an X in appropriate space.*

_____Categorical Exclusion without Environmental Action Statement
_____Categorical Exclusion and Environmental Action Statement
___X___Environmental Assessment and Finding of No Significant Impact
_____Environmental Impact Statement and Record of Decision

Mandatory 10- or 15-Year Re-evaluation Date: September 2020

Description of Use: *Hunting*

Hunting has been permitted as a compatible public use activity on Dahomey refuge since acquisition. The original hunting plan was completed, reviewed by the public, and approved in 1994. Refuge hunting seasons generally coincide with the State's hunting seasons and require only minor changes annually. Portions of the refuge are closed annually to all uses except those for disabled hunters. Due to overlapping hunting seasons, hunting of one type of game may be closed for the duration of hunting of a different type of game. All hunting activities are permitted with a valid refuge hunt permit and appropriate State licenses.

The refuge hunts are excellent wildlife management and public relations tools that provide quality recreational opportunities for the general public while regulating specific animal populations at desired levels. The refuge hunting plan was developed to ensure the associated public recreation and wildlife management objectives are met in a responsible and consistent manner.

Hunting, a wildlife-dependent recreational pursuit, has been identified in the National Wildlife Refuge System Improvement Act of 1997 as a priority public use provided it is compatible with the purpose for which the refuge was established.

The entire 9,691-acre refuge is open to public hunting. Note, however, a 160-acre tract immediately north and east of the refuge headquarters is only open to disabled hunters.

All hunting seasons are established annually through coordination with the Mississippi Department of Wildlife, Fisheries and Parks.

Public hunting opportunities in the northwest delta portion of the Yazoo Basin are limited with Service managed refuges and State managed wildlife management areas representing virtually all the public lands open to hunting. Private lands offer hunting opportunities only to those willing and able to purchase hunting rights through long-term leases or private ownership. The demand for public hunting areas in this portion of Mississippi is increasing as the area shifts toward a more urbanized society, and refuges are expected to meet an increasing part of this demand.

Availability of Resources: Funding for the hunting program is borne by annual operation and maintenance funds, which support activities involving the public such as fishing, photography, environmental education and interpretation, and wildlife observation. The cost of operating and maintaining the present small game, big game, turkey, and migratory waterfowl seasons would be approximately $17,500 annually within the annual North Mississippi National Wildlife Refuges Complex budget of approximately $750,000. Therefore, the program is in compliance with specific funding requirements of the Refuge Recreation Act.

Special equipment, facilities, or improvements necessary to support the use: $5,000

Maintenance costs: $1,500

Permit sales: $1,000

Law enforcement costs: $8,500

Monitoring costs: $1,500

Offsetting revenues: $7,500

The refuge is a participant in the Recreational Fee Demonstration Project, which currently returns 80 percent of fees generated from recreational activities back to the refuge. The offsetting revenues are from the sale of hunting and fishing permits.

Anticipated Impacts of the Use:

Short-term impacts:

Dahomey refuge has been open to hunting since its establishment in 1991 with no documented disturbance to refuge habitats and no noticeable impact on the abundance of species hunted or other associated wildlife. While managed hunting opportunities may result in localized disruption of individual animals' daily routines, no noticeable effect on populations has been noticed or documented. Restrictions within the hunting program, notably the closure of small game hunting during the general gun deer hunt, the requirement that all hunters, except those hunting turkey or waterfowl, wear fluorescent orange-colored material above the waistline while actually hunting, and the prohibition of hunting or shooting across any open field from ground level have been implemented due to safety concerns. These restrictions will be closely monitored for effectiveness.

Long-term impacts:

Prior to Service ownership of Dahomey refuge, the forested wetland that constitutes the refuge was a private hunting club with a large membership. Discussions with members of this hunting club indicate that deer and turkeys were the game most heavily hunted. While deer and turkey along with squirrel are still the game most heavily hunted, there is no indication of adverse biological impacts associated with the activities. Should, however, it become necessary, the refuge has the latitude to adjust hunting seasons and bag limits annually, or even close the refuge entirely if safety or habitat concerns merit such actions. This latitude, coupled with monitoring of wildlife populations and habitat conditions by the Service and the Mississippi Department of Wildlife, Fisheries and Parks, will ensure that long-term negative impacts to either wildlife populations and/or habitats on the refuge are unlikely.

Should hunting pressure continue to increase on the refuge, alternatives such as quota hunts, a reduction in the number of days of hunting, or restrictions on that part of the refuge open to hunting can be utilized to limit impacts.

Cumulative impacts:

The timing and duration of the refuge's hunting program do not coincide with most other public uses of the refuge and would not result in cumulative impacts to refuge resources.

Public Review and Comment: The period of public review and comment began on September 9, 2004 and ended on October 21, 2004. The following methods were used to solicit public review and comment:

Posted notice at refuge headquarters
Public notice in newspapers with wide local distribution
Public meeting(s)

This compatibility determination was part of the Draft North Mississippi National Wildlife Refuges Complex Comprehensive Conservation Plan and Environmental Assessment, which was announced in the *Federal Register* and made available for public comment for 30 days.

Determination (check one below):

   X   Compatible with the following stipulations

      Not Compatible

Stipulations Necessary to Ensure Compatibility: Hunting seasons and bag limits are established annually as agreed upon during the annual hunt coordination with State personnel. These generally fall within the State framework. The refuge can, and has, established more restrictive seasons and bag limits to prevent over-harvest of individual species on the refuge. All hunters are required to purchase and possess a refuge hunting permit while participating in refuge hunts. This permit, which augments the State hunting regulations, explains not only the general hunt regulations but the refuge-specific regulations as well. Law enforcement patrols are frequently conducted throughout the hunting season to ensure compliance with refuge laws and regulations. The refuge has included a Refuge Operating Needs System (RONS) project for a fulltime officer to ensure compatibility long term.

Justification: Hunting has shown to be a viable management tool for controlling wildlife populations. Allowing these uses to continue is consistent with the refuge's establishing purpose, management objectives, and follows current Service policy.

NEPA Compliance for Refuge Use Description: *Place an X in appropriate space.*

      Categorical Exclusion without Environmental Action Statement
      Categorical Exclusion and Environmental Action Statement
   X   Environmental Assessment and Finding of No Significant Impact
      Environmental Impact Statement and Record of Decision

Mandatory 10- or 15-Year Re-evaluation Date: September 2020

Description of Use: *Off-Road Vehicles*

Off-road vehicle (4-wheel all-terrain) use is not a priority public use; however, it can occur on the refuge provided it is compatible with the purpose for which the refuge was established.
The general public could participate in the proposed use of off-road vehicles year-round from sunrise to sunset on Dahomey refuge, an area of approximately 9,600 acres southwest of Cleveland, Mississippi.

Off-road vehicles may be used on unimproved dirt roads, fire breaks, and logging roads by visitors who possess a valid hunting and fishing permit and who are gaining access to interior portions of the refuge for hunting and fishing opportunities.

The use of off-road vehicles is proposed in response to questions raised during the scoping process. These questions centered on opportunities to provide visitors who possess a valid hunting and fishing permit off-road vehicle access to internal areas of the refuge for the purpose of hunting and fishing.

Availability of Resources: Funding for this program would be borne by annual operation and maintenance funds, which support activities involving the public, such as interpretation, environmental education, wildlife photography, and refuge hunting and fishing programs. The North Mississippi National Wildlife Refuges Complex would spend approximately $37,500 of an annual budget of approximately $750,000 in direct support of this program on Dahomey refuge.

Special equipment, facilities, or improvements to support the use: $10,000

Maintenance costs: $20,000

Law enforcement costs: $12,500

Monitoring costs: $2,500

Offsetting revenues: $2,000

The refuge does not have the resources to administer this use. Currently, the North Mississippi National Wildlife Refuges Complex does not have law enforcement personnel to monitor this activity. The Complex has included a Refuge Operating Needs System (RONS) package for a fulltime law enforcement officer for Dahomey refuge. Additionally, this activity would require considerable operation and maintenance funds to maintain the existing unimproved dirt roads, fire breaks, and logging roads. It is expected that $2,000 of offsetting revenues would be generated by the sale of hunting and fishing permits to visitors who would not use the refuge unless they could also use off-road vehicles while accessing hunting and fishing areas.

Anticipated Impacts of the Use:

Short-term impacts:

Adverse impacts to unimproved roads, fire breaks, and logging roads by the repeated use of off-road vehicles are well documented and disturbance to wildlife, plants, and their habitats would occur. Such use would be limited to the hunting and fishing seasons, which also coincide with extended periods of heavy rainfall. As use continues, the unimproved roads, fire breaks, and logging roads used for access become wallowed out and rainfall would accumulate in these "wet" areas. Repeated use exacerbates this condition. Conflicts would occur between those hunters and anglers who use off-road vehicles and those who object to the disturbance and noise associated with the vehicles.

Long-term impacts:

Long-term impacts from the repeated use of off-road vehicles by the public would be compounded over time. Unimproved roads, fire breaks, and logging roads would continue to deteriorate and annual maintenance costs would increase. Additional damage to plants and habitats would be experienced as access for the heavy equipment required to maintain these access routes is developed. Conflicts between hunters who use off-road vehicles and those who object to the associated disturbance and noise would continue.

Cumulative impacts:

No cumulative impacts are expected because other forms of public use on the unimproved roads, fire breaks, and logging roads would be limited to persons bicycling or walking. The "footprint" left by these other forms of use is very minimal. As the facilities and road networks at the refuge are improved, general outdoor recreation would likely increase. With this increase in use, conflicts would also increase between hunters who use off-road vehicles and those visitors using the refuge who object to disturbance and noise.

Public Review and Comment: The period of public review and comment began on September 9, 2004 and ended on October 21, 2004. The following methods were used to solicit public review and comment:

> Posted notice at refuge headquarters
> Public notice in newspapers with wide local distribution
> Public meeting(s)

This compatibility determination was part of the Draft North Mississippi National Wildlife Refuges Complex Comprehensive Conservation Plan and Environmental Assessment, which was announced in the *Federal Register* and made available for public comment for 30 days.

Determination (check one below):

_____Compatible with the following stipulations

__X__Not Compatible

Stipulations Necessary to Ensure Compatibility: None

Justification: To provide hunter access, a series of all-weather roads have been constructed. Additional all-weather roads are planned. In addition, approximately 23 miles of fire breaks and old logging roads are maintained obstruction free to facilitate the use of hand held carts, bicycles, wagons, etc., for the purpose of retrieving deer. Additional obstruction-free unimproved dirt roads also occur on the refuge. These facilities eliminate the need for the average hunter to use off-road vehicles on the refuge and prevent the inevitable habitat destruction that accompanies this type of usage. Off-road vehicle usage is an activity that is not compatible with refuge objectives.

NEPA Compliance for Refuge Use Description: *Place an X in appropriate space.*

_____Categorical Exclusion without Environmental Action Statement
_____Categorical Exclusion and Environmental Action Statement
__X__Environmental Assessment and Finding of No Significant Impact
_____Environmental Impact Statement and Record of Decision

Mandatory 10- or 15-Year Re-evaluation Date: September 2015

Description of Use: *Resource Research Studies*

This activity would allow university professors and their students, nongovernmental researchers, and governmental scientists access to Dahomey refuge's natural environment to conduct both short- and long-term research projects and surveys. The outcome of this research would result in better knowledge of our natural resources and improved methods to manage, monitor, and protect the refuge resources.

Resource research studies are not a priority public use within the Service, but do support the mission of the Service in gathering good scientific data to make management decisions.

These activities would be conducted throughout the refuge in a variety of habitats. Activities carried out during approved research projects and surveys may be limited to avoid unnecessary disturbance to refuge resources or ongoing management activities.

The activities would vary in scope and duration to satisfy the requirement of the research project or survey. Projects may involve everything from a limited one-time sampling or survey to long-term study plots.

Research projects and surveys would be conducted by universities, state and federal government representatives, and rarely by private individuals. The refuge would act solely in a supportive role, providing minimal assistance in most cases.

Furthering the knowledge of the impacts and benefits of management decisions, life histories of wildlife species utilizing the refuge, and interrelationships of habitats and wildlife occurring on the refuge is crucial to effective management. The refuge provides secure sites for long-term evaluation of management actions, population trends, and ecological functions within the bottomland hardwood ecosystems in northwest Mississippi.

Availability of Resources: This program is borne by annual operation and maintenance funds, which support activities involving the public, such as recreation, interpretation, environmental education, and refuge hunting and fishing programs. The North Mississippi National Wildlife Refuges Complex spends approximately $3,600 of an annual budget of approximately $750,000 in direct support of these programs on Dahomey refuge. Therefore, the program is in compliance with specific funding provisions of the Refuge Recreation Act.

Special equipment, facilities or improvement necessary to support the use: None

Maintenance costs: $1,000

Monitoring costs: $2,600

Offsetting revenues: None

Anticipated Impacts of the Use:

Short-term impacts:

There should be no significant adverse impacts from scientific research on the refuge. The knowledge gained from the research would provide information to improve management techniques for trust resource species. Impacts such as trampling vegetation, removal of small numbers of plants and/or animals, and temporary disturbance to wildlife could occur, but should not be significant. The small number of individual plants and animals that may be collected for further study would not have a significant effect on the refuge plant and animal populations, and would require management approval prior to collection.

Long-term impacts:

Long-term benefits associated with improved management techniques developed through research or surveys would far outweigh any negative impacts, which may occur.

Cumulative impacts:

No adverse cumulative effects are anticipated.

Public Review and Comment: The period of public review and comment began on September 9, 2004 and ended on October 21, 2004. The following methods were used to solicit public review and comment:

> Posted notice at refuge headquarters
> Public notice in newspapers with wide local distribution
> Public meeting(s)

This compatibility determination was part of the Draft North Mississippi National Wildlife Refuges Complex Comprehensive Conservation Plan and Environmental Assessment, which was announced in the *Federal Register* and made available for public comment for 30 days.

Determination (check one below):

> __X__Compatible with the following stipulations

> _____Not Compatible

Stipulations Necessary to Ensure Compatibility: Each request for use of the refuge for research or survey would be examined on its individual merit. Questions of who, what, when, where, and why, would be asked to determine if the requested research could contribute to the refuge purposes and could best be conducted on the refuge without significantly affecting the resources. If so, the researcher would be issued a Special Use Permit that would clearly define allowed activities. Progress would be monitored and the researcher would be required to submit annual progress reports and copies of all publications derived from the research.

Justification: The benefits derived from sound research provide a better understanding of species and the environmental communities present on the refuge. Research projects would be designed to minimize impacts and disturbance.

NEPA Compliance for Refuge Use Description: *Place an X in appropriate space.*

_____Categorical Exclusion without Environmental Action Statement
_____Categorical Exclusion and Environmental Action Statement
__X__Environmental Assessment and Finding of No Significant Impact
_____Environmental Impact Statement and Record of Decision

Description of Use: *Wildlife Observation and Photography*

Wildlife observation and photography have been identified in the National Wildlife Refuge System Improvement Act of 1997 as priority wildlife-dependent recreational uses provided they are compatible with the purpose for which the refuge was established.

Wildlife photography, including other image-capturing activities, such as videography, has occurred on the refuge. There are no photography blinds or platforms on the refuge and none are proposed at this time. However, opportunities exist for photography on the refuge. This compatibility determination applies to personal photography only. Commercial photography or videography, if allowed, would require a special use permit by the refuge and would include specific restrictions.

The general public could participate in wildlife observation and photography year-round from sunrise to sunset on Dahomey refuge, an area approximately 9,600 acres west of Cleveland, Mississippi,

Wildlife observation and photography could be accomplished while driving or walking on refuge roads open to public vehicular traffic. Also, these priority public uses could be accomplished by walking the 23 miles of old trails/logging roads or by boating on refuge waters.

The National Wildlife Refuge System Improvement Act of 1997 identifies wildlife observation and photography as priority public uses for national wildlife refuges, along with hunting, fishing, and environmental education and interpretation. As expressed priority uses of the Refuge System, these uses take precedence over other potential public uses in refuge planning and management. The Service strives to provide priority public uses when compatible with the purposes of the refuge and the mission of the National Wildlife Refuge System.

Availability of Resources: Funding for this operation is borne by annual operation and maintenance funds, which supports activities involving the public, such as outdoor recreation, environmental education and interpretation, and the conduct of refuge hunting and fishing programs. The North Mississippi National Wildlife Refuges Complex spends approximately $8,000 of an annual budget of approximately $750,000 in direct support of these programs on Dahomey refuge. Therefore, the program is in compliance with specific funding requirements of the Refuge Recreation Act.

Special equipment, facilities, or improvements necessary to support the use: $4,000

Maintenance costs: $3,000

Monitoring costs: $1,000

Anticipated Impacts of the Use:

Short-term impacts:

The refuge provides habitat for resident and migratory wildlife. As a result of these activities, individual animals may be disturbed by human contact to varying degrees. Examples of potential disturbance could include flushing of birds from feeding, resting, or nesting areas, and trampling of plants from observers and photographers wandering off designated roads in order to get closer to subjects. Disturbance to trust species is expected to be minimal. Short-term impacts to facilities, such as roads and trails, could be avoided by special closures due to unsafe conditions. The wildlife observation and photography programs have been designed to avoid or minimize impacts on refuge resources and visitors.

Long-term impacts:

The vast majority of the activities associated with this use would be during the fall and early winter. Due to the recovery time between periods of expected use, no long-term impacts are expected.

Cumulative impacts:

No cumulative adverse impacts are anticipated. However, programs could be modified in the future to mitigate unforeseen impacts.

Public Review and Comment: The period of public review and comment began on September 9, 2004 and ended on October 21, 2004. The following methods were used to solicit public review and comment:

> Posted notice at refuge headquarters
> Public notice in newspapers with wide local distribution
> Public meeting(s)

This compatibility determination was part of the Draft North Mississippi National Wildlife Refuges Complex Comprehensive Conservation Plan and Environmental Assessment, which was announced in the *Federal Register* and made available for public comment for 30 days.

Determination (check one below):

> __X__Compatible with the following stipulations

> _____Not Compatible

Stipulations Necessary to Ensure Compatibility: The 160-acre tract located northeast of the refuge headquarters is only open to disabled persons. Two hunting blinds are located on this 160-acre tract. Although established as barrier free hunting blinds for disabled hunters, these blinds provide an excellent opportunity for disabled persons to participate in wildlife observation and photography.

Justification: These wildlife-dependent uses are priority public uses of the National Wildlife Refuge System. Wildlife observation and photography would provide an excellent forum for allowing public access and increasing understanding of refuge resources. The stipulations outlined above should minimize potential impacts relative to wildlife/human interactions. These wildlife dependent uses would not conflict with the national policy to maintain the biological diversity, integrity, and environmental health of the refuge.

NEPA Compliance for Refuge Use Description: Place an X in appropriate space.

_____Categorical Exclusion without Environmental Action Statement
_____Categorical Exclusion and Environmental Action Statement
___X___Environmental Assessment and Finding of No Significant Impact
_____Environmental Impact Statement and Record of Decision

Mandatory 10- or 15-Year Re-evaluation Date: September 2020

Refuge Name: Tallahatchie National Wildlife Refuge

Uses: Several uses were evaluated to determine their compatibility with the Refuge System and mission and purposes of the refuge: 1) Bicycling; 2) Environmental Education and Interpretation; 3) Farming; 4) Fishing; 5) Hunting; 6) Off-Road Vehicle Use; 7) Resource Research Studies; and 8) Wildlife Observation and Photography.

Location: Grenada and Tallahatchie Counties, Mississippi

Establishing and Acquisition Authorities: Migratory Bird Conservation Act, Consolidated Farm and Rural Development Act

Refuge Purposes: "...for use as an inviolate sanctuary, or for any other management purpose, for migratory birds." 16 U.S.C. § 751d (Migratory Bird Conservation Act)

"...for conservation purposes..." 7 U.S.C. § 2002 (Consolidated Farm and Rural Development Act)

National Wildlife Refuge System Mission: The mission of the National Wildlife Refuge System is "to administer a national network of lands and waters for the conservation, management, and where appropriate, restoration of the fish, wildlife, and plant resources and their habitats within the United States for the benefit of present and future generations of Americans."

Description of Use: *Bicycling*

The use is bicycling to facilitate travel for the priority public uses on Tallahatchie National Wildlife Refuge. Priority public uses as identified in the National Wildlife Refuge System Improvement Act of 1997 include hunting, fishing, wildlife observation, wildlife photography, and environmental education and interpretation.

The general public could participate in the proposed public use on Tallahatchie National Wildlife Refuge, an area of approximately 4,000 acres west of Holcomb, Mississippi.

Bicycles may be used on designated motorized vehicle access roads. Additionally, bicycles may be used on unimproved dirt roads, fire breaks, and logging roads.

To promote safety, bicycling would be permitted from sunrise to sunset. Additionally, during the deer gun-hunting season, bicycling would only be allowed to facilitate hunter access. During the deer gun-hunting season, bicyclists would need to possess a valid hunting and fishing permit. During other refuge hunting seasons, bicycle travel for non-consumptive priority public uses would be allowed.

Bicycling to facilitate non-consumptive priority public uses would involve observing the natural landscape from a bicycle. Riders would stop to observe associated animals and plant communities. The use would mainly occur in groups with an average size of 2-4 riders. Regarding consumptive uses, anglers could access refuge lands for fishing by bicycle travel on designated roads and trails. Hunters could do the same to access game. To promote safety with other users, prevent conflicts, and promote a quality wildlife observation environment, group size would be limited to 10 bicyclists. Groups of more than 10 would have to contact the refuge office for a special use permit prior to using the refuge. This would help protect refuge resources and ensure that larger groups would not conflict with concurrent public uses.

Bicycle travel on the refuge would be conducted in accordance with the stipulations necessary to ensure compatibility. Travel would be limited to designated roads and trails.

Bicycle travel on the refuge would provide increased opportunity for public participation in priority public uses. It is an alternative method of travel to view the refuge's diverse biological assets and could be less physically demanding than pedestrian travel.

Availability of Resources: Funding for these programs is borne by annual operation and maintenance funds, which support activities involving the public, such as recreation, environmental education and interpretation, and hunting and fishing programs. The North Mississippi National Wildlife Refuges Complex spends approximately $3,000 of an annual budget of approximately $750,000 in direct support of these programs on Tallahatchie refuge. Therefore, the program is in compliance with specific funding provisions of the Refuge Recreation Act.

Special equipment, facilities, or improvements necessary to support the use: $1,000

Maintenance costs: $1,000

Monitoring costs: $1,000

Anticipated Impacts of the Use:

Short-term impacts:

Bicycle use can cause soil compaction, particularly when soils are wet, which can degrade plant communities. Soil compaction can diminish the soil porosity, aeration, and nutrient availability.

It is anticipated that bicycle use could alter drainage features of roads and trails through erosion and compaction. Tires may create trail incision causing increased water channeling and erosion during wet conditions. These problems would be minimized because routes designated for bicycle use are existing improved roads, logging trails, and fire breaks. Based on current levels of use and conditions of designated routes, changes to hydrology because of this use are likely to be insignificant.

Anticipated impacts of bicycle use on wildlife include temporal disturbances to species using habitat on the trail or directly adjacent to the trail. These disturbances are likely to be short-term and infrequent based on current level of use.

Disturbances to trust species are minimal due to the locations of the designated gravel roads and unimproved roads and fire breaks. Short-term impacts to facilities, such as roads and trails, can be avoided by special closures.

Long-term impacts:

No long-term impacts are anticipated.

Cumulative impacts:

No cumulative adverse impacts are anticipated. However, programs could be modified in the future to mitigate unforeseen impacts.

Public Review and Comment: The period of public review and comment began on September 9, 2004 and ended on October 21, 2004. The following methods were used to solicit public review and comment:

> Posted notice at refuge headquarters
> Public notice in newspapers with wide local distribution
> Public meeting(s)

This compatibility determination was part of the Draft North Mississippi National Wildlife Refuges Complex Comprehensive Conservation Plan and Environmental Assessment, which was announced in the *Federal Register* and made available for public comment for 30 days.

Determination (check one below):

> __X__ Compatible with the following stipulations

> _____ Not Compatible

Stipulations Necessary to Ensure Compatibility: At the present time, public entry to include visitors involved in bicycling is not permitted on that part of the refuge located north of Highway 8 except by special use permit. Bicycling, except for hunting use, is not permitted during the deer gun-hunting season. Hunters are allowed to use bicycles but they must remain on designated roads and trails. Bicycle group size is limited to 10 bicyclists, to promote public safety, accommodate other users, and provide a positive wildlife viewing experience. Group size greater than 10 requires a special use permit issued by the refuge manager.

Justification: That part of Tallahatchie refuge located north of Highway 8 is divided by the Tippo Bayou. There is no legal access for general public use of the northeast section of the refuge. The remaining refuge lands north of Highway 8 are enrolled in the cooperative farming program or established as waterfowl management units. Management efforts are successful with large numbers of migratory waterfowl using the refuge from October to March. Experience has shown that birds using the refuge are susceptible to disturbance.

Bicycling has been determined to be compatible provided the above stipulations are implemented. Bicycle use, as identified in this compatibility determination, is not expected to materially interfere with, or detract from, the mission of the National Wildlife Refuge System or the purposes for which the refuge was established. The use of bicycles to facilitate the priority public use is a reasonable mode of access on designated roads and trails. Monitoring would be conducted to ensure this use remains compatible. If significant impacts are found, corrective actions would be taken to protect refuge resources.

NEPA Compliance for Refuge Use Description: *Place an X in appropriate space.*

_____ Categorical Exclusion without Environmental Action Statement
_____ Categorical Exclusion and Environmental Action Statement
__X__ Environmental Assessment and Finding of No Significant Impact
_____ Environmental Impact Statement and Record of Decision

Mandatory 10- or 15-Year Re-evaluation Date: September 2015

Description of Use: *Environmental Education and Interpretation*

Environmental education and interpretation would consist primarily of teacher workshops, visitor education, teaching students, and interpretation.

Those activities seek to increase the public's knowledge and understanding of wildlife and contribute to the conservation of such wildlife. Activities would include traditional environmental education, such as teacher or staff-led on-site field trips, off-site programs in classrooms, nature study such as teacher and student workshops, and interpretation of the wildlife resources incorporated in support of facilities, such as interpretive trails, kiosks, and visitor contact stations.

Environmental education and interpretation have been identified in the National Wildlife Refuge System Improvement Act of 1997 as priority public uses provided they are compatible with the purpose for which the refuge was established.

All that portion of the refuge south of Highway 8 has the potential to be utilized for environmental education and interpretation.

Environmental education and interpretation are year-round activities, conducted on an as requested basis. Although these activities do not require a special use permit, they are most often closely coordinated with the refuge manager.

The refuge would serve as an outdoor classroom for a variety of audiences with an interest in wildlife conservation and management. Typically, teachers, students, and other groups would learn from hands-on demonstrations, projects, and activities delivered by refuge staff. Activities would be conducted on-site utilizing existing refuge facilities. Group size would typically be limited to ensure effective presentation of desired materials, which may be specifically tailored to meet the educational needs of the group.

Environmental education and interpretation are utilized to encourage understanding in citizens of all ages to develop land ethics, foster public support, increase visibility, and improve the image of the Service.

Availability of Resources: Funding for these activities is borne by annual operation and maintenance funds, which support activities involving the public, such as outdoor recreation, wildlife photography, and the refuge hunting and fishing programs. The North Mississippi National Wildlife Refuges Complex spends approximately $3,600 of an annual budget of approximately $750,000 in direct support of these programs on Tallahatchie refuge. Therefore, the program is in compliance with specific funding provisions of the Refuge Recreation Act.

Currently, these activities are conducted as time and resources permit. Developing a volunteer organization for the refuge would provide for the future of these programs by providing additional personnel to deliver the programs.

Facilities (including kiosks, interpretive signs and brochures): $2000

On-site activities: $1000

Maintenance costs: $2000

Monitoring costs: $1,000

Offsetting revenues: None

Anticipated Impacts of the Use:

Short-term impacts:

The use of on-site, hands-on, action-oriented activities by groups of teachers/students to accomplish environmental education objectives may impose a low level impact on those sites used for these activities. Impacts may include trampling of vegetation and temporary disturbance to wildlife species in the immediate vicinity during the activities. Since most activities would take place on existing roads, trails, and at other facilities, impacts would be minimal.

Long-term impacts:

Current utilization of these uses is incidental to overall refuge programs and no long-term adverse impacts have been experienced. Long-term beneficial impacts include the furthering of the refuge mission through the education of the general public.

Cumulative impacts:

No adverse cumulative impacts are anticipated.

Public Review and Comment: The period of public review and comment began on September 9, 2004 and ended on October 21, 2004. The following methods were used to solicit public review and comment:

> Posted notice at refuge headquarters
> Public notice in newspapers with wide local distribution
> Public meeting(s)

This compatibility determination was part of the Draft North Mississippi National Wildlife Refuges Complex Comprehensive Conservation Plan and Environmental Assessment, which was announced in the *Federal Register* and made available for public comment for 30 days.

Determination (check one below):

> __X__ Compatible with the following stipulations

> _____ Not Compatible

Stipulations Necessary to Ensure Compatibility: On-site activities should be held where minimal impact would occur. Evaluations of sites and programs should be conducted periodically to assess if objectives are being met and that natural resources are not being degraded. If evidence of unacceptable adverse impacts begin to appear, it may be necessary to change the location of the outdoor activities.

Justification: Environmental education and interpretation are used to encourage an understanding in citizens of all ages to act responsibly in protecting a healthy ecosystem. They are tools to use in building land ethic, developing support of the refuge, and decreasing wildlife violations. Environmental education and interpretation are methods of increasing visibility in the community and improving the image of the Service.

Environmental education at the refuge is incidental to other programs since there is no full-time staff to conduct these activities. However, the program is important and provides visitors with an awareness of refuge-specific issues such as wetland ecology, migratory bird management, and issues relating to the entire Refuge System. Environmental education and interpretation activities are expected to increase while ensuring compatibility with the purpose for which the refuge was established.

NEPA Compliance for Refuge Use Description: *Place an X in appropriate space.*

_____Categorical Exclusion without Environmental Action Statement
_____Categorical Exclusion and Environmental Action Statement
__X__Environmental Assessment and Finding of No Significant Impact
_____Environmental Impact Statement and Record of Decision

Mandatory 10- or 15-Year Re-evaluation Date: September 2020

Description of Use: *Farming*

Cooperative farming has been a management tool on Tallahatchie refuge since 1991. Primarily serving as a supplement to natural food resources, this program is designed to assist the refuge in meeting wintering waterfowl goals. Cooperative agreements with farmers are entered into annually prior to the planting season. These agreements describe the location and amount of acreage to be planted during the coming year. The agreement is then signed by the cooperative farmer and the Service representative (refuge manager). Shares are acreage based with a 75 percent cooperator's share and a 25 percent refuge share. The cooperator assumes responsibility for all associated costs for the crops raised. Modifications to the original contract may occur throughout the farming season with amendments agreed upon and signed by all parties involved. Currently, cooperative farming occurs on 721 acres.

In addition to providing winter food resources, this program may be utilized to maintain a newly acquired tract of land in an open condition until decisions are made concerning the tract's ultimate vegetative community.

Farming is used to complement natural food production on the refuge and assist in meeting the minimum waterfowl maintenance objectives, as determined in cooperation with the Lower Mississippi Valley Joint Venture Office of the North American Waterfowl and Wetlands Plan. Providing wintering and migrating habitat can be achieved, in part, through a successful cropland program. By incorporating a system of impoundments with the cropland program, the waterfowl maintenance objectives can be more easily met. Preferred waterfowl crops include corn, milo, rice, millet, soybeans, and natural (moist-soil) foods. By planting crops such as rice and milo in the impoundment areas and using wells to flood the areas during the wintering season, food availability for waterfowl is enhanced.

Farming is not a priority public use within the Service.

Cooperative farming is confined to those agricultural fields north of Highway 8 that were acquired as part of the refuge and have not been reforested or maintained in other vegetative communities. Tracts acquired in the future that include agricultural fields may also be farmed prior to determining ultimate vegetative communities.

Cooperative farming agreements are entered into annually, usually prior to April 15th and extend until the end of the harvest season.

Cooperative farming is conducted through a cooperative agreement wherein the cooperator provides all materials, equipment, and labor to fulfill the requirements of the contract. Facilities such as roads, gates, and access points are maintained by the refuge staff.

This use is necessary to fulfill refuge obligations to provide for the wintering needs of migratory waterfowl. While agricultural lands are abundant off the refuge, they do not provide a secure habitat for wintering waterfowl.

Availability of Resources: The North Mississippi National Wildlife Refuges Complex currently spends approximately $3,600 of an annual budget of approximately $750,000 in the administration of the refuge cooperative farming program. In order for the refuge to conduct the farming program in-house, specialized equipment would have to be acquired and maintained. It is estimated that utilizing refuge staff and equipment would cost approximately $73,000 per year.

Special equipment, facilities, or improvements necessary to support the use: None

Maintenance of roads, gates, and access points for cooperative farmers: $2,600

Monitoring costs: $1,000

Offsetting revenues: None

Anticipated Impacts of the Use:

Short-term impacts:

Soil disturbance is likely to occur when the areas are disked during the spring planting season. These impacts are lessened by the implementation of no-till and conservation tillage farming methods. Buffer strips adjacent to water bodies and other sensitive areas help trap sediments and hold agricultural run-off.

The application of pesticides is controlled by the Service and only used after Pesticide Use Proposals submitted by the refuge manager are approved. Pesticide amounts, kinds, and methods of application are controlled by the Service. Impacts are unknown but would be short term.

Monotypic stands of agricultural crop reduce the diversity and suitability of refuge lands for a variety of migratory and resident wildlife species.

Long-term impacts:

None

Cumulative impacts:

The cumulative impacts should be minimal due to limits on the use and kinds of pesticides, no-till and conservation tillage farming practices and the use of buffer strips adjacent to water bodies and other sensitive areas.

Public Review and Comment: The period of public review and comment began on September 9, 2004 and ended on October 21, 2004. The following methods were used to solicit public review and comment:

     Posted notice at refuge headquarters
     Public notice in newspapers with wide local distribution
     Public meeting(s)

This compatibility determination was part of the Draft North Mississippi National Wildlife Refuges Complex Comprehensive Conservation Plan and Environmental Assessment, which was announced in the *Federal Register* and made available for public comment for 30 days.

Determination (check one below):

     __X__Compatible with the following stipulations

     _____Not Compatible

Stipulations Necessary to Ensure Compatibility: Cooperators must meet conditions outlined in the Cooperative Farming Agreements, which are contractual agreements between the refuge and local farmers. Additionally, cooperators must follow conditions outlined under integrated pest management and within the Service's Pesticide Use Proposal process. Cooperators are subject to dismissal for not meeting these conditions.

Justification: Section 6 RM 4.1 of the National Wildlife Refuge System Refuge Manual states, "Service policy is to use the most natural means available to meet wildlife objectives. In situations where objectives cannot be met through maintenance of natural ecosystems, the artificial and intensive method of cropland management may be employed. The acreage devoted to croplands will be that required to meet minimum habitat objectives." The specific objective is as follows:

Using food as an index to carrying capacity, provide wintering waterfowl habitat for:

     Ducks -1.2 million duck-use days
     Geese - 0.35 million duck-use days

Since establishment in 1991, the acreage of agricultural lands at Tallahatchie refuge has been reduced from 1,980 acres to 600 acres. Almost all of the 1,680 acres of former agricultural fields has been reforested. Complete water management through the use of wells is available on the remaining 600 acres of agricultural lands. Augmented with 718 acres of moist-soil areas, the existing agricultural lands fail to meet the food requirements for duck-use days as specified in the North American Waterfowl and Wetland Plan.

Although cropland management will be directed primarily to satisfy certain habitat and life requirements of wintering waterfowl, other bird and mammal species will also benefit. The production of crops is essential for waterfowl management to meet the primary objectives for which the refuge was established. Farming is an essential management tool for providing "hot" foods for migratory birds.

The annual Cooperative Farming agreement addresses the management of the refuge farm fields. These fields are farmed by a cooperator under an agreement with the refuge. Under this agreement, the refuge receives a 25 percent share of each cooperative farmer's allotment where 1 acre out of 4 is planted for waterfowl food production. For his 75 percent share, the cooperative farmer plants rice, soybeans, corn, or milo.

NEPA Compliance for Refuge Use Description: *Place an X in appropriate space.*

_____Categorical Exclusion without Environmental Action Statement
_____Categorical Exclusion and Environmental Action Statement
___X__Environmental Assessment and Finding of No Significant Impact
_____Environmental Impact Statement and Record of Decision

Mandatory 10- or 15-Year Re-evaluation Date: September 2015

Description of Use: *Fishing*

Fishing was a traditional recreational use of Tallahatchie refuge prior to its inclusion in the National Wildlife Refuge System and continues to be a popular recreational pursuit. The refuge provides additional public fishing opportunities in an area that is lacking sufficient amounts of natural stream fishing open to the public, and current fish populations currently support a sustainable harvest under a regulated fishing program.

Fishing is permitted on that part of Tippo Bayou south of Highway 8 that basically forms the eastern boundary of the refuge for about 4 miles, and on Long Lake, an old channel of Tippo Bayou that is about 2 miles long and totally within the refuge. The refuge maintains a boat ramp on each of these water bodies that is open to the public with the purchase of an annual hunting and fishing permit. During high water periods in the late winter and spring, catfish, bluegill, and crappie are present in numbers to attract local anglers. However, during late summer and early fall, water levels and dissolved oxygen levels are sufficiently low that fish sampling has shown fish populations are dominated by shad, carp, and gar. Few anglers fish on the refuge during these time periods.

Fishing, a wildlife-dependent recreational pursuit, has been identified in the National Wildlife Refuge System Improvement Act of 1997 as a priority public use provided it is compatible with the purpose for which the refuge was established.

Fishing is permitted, year-round from sunrise to sunset, on that portion of Tippo Bayou south of Highway 8 that forms the eastern boundary of the refuge, and on about 2 miles of Long Lake, an old channel of Tippo Bayou that is entirely within the refuge.

Fishing is conducted on the refuge subject to regulations established by the Mississippi Department of Wildlife, Fisheries and Parks. Fishing is further restricted by regulations which prohibit commercial fishing on the refuge, prohibit the use of certain fishing methods, and prohibit access after dark. The purchase of an annual hunting and fishing permit is required to fish on the refuge.

Fishing is conducted to provide fishable waters to the public in an area where public fishing opportunities in natural stream habitats are limited and to utilize a sustainable natural resource.

Availability of Resources: Funding for the fishing program is borne by annual operation and maintenance funds, which support activities involving the public, such as recreation, interpretation, environmental education, and refuge hunting and fishing programs. The North Mississippi National Wildlife Refuges Complex spends approximately $7,000 of a budget of approximately $750,000 in direct support of the fishing program on the refuge. Therefore, the program is in compliance with specific funding requirements of the Refuge Recreation Act.

Special equipment, facilities, or improvements necessary to support the use: None

Maintenance costs: $5,000

Monitoring costs: $2,000

Offsetting revenues: $200

Anticipated Impacts of the Use:

Short-term impacts:

Minor impacts such as litter and gasoline contamination could occur but not at a level that would cause great concern.

Long-term impacts:

Since the number of persons fishing on the refuge is small and the activity occurs primarily during high water periods in the spring, no long-term impacts are expected.

Cumulative impacts:

No cumulative impacts are known to occur.

Public Review and Comment: The period of public review and comment began on September 9, 2004 and ended on October 21, 2004. The following methods were used to solicit public review and comment:

> Posted notice at refuge headquarters
> Public notice in newspapers with wide local distribution
> Public meeting(s)

This compatibility determination was part of the Draft North Mississippi National Wildlife Refuges Complex Comprehensive Conservation Plan and Environmental Assessment, which was announced in the *Federal Register* and made available for public comment for 30 days.

Determination (check one below):

> __X__ Compatible with the following stipulations

> _____ Not Compatible

Stipulations Necessary to Ensure Compatibility: Commercial fishing and possession or use of jugs, seines, nets, hand-grab baskets, or any other similar devices are prohibited. Persons are prohibited from accessing the refuge after dark.

Justification: While the number of participants is limited, fishing has been an important activity on the refuge resulting in only very temporary disturbance to refuge habitats and wildlife populations, and has caused no noticeable impact on the abundance of species sought or other wildlife affected by angler disturbance. Current regulations limit the impacts to trust species and provide a safe and rewarding experience for the refuge visitor.

NEPA Compliance for Refuge Use Description: *Place an X in appropriate space.*

_____Categorical Exclusion without Environmental Action Statement
_____Categorical Exclusion and Environmental Action Statement
___X___Environmental Assessment and Finding of No Significant Impact
_____Environmental Impact Statement and Record of Decision

Mandatory 10- or 15-Year Re-evaluation Date: September 2020

Description of Use: *Hunting*

Hunting has been permitted as a compatible public use activity on Tallahatchie refuge since acquisition. The original hunting plan was completed, reviewed by the public, and approved in 1994. Refuge hunting seasons generally coincide with the State hunting seasons and require only minor changes annually. Only that part of the refuge south of Highway 8 is open to public hunting. Due to overlapping hunting seasons, hunting of one type of game may be closed for the duration of hunting of a different type of game. All hunting activities are permitted with a valid refuge hunt permit and appropriate State licenses.

The refuge hunting program is an excellent wildlife management and public relations tool that provides quality recreational opportunities for the general public while regulating specific animal populations at desired levels. The refuge hunting plan was developed to ensure that associated public recreation and wildlife management objectives are met in a responsible and consistent manner.

Hunting, a wildlife-dependent recreational pursuit, has been identified in the National Wildlife Refuge System Improvement Act of 1997 as a priority public use provided it is compatible with the purpose for which the refuge was established.

The general public can participate in hunting on Tallahatchie refuge, an area of approximately 4,000 acres west of Holcomb, Mississippi.

All hunting seasons are established annually through coordination with the Mississippi Department of Wildlife, Fisheries and Parks.

Public hunting opportunities in the northwest delta portion of the Yazoo Basin are limited with Service managed refuges and State managed wildlife management areas representing virtually all the public lands open to hunting. Private lands offer hunting opportunities only to those willing and able to purchase hunting rights through long-term leases or private ownership. The demand for public hunting areas in this portion of Mississippi is increasing as there is a shift towards a more urbanized society, and refuges are expected to meet an increasing part of this demand.

Availability of Resources: Funding for the hunting program is borne by annual operation and maintenance funds, which support activities involving the public such as fishing, photography, environmental education and interpretation, and wildlife observation. The cost of operating and maintaining the present small game, big game, turkey, and migratory waterfowl seasons would be approximately $17,500 annually within the annual North Mississippi National Wildlife Refuges Complex budget of approximately $750,000. Therefore, the program is in compliance with specific funding requirements of the Refuge Recreation Act.

Special equipment, facilities or improvements necessary to support the use: $5,000

Maintenance costs: $1,500

Permit sales: $1,000

Law enforcement costs: $8,500

Monitoring costs: $1,500

Offsetting revenues: $7,500

The refuge is a participant in the Recreational Fee Demonstration Project which currently returns 80 percent of fees generated from recreational activities back to the refuge. The offsetting revenues are from the sale of hunting and fishing permits.

Anticipated Impacts of the Use:

Short-term impacts:

That part of Tallahatchie refuge south of Highway 8 has been open to hunting since its establishment in 1992, with no documented disturbance to refuge habitats and no noticeable impact on the abundance of species hunted or other associated wildlife. While managed hunting opportunities may result in localized disruption of an individual animal's daily routine, no noticeable effect on populations has been noticed or documented. Restrictions within the hunting program, notably the closure of small game hunting during the general gun deer hunt, the requirement that all hunters, except those hunting turkey or waterfowl, wear fluorescent orange-colored material above the waistline while actually hunting, and the prohibition of hunting or shooting across any open field from ground level have been implemented due to safety concerns. These restrictions will be closely monitored for effectiveness.

Long-term impacts:

Prior to Service ownership of Tallahatchie refuge, the area south of Highway 8 was in several ownerships. Hunting was an activity that occurred on each individual parcel either by the owners or by the person or persons who leased the hunting rights from the owners. Deer and migratory waterfowl were the most heavily hunted species. While deer and migratory waterfowl are still the game most heavily hunted, hunters also pursue squirrel and rabbits. To date, there is no indication of adverse biological impacts associated with the activities. Should it become necessary, the refuge has the latitude to adjust hunting seasons and bag limits annually, and to close the refuge entirely if safety or habitat issues become concerns. This latitude, coupled with monitoring of wildlife populations and habitat conditions by the Service and the State Department of Wildlife, Fisheries and

Parks, will ensure that long-term negative impacts to either wildlife populations and/or habitats on the refuge are unlikely.

Should hunting pressure continue to increase on the refuge, alternatives such as quota hunts, a reduction in the number of days of hunting, or restrictions on that part of the refuge open to hunting can be utilized to limit impacts.

Cumulative impacts:

The timing and duration of the refuge's hunting program does not coincide with most other public uses of the refuge and would not result in cumulative impacts to refuge resources.

Public Review and Comment: The period of public review and comment began on September 9, 2004 and ended on October 21, 2004. The following methods were used to solicit public review and comment:

> Posted notice at refuge headquarters
> Public notice in newspapers with wide local distribution
> Public meeting(s)

This compatibility determination was part of the Draft North Mississippi National Wildlife Refuges Complex Comprehensive Conservation Plan and Environmental Assessment, which was announced in the *Federal Register* and made available for public comment for 30 days.

Determination (check one below):

> __X__Compatible with the following stipulations

> _____Not Compatible

Stipulations Necessary to Ensure Compatibility: At the present time, public entry to include visitors involved in hunting is not permitted on that part of the refuge located north of Highway 8 except by special use permit.

Hunting seasons and bag limits are established annually as agreed upon during the annual hunt coordination with State personnel. These generally fall within the State framework. The refuge can, and has, established more restrictive seasons and bag limits to prevent over-harvest of individual species on the refuge. All hunters are required to purchase and possess a refuge hunting permit while participating in refuge hunts. This permit, which augments the State hunting regulations, explains not only the general hunt regulations but also the refuge-specific regulations. Law enforcement patrols are frequently conducted throughout the hunting season to ensure compliance with refuge laws and regulations. The refuge has included a RONS project for a fulltime officer to ensure compatibility long term.

Justification: That part of Tallahatchie refuge located north of Highway 8 is divided by the Tippo Bayou. There is no legal access for general public use to the northeast section of the refuge. The remaining refuge lands north of Highway 8 are either enrolled in the cooperative farming program or established waterfowl management units. Management efforts are successful with large numbers of migratory waterfowl using the refuge from October to March. Experience has shown that birds using the refuge are susceptible to disturbance.

Hunting has shown to be a viable management tool for controlling wildlife populations. Allowing these uses to continue is consistent with the refuge's establishing purpose and management objectives, and follows current Service policy.

NEPA Compliance for Refuge Use Description: *Place an X in appropriate space.*

_____Categorical Exclusion without Environmental Action Statement
_____Categorical Exclusion and Environmental Action Statement
__X__Environmental Assessment and Finding of No Significant Impact
_____Environmental Impact Statement and Record of Decision

Mandatory 10- or 15-Year Re-evaluation Date: September 2020

Description of Use: *Off-Road Vehicle Use*

Off-road vehicle (4-wheel all-terrain) use is not a priority public use; however, it can occur on the refuge provided it is compatible with the purpose for which the refuge was established. The general public could participate in the proposed use of off-road vehicles year-round from sunrise to sunset on Tallahatchie refuge, an area of approximately 4,000 acres west of Holcomb, Mississippi.

Off-road vehicles could be used on unimproved dirt roads, fire breaks, and logging roads by visitors who possess a valid hunting and fishing permit and who are gaining access to interior portions of the refuge for hunting and fishing opportunities.

The use of off-road vehicles is proposed in response to questions raised during the scoping process. These questions centered on opportunities to provide visitors who possess a valid hunting and fishing permit off-road vehicle access to internal areas of the refuge for the purpose of hunting and fishing.

Availability of Resources: Funding for this program would be borne by annual operation and maintenance funds which support activities involving the public such as interpretation, environmental education, wildlife photography, and hunting and fishing programs. The North Mississippi National Wildlife Refuges Complex would spend approximately $27,500 of an annual budget of approximately $750,000 in direct support of this program on Tallahatchie refuge.

Special equipment, facilities, or improvements necessary to support the use: $10,000

Maintenance costs: $10,000

Law enforcement costs: $5,000

Monitoring costs: $2,500

Offsetting revenues: $1,000

The refuge does not have the resources to administer this use. Currently, the North Mississippi National Wildlife Refuges Complex does not have law enforcement personnel to monitor this activity. The Complex has included a Refuge Operating Needs System (RONS) package for a fulltime law enforcement officer for Tallahatchie refuge. Additionally, this activity would require considerable operation and maintenance funds to maintain the existing unimproved dirt roads, fire breaks, and logging roads. It is expected that $1,000 of offsetting revenues would be generated by the sale of hunting and fishing permits to visitors who would not use the refuge unless they could also use off-road vehicles while accessing hunting and fishing areas.

Anticipated Impacts of the Use:

Short-term impacts:

Adverse impacts to unimproved roads, fire breaks, and logging roads by the repeated use of off-road vehicles are well documented and disturbance to wildlife, plants and their habitats would occur. Such use would be limited to the hunting and fishing season which also coincides with extended periods of heavy rainfall. As use continues, the unimproved roads and fire breaks used for access become wallowed out and rainfall would accumulate in these "wet" areas. Repeated use exacerbates this condition. Conflicts would occur between those hunters and anglers who use off-road vehicles and those who object to the disturbance and noise associated with the vehicles.

Long-term impacts:

Long-term impacts from the repeated use of off-road vehicles by the public would be compounded over time. Unimproved roads and fire breaks would continue to deteriorate and annual maintenance costs would increase. Additional damage to plants and habitats would be experienced as access for the heavy equipment required to maintain these access routes is developed. Conflicts between hunters who use off-road vehicles and those who object to the associated disturbance and noise would continue.

Cumulative impacts:

No cumulative impacts are expected because other forms of public use on the unimproved roads, fire breaks, and logging roads would be limited to persons bicycling or walking. The "footprint" left by these other forms of use is very minimal. As the facilities and road network at the refuge are improved, general outdoor recreation would likely increase. With this increase in use, conflicts would also increase between hunters who use off-road vehicles and those visitors using the refuge who object to disturbance and noise.

Public Review and Comment: The period of public review and comment began on September 9, 2004 and ended on October 21, 2004. The following methods were used to solicit public review and comment:

> Posted notice at refuge headquarters
> Public notice in newspapers with wide local distribution
> Public meeting(s)

This compatibility determination was part of the Draft North Mississippi National Wildlife Refuges Complex Comprehensive Conservation Plan and Environmental Assessment, which was announced in the *Federal Register* and made available for public comment for 30 days.

Determination (check one below):

_____Compatible with the following stipulations

__X__Not Compatible

Stipulations Necessary to Ensure Compatibility: None

Stipulations Necessary to Ensure Compatibility: None

Justification: To provide hunter access, a series of all-weather roads have been constructed. Additional all-weather roads are planned. In addition, the unimproved roads and fire breaks are maintained obstruction free to facilitate the use of hand held carts, bicycles, wagons, etc., for the purpose of retrieving deer. These facilities eliminate the need for the average hunter to use off-road vehicles on the refuge and prevent the inevitable habitat destruction that accompanies this usage type. Off-road vehicle usage is an activity which is not compatible with refuge objectives.

NEPA Compliance for Refuge Use Description: *Place an X in appropriate space.*

_____Categorical Exclusion without Environmental Action Statement
_____Categorical Exclusion and Environmental Action Statement
__X__Environmental Assessment and Finding of No Significant Impact
_____Environmental Impact Statement and Record of Decision

Mandatory 10- or 15-Year Re-evaluation Date: September 2015

Description of Use: *Resource Research Studies*

This activity would allow university professors and their students, nongovernmental researchers, and governmental scientists access to the Tallahatchie refuge natural environment to conduct both short- and long-term research projects and surveys. The outcome of this research would result in better knowledge of our natural resources and improved methods to manage, monitor, and protect the refuge resources.

Resource research studies are not a priority public use within the Service, but do support the mission of the Service in gathering good scientific data to make management decisions.

These activities would be conducted throughout the refuge in a variety of habitats. Activities carried out during approved research projects and surveys may be limited to avoid unnecessary disturbance to refuge resources or ongoing management activities.

The activities would vary in scope and duration to satisfy the requirement of the research project or survey. Projects may involve everything from a limited one-time sampling or survey to long-term study plots.

Research projects and surveys would be conducted by universities, state and federal government representatives, and rarely by private individuals. The refuge would act solely in a supportive role, providing minimal assistance in most cases.

Furthering the knowledge of the impacts and benefits of management decisions, life histories of wildlife species utilizing the refuge, and interrelationships of habitats and wildlife occurring on the refuge is crucial to the effective management of the refuge. The refuge provides secure sites for long-term evaluation of management actions, population trends and ecological functions within the bottomland hardwood ecosystems in northwest Mississippi.

Availability of Resources: Funding for this program is borne by annual operation and maintenance funds which support activities involving the public such as recreation, interpretation, environmental education, and refuge hunting and fishing programs. The North Mississippi National Wildlife Refuges Complex spends approximately $3,600 of an annual budget of approximately $750,000 in direct support of these programs on Tallahatchie refuge. Therefore, the program is in compliance with specific funding requirements of the Refuge Recreation Act.

Special equipment, facilities or improvement necessary to support the use: None

Maintenance costs: $1,000

Monitoring costs: $2,600

Offsetting revenues: None

Anticipated Impacts of the Use:

Short-term impacts:

There should be no significant adverse impacts from scientific research on the refuge. The knowledge gained from the research would provide information to improve management techniques for trust resource species. Impacts such as trampling vegetation, removal of small numbers of plants and/or animals and temporary disturbance to wildlife could occur, but should not be significant. The small number of individual plants and animals that may be collected for further study would not have a significant effect on the refuge plant and animal populations, and would require management approval prior to collecting.

Long-term impacts:

Long-term benefits associated with improved management techniques developed through research or surveys would far outweigh any negative impacts which may occur.

Cumulative impacts:

No adverse cumulative effects are anticipated.

Public Review and Comment: The period of public review and comment began on September 9, 2004 and ended on October 21, 2004. The following methods were used to solicit public review and comment:

> Posted notice at refuge headquarters
> Public notice in newspapers with wide local distribution
> Public meeting(s)

This compatibility determination was part of the Draft North Mississippi National Wildlife Refuges Complex Comprehensive Conservation Plan and Environmental Assessment, which was announced in the *Federal Register* and made available for public comment for 30 days.

Determination (check one below):

   _X_ Compatible with the following stipulations

   _____ Not Compatible

Stipulations Necessary to Ensure Compatibility: Each request for use of the refuge for research or survey would be examined on its individual merit. Questions of who, what, when, where, and why, would be asked to determine if the requested research contributed to the refuge purposes and could best be conducted on the refuge without significantly affecting the resources. If so, the researcher would be issued a Special Use Permit that would clearly define allowed activities. Progress would be monitored and the researcher would be required to submit annual progress reports and copies of all publications derived from the research.

Justification: The benefits derived from sound research provide a better understanding of species and the environmental communities present on the refuge. Research projects would be designed to minimize impacts and disturbance.

NEPA Compliance for Refuge Use Description: *Place an X in appropriate space.*

_____ Categorical Exclusion without Environmental Action Statement
_____ Categorical Exclusion and Environmental Action Statement
_X_ Environmental Assessment and Finding of No Significant Impact
_____ Environmental Impact Statement and Record of Decision

Mandatory 10- or 15-Year Re-evaluation Date: September 2015

Description of Use: *Wildlife Observation and Photography*

Wildlife observation and photography have been identified in the National Wildlife Refuge System Improvement Act of 1997 as priority wildlife-dependent recreational uses provided they are compatible with the purpose for which the refuge was established.

Wildlife photography, including other image-capturing activities such as videography, has occurred on the refuge. There are no photography blinds or platforms on the refuge and none are proposed at this time. However, opportunities exist for photography on the refuge. This compatibility determination applies to personal photography only. Commercial photography or videography, if allowed, would require a special use permit by the refuge with specific restrictions.

The general public can participate in wildlife observation and photography year-round from sunrise to sunset on Tallahatchie refuge, an area of approximately 4,000 acres west of Holcomb, Mississippi.

Wildlife observation and photography can be accomplished while driving or walking on refuge roads open to public vehicular traffic. Also, these priority public uses can be accomplished by boating on refuge waters or walking the unimproved roads and fire breaks.

The National Wildlife Refuge System Improvement Act of 1997 identifies wildlife observation and photography as priority public uses for national wildlife refuges, along with hunting, fishing, and environmental education and interpretation. As expressed priority uses of the Refuge System, these uses take precedence over other potential public uses in refuge planning and management. The Service strives to provide priority public uses when compatible with the purposes of the refuge and the mission of the National Wildlife Refuge System.

Availability of Resources: Funding for this operation is borne by annual operation and maintenance funds which support activities involving the public, such as environmental education, interpretation, hunting and fishing programs. The North Mississippi National Wildlife Refuges Complex spends approximately $6,000 of an annual budget of approximately $750,000 in direct support of these programs on Tallahatchie refuge. Therefore, the program is in compliance with specific funding requirements of the Refuge Recreation Act.

Special equipment, facilities, or improvements necessary to support the use: $3,000

Maintenance costs: $2,000

Monitoring costs: $1,000

Anticipated Impacts of the Use:

Short-term impacts:

The refuge provides habitat for resident and migratory wildlife. As a result of these activities, individual animals may be disturbed by human contact to varying degrees. Examples of potential disturbance include flushing of birds from feeding, resting, or nesting areas, and trampling of plants from observers and photographers wandering off designated roads in order to get closer to subjects. Disturbance to trust species are expected to be minimal. Short-term impacts to facilities such as roads and trails can be avoided by special closures due to unsafe conditions. The wildlife observation and photography programs have been designed to avoid or minimize impacts to refuge resources and visitors.

Long-term impacts:

Due to the recovery time between periods of expected use, no long-term impacts are expected.

Cumulative impacts:

No cumulative adverse impacts are anticipated. However, programs can be modified in the future to mitigate unforeseen impacts.

Public Review and Comment: The period of public review and comment began on September 9, 2004 and ended on October 21, 2004. The following methods were used to solicit public review and comment:

    Posted notice at refuge headquarters
    Public notice in newspapers with wide local distribution
    Public meeting(s)

This compatibility determination was part of the Draft North Mississippi National Wildlife Refuges Complex Comprehensive Conservation Plan and Environmental Assessment, which was announced in the *Federal Register* and made available for public comment for 30 days.

Determination (check one below):

    __X__Compatible with the following stipulations

    _____Not Compatible

Stipulations: At the present time, public entry to include visitors involved in wildlife observation and photography is not permitted on that part of the refuge located north of Highway 8 except by special use permit.

Justification: That part of Tallahatchie refuge located north of Highway 8 is divided by the Tippo Bayou. There is no legal access for general public use to the northeast section of the refuge. The remaining refuge lands north of Highway 8 are either enrolled in the cooperative farming program or established waterfowl management units. Management efforts are successful with large numbers of migratory waterfowl using the refuge from October to March. Experience has shown that birds using the refuge are susceptible to disturbance. The northwest section of the refuge is bisected by a public county road which offers an excellent opportunity for wildlife observation and photography.

These wildlife-dependent uses are priority public uses of the National Wildlife Refuge System. Providing opportunities for wildlife observation and photography would contribute toward fulfilling provisions of the National Wildlife Refuge System Administration Act, as amended in 1997. Wildlife observation and photography would provide an excellent forum for allowing public access and increasing understanding of refuge resources. The stipulations outlined above should minimize potential impacts relative to wildlife/human interactions. In our opinion, these wildlife dependent uses will not conflict with the national policy to maintain the biological diversity, integrity, and environmental health of the refuge.

NEPA Compliance for Refuge Use Description: *Place an X in appropriate space.*

_____Categorical Exclusion without Environmental Action Statement
_____Categorical Exclusion and Environmental Action Statement
___X___Environmental Assessment and Finding of No Significant Impact
_____Environmental Impact Statement and Record of Decision

Mandatory 10- or 15-Year Re-evaluation Date: September 2020

Approval of Compatibility Determinations:

The signature of approval covers all the compatibility determinations considered within the Comprehensive Conservation Plan for the North Mississippi National Wildlife Refuges Complex. If one of the descriptive uses is considered for compatibility outside of the plan, the approval signatures become part of that determination.

Signature: _____ 9/20/05
     Project Leader   Date

Review: _____ 9SEP05
   Regional Compatibility Coordinator   Date

Review: _____ 9/9/05
   Refuge Supervisor   Date

Concurrence: _____ Acting 9-16-05
   Regional Chief   Date
   National Wildlife Refuge System
   Southeast Region

Appendix E: Species Lists

MASTER LIST OF BIRD SPECIES*

Common Name	Scientific Name
Pied-billed grebe	*Podilymbus podiceps*
Horned grebe	*Podiceps auritus*
Eared grebe	*Podiceps nigricollis*
American white pelican	*Pelecanus erythrorhynchus*
Anhinga	*Anhinga anhinga*
Double-crested cormorant	*Phalacrocorax auritus*
Least bittern	*Ixobrychus exilis*
American bittern	*Botarus lentiginosus*
Black-crowned night-heron	*Nycticorax nycticorax*
Yellow-crowned night-heron	*Nyctanassa violacea*
Green heron	*Butorides striatus*
Tricolored heron	*Egretta tricolor*
Little blue heron	*Egretta caerulea*
Cattle egret	*Bubulcus ibis*
Snowy egret	*Egretta thula*
Great egret	*Casmerodius albus*
Great blue heron	*Ardea herodia*
Wood stork	*Mycteria americana*
Glossy ibis	*Plegadis falcinellus*
White-faced ibis	*Plegadis chihi*
White ibis	*Eudocimus albus*
Roseate spoonbill	*Ajaia ajaja*
Sandhill crane	*Grus canadensis*
Greater white-fronted goose	*Anser albifrons*
Snow goose	*Chen caerulescens*
Ross' goose	*Chen rossii*
Canada goose	*Branta canadensis*
Mallard	*Anas platyrhynchos*
American black duck	*Anas rubripes*
Gadwall	*Anas strepera*
American green-winged teal	*Anas crecca*

Common Name	Scientific Name
American wigeon	*Anas americana*
Northern pintail	*Anas acuta*
Northern shoveler	*Anas clypeata*
Blue-winged teal	*Anas discors*
Ruddy duck	*Oxyura jamaicensis*
Fulvous whistling-duck	*Dendrocygna bicolor*
Wood duck	*Aix sponsa*
Canvasback	*Aythya valisineria*
Redhead	*Aythya americana*
Ring-necked duck	*Aythya collaris*
Greater scaup	*Aythya marila*
Lesser scaup	*Aythya affinis*
Oldsquaw	*Clangula hyemalis*
Common goldeneye	*Bucephala clangula*
Bufflehead	*Bucephala albeola*
Common merganser	*Mergus merganser*
Red-breasted merganser	*Mergus serrator*
Hooded merganser	*Lophodytes cucullatus*
King rail	*Rallus elegans*
Virgina rail	*Rallus limicola*
Sora	*Porzana carolina*
Yellow rail	*Coturnicops noveborasensis*
Purple gallinule	*Porphyrula martinica*
Common moorhen	*Gallinula chloropus*
American coot	*Fulica americana*
American avocet	*Recurvirostra americana*
Black-necked stilt	*Himantopus mexicanus*
Wilson's plover	*Charadrius wilsonia*
Semipalmated plover	*Charadrius semipalmatus*
Killdeer	*Charadrius vociferous*
Black-bellied plover	*Pluvialis squatrola*
American golden plover	*Pluvialis dominica*
Marbled godwit	*Limosa fedoa*
Hudsonian godwit	*Limosa haemastica*
Whimbrel	*Numenius phaeopus*

Common Name	Scientific Name
Willet	*Catoptrophorus semipalmatus*
Greater yellowlegs	*Tringa melanoleuca*
Lesser yellowlegs	*Tringa flavipes*
Solitary sandpiper	*Tringa solitaria*
Spotted sandpiper	*Actitis macularia*
Wilson's phalarope	*Phalaropus tricolor*
Red-necked phalarope	*Phalaropus lobatus*
Red phalarope	*Phalaropus fulicaria*
Short-billed dowitcher	*Limnodromus griseus*
Long-billed dowitcher	*Limnodromus scolopaceus*
Stilt sandpiper	*Calidris himantopus*
Common snipe	*Gallinago gallinago*
American woodcock	*Scolopax minor*
Ruddy turnstone	*Arenaria interpres*
Dunlin	*Calidris alpina*
Sanderling	*Calidris alba*
Semipalmated sandpiper	*Calidris pusilla*
Western sandpiper	*Calidris mauri*
Least sandpiper	*Calidris minutilla*
White-rumped sandpiper	*Calidris fuscicollis*
Baird's sandpiper	*Calidris bairdii*
Pectoral sandpiper	*Calidris melanotos*
Ruff	*Philomachus pugnax*
Upland sandpiper	*Bartramia longicauda*
Buff-breasted sandpiper	*Tryngites subruficollis*
Franklin's gull	*Larus pipixcan*
Laughing gull	*Larus atricilla*
Bonaparte's gull	*Larus philadelphia*
Ring-billed gull	*Larus delawarensis*
Herring gull	*Larus argentatus*
Common tern	*Sterna hirundo*
Forster's tern	*Sterna forsteri*
Least tern	*Sterna antillarum*
Black tern	*Chlidonias niger*
Caspian tern	*Sterna caspia*

Common Name	Scientific Name
Turkey vulture	*Cathartes aura*
Black vulture	*Coragyps atratus*
Golden eagle	*Aquila chrysaetos*
Bald eagle	*Haliaeetus leucocephalus*
Mississippi kite	*Ictinia mississippiensis*
American swallow-tailed kite	*Elanoides forficatus*
Northern harrier	*Circus cyaneus*
Sharp-shinned hawk	*Accipiter striatus*
Cooper's hawk	*Accipiter cooperii*
Red-shouldered hawk	*Buteo lineatus*
Broad-winged hawk	*Buteo platypterus*
Red-tailed hawk	*Buteo jamaicensis*
Osprey	*Pandion haliaetus*
American kestrel	*Falco sparverius*
Merlin	*Falco columbarius*
Peregrine falcon	*Falco peregrinus*
Northern bobwhite	*Colinus virginianus*
Wild turkey	*Meleagris gallopavo*
Rock dove	*Columba livia*
Mourning dove	*Zenaida macroura*
Common ground-dove	*Columbina passerine*
Yellow-billed cuckoo	*Coccyzus americanus*
Barn owl	*Tyto alba*
Short-eared owl	*Asio flammeus*
Great horned owl	*Bubo virginianus*
Barred owl	*Strix varia*
Eastern screech owl	*Otus asio*
Chuck-will's-widow	*Caprimulgus carolinensis*
Whip-poor-will	*Caprimulgus vociferous*
Common nighthawk	*Chordeiles minor*
Chimney swift	*Chaetura pelagica*
Ruby-throated hummingbird	*Archilochus colubris*
Belted kingfisher	*Ceryle alcyon*
Red-bellied woodpecker	*Melanerpes carolinus*
Northern flicker	*Colaptes auratus*

Common Name	Scientific Name
Red-headed woodpecker	*Melanerpes erythrocephalus*
Yellow-bellied sapsucker	*Sphyrapicus varius*
Downy woodpecker	*Picoides pubescens*
Hairy woodpecker	*Picoides villosus*
Pileated woodpecker	*Dryocopus pileatus*
Eastern kingbird	*Tyrannus tryrannus*
Scissor-tailed flycatcher	*Tyrannus forficatus*
Great crested flycatcher	*Myiarchus crinitus*
Olive-sided flycatcher	*Contopus borealis*
Eastern wood-pewee	*Contopus virens*
Eastern phoebe	*Sayornis phoebe*
Acadian flycatcher	*Empidonax virescens*
Willow flycatcher	*Empidonax traillii*
Horned lark	*Eremophilia alpestris*
Tree swallow	*Tachycineta bicolor*
Purple martin	*Progne subis*
Bank swallow	*Riparia riparia*
Northern rough-winged swallow	*Stelgidopteryx serripennis*
Cliff swallow	*Hirundo pyrrhonota*
Barn swallow	*Hirundo rustica*
Blue jay	*Cyanocitta cristata*
American crow	*Corvus brachyrhynchos*
Fish crow	*Corvus ossifragus*
Tufted titmouse	*Parus bicolor*
Carolina chickadee	*Parus carolinensis*
Brown creeper	*Certhia americana*
White-breasted nuthatch	*Sitta carolinensis*
Red-breasted nuthatch	*Sitta canadensis*
House wren	*Troglodytes aedon*
Winter wren	*Troglodytes troglodytes*
Carolina wren	*Thryothorus ludovicianus*
Bewick's wren	*Thryomanes bewickii*
Marsh wren	*Cistothorus palustris*
Sedge wren	*Cistothorus platensis*
Golden-crowned kinglet	*Regulus satrapa*

Common Name	Scientific Name
Ruby-crowned kinglet	*Regulus calendula*
Blue-gray gnatcatcher	*Polioptila caerulea*
Eastern bluebird	*Sialia sialis*
Wood thrush	*Hylocichla mustelina*
Veery	*Catharus fuscescens*
Swainson's thrush	*Catharus ustulatus*
Gray-cheeked thrush	*Catharus minimus*
Hermit thrush	*Catharus guttatus*
American robin	*Turdus migratorius*
Loggerhead shrike	*Lanius ludovicianus*
Gray catbird	*Dumetella carolinensis*
Northern mockingbird	*Mimus polyglottos*
Brown thrasher	*Toxostoma rufum*
American pipit	*Anthus rubescens*
Cedar waxwing	*Bombycilla cedrorum*
European starling	*Sturnus vulgaris*
White-eyed vireo	*Vireo griseus*
Yellow-throated vireo	*Vireo flavifrons*
Red-eyed vireo	*Vireo olivaceus*
Warbling vireo	*Vireo gilvus*
Philadelphia vireo	*Vireo philadelphicus*
Prothonotary warbler	*Protonotaria citrea*
Blue-winged warbler	*Vermivora pinus*
Tennessee warbler	*Vermivora peregrine*
Northern parula	*Parula americana*
Black-and-white warbler	*Mniotilta varia*
Cerulean warbler	*Dendroica cerulean*
Blackburnian warbler	*Dendroica fusca*
Magnolia warbler	*Dendroica magnolia*
Yellow-rumped warbler	*Dendroica coronata*
Black-throated green warbler	*Dendroica virens*
Yellow-throated warbler	*Dendroica dominica*
Bay-breasted warbler	*Dendroica castanea*
Blackpoll warbler	*Dendroica striata*
Pine warbler	*Dendroica pinus*

Common Name	Scientific Name
Palm warbler	*Dendroica palmarum*
Yellow warbler	*Dendroica petechia*
Canada warbler	*Wilsonia canadensis*
Willson's warbler	*Wilsonia pusilla*
Hooded warbler	*Wilsonia citrine*
Worm-eating warbler	*Helmitheros vermivorus*
Swainson's warbler	*Limnothlypis swainsonii*
Ovenbird	*Seiurus aurocapillus*
Louisiana waterthrush	*Seiurus motacilla*
Northern waterthrush	*Seiurus noveboracensis*
Common yellowthroat	*Geothlypis trichas*
Yellow-breasted chat	*Icteria virens*
American redstart	*Setophaga ruticilla*
Rose-breasted grosbeak	*Pheucticus ludovicianus*
Northern cardinal	*Cardinalis cardinalis*
Blue grosbeak	*Guiraca caerulea*
Indigo bunting	*Passerina cyanea*
Painted bunting	*Passerina ciris*
Rufous-sided towhee	*Pipilo erythrophthalmus*
Grasshopper sparrow	*Ammodramus savannarum*
Le Conte's sparrow	*Ammodramus leconteii*
Vesper sparrow	*Pooecetes gramineus*
Savannah sparrow	*Passerculus sandwichensis*
Song sparrow	*Melospiza melodia*
Field sparrow	*Spizella pusilla*
Chipping sparrow	*Spizella passerine*
Dark-eyed junco	*Junco hyemalis*
White-throated sparrow	*Zonotrichia albicollis*
White-crowned sparrow	*Zonotrichia leucophrys*
Fox sparrow	*Passerella iliaca*
Lincoln's sparrow	*Melospiza lincolnii*
Swamp sparrow	*Melospiza georgiana*
Dickcissel	*Spiza americana*
Bobolink	*Dolichonyx oryzivorus*
Eastern meadowlark	*Sturnella magna*

Common Name	Scientific Name
Yellow-headed blackbird	*Xanthocephalus xanthocephalus*
Red-winged blackbird	*Agelaius phoeniceus*
Rusty blackbird	*Euphagus carolinus*
Brewer's blackbird	*Euphagus cyanocephalus*
Brown-headed cowbird	*Molothrus ater*
Common grackle	*Quiscalus quiscula*
Orchard oriole	*Icterus spurius*
Baltimore oriole	*Icterus galbula*
Scarlet tanager	*Piranga olivacea*
Summer tanager	*Piranga rubra*
House sparrow	*Passer domesticus*
Pine siskin	*Carduelis pinus*
American goldfinch	*Carduelis tristis*
Purple finch	*Carpodacus purpureus*
House finch	*Carpodacus mexicanus*

*Birds documented on at least one of the three refuges in the Complex

MASTER LIST OF MAMMALS SPECIES*

Scientific Name	Common Name
Order Marsupialia	
Family Didelphidae	
Didelphis virginiana	Virginia opossum
Family Soricidae	
Sorex logirostris	southeastern shrew
Blarina carolinensis	southern short-tailed shrew
Cryptotis parva	least shrew
Family Talpidae	
Scalopus aquaticus	eastern mole
Order Chiroptera	
Family Vespertilionidae	
Myotis austroriparius	southeastern myotis
Myotis grisescens	gray myotis
Myotis lucifugus	little brown bat
Myotis septentrionalis	northern myotis
Myotis sodalis	Indiana myotis
Lasionycteris noctivagans	silver-haired bat
Pipistrellus subflavus	eastern pipistrelle
Eptesicus fuscus	big brown bat
Lasiurus borealis	eastern red bat
Lasiurus cinereus	hoary bat
Lasiurus intermedius	northern yellow bat
Lasiurus seminolus	Seminole bat
Nycticeius humeralis	evening bat
Plecotus rafinesquii	Rafinesque's big-eared bat
Family Molossidae	
Tadarida brasiliensis	Brazilian free-tailed bat

Scientific Name	Common Name
Order Xenarthra	
Family Dasypodidae	
Dasypus novemcinctus	nine-banded armadillo
Order Lagomorpha	
Family Leporidae	
Sylvilagus aquaticus	swamp rabbit
Sylvilagus floridanus	eastern cottontail
Order Rodentia	
Family Sciuridae	
Tamias striatus	eastern chipmunk
Marmota monax	woodchuck
Sciurus carolinensis	gray squirrel
Sciurus niger	fox squirrel
Glaucomys volans	eastern flying squirrel
Family Castoridae	
Castor canadensis	beaver
Family Cricetidae	
Oryzomys palustris	marsh rice rat
Reithrodontomys fulvescens	fulvous harvest mouse
Reithrodontomys humulis	eastern harvest mouse
Peromyscus gossypinus	cotton mouse
Peromyscus leucopus	white-footed mouse
Peromyscus maniculatus	deer mouse
Peromyscus polionotus	oldfield mouse
Ochrotomys nuttalli	golden mouse
Sigmodon hispidus	hispid cotton rat
Neotoma floridana	eatern woodrat
Microtus pinetorum	woodland vole
Ondatra zibethicus	Muskrat

Scientific Name	Common Name
Family Muridae	
Rattus norvegicus	Norway rat
Rattus rattus	roof rat
Mus musculus	house mouse
Family Zapodidae	
Zapus hudsonius	meadow jumping mouse
Family Myocastoridae	
Myocastor coypus	nutria
Order Carnivora	
Family Canidae	
Canis familiaris	domestic dog
Canis latrans	coyote
Canis rufus	red wolf
Vulpes vulpes	red fox
Urocyon cinereoargenteus	gray fox
Family Ursidae	
Ursus americanus	black bear
Family Procyonidae	
Procyon lotor	raccoon
Family Mustelidae	
Mustela frenata	long-tailed weasel
Mustela vison	mink
Spilogale putorius	eastern spotted skunk
Mephitis mephitis	striped skunk
Lutra canadensis	river otter
Family Felidae	
Felis catus	domestic cat
Felis concolor	mountain lion
Lynx rufus	Bobcat

Scientific Name	Common Name
Order Artiodactyla	
Family Suidae	
Sus scrofa	wild pig
Family Cervidae	
Odocoileus virginianus	white-tailed deer

* at least one refuge in the Complex is within the historic
range of the species

MASTER LIST OF AMPHIBIANS AND REPTILES*

Common Name	Scientific Name	CWR	DAH	TAL
Spadefoot toads	**Pelobatidae**			
Eastern spadfoot toad	*Scaphiopus holbrookii*			
Narrowmouth toads	**Microhylidae**			
Eastern narrowmouth toad	*Gastrophryne carolinensis*	X	X	X
Toads	**Bufonidae**			
American toad	*Bufo americanus*		X	X
Southern toad	*Bufo terrestris*			
Fowler's toad	*Bufo woodhousii fowleri*	X	X	X
Treefrogs	**Hylidae**			
Green treefrog	*Hyla cinerea*	X	X	X
Bird-voiced treefrog	*Hyla avivoca*			X
Gray treefrog	*Hyla versicolor*			
Cope's gray treefrog	*Hyla chrysoscelis*			
Gray treefrog species	*Hyla versicolor/chrysoscelis*	X	X	X
Upland chorus frog	*Pseudacris triseriata feriarum*	X		
Northern spring peeper	*Pseudacris crucifer*	X	X	
Northern cricket frog	*Acris crepitans*	X	X	X
Southern cricket frog	*Acris gryllus*	X		X
True frogs	**Ranidae**			
Bronze frog	*Rana clamitans*	X	X	X
Bullfrog	*Rana catesbeiana*	X	X	X
Southern leopard frog	*Rana utricularia*	X	X	X
Northern crawfish frog	*Rana areolata*			
Pickerel frog	*Rana palustris*	X		
Sirens	**Sirenidae**			
Western lesser siren	*Siren intermedia*		X	
Amphiumas	**Amphiumidae**			
Three-toed amphiuma	*Amphiuma tridactylum*			X
Newts	**Salamandridae**			
Central newt	*Notophthalmus viridescens*		X	

Common Name	Scientific Name	CWR	DAH	TAL
Mole salamanders	**Ambystomatidae**			
Mole salamander	Ambystoma talpoideum		X	
Smallmouth salamander	Ambystoma texanum			
Spotted salamander	Ambystoma maculatum			
Marbled salamander	Ambystoma opacum		X	
Lungless salamanders	**Plethodontidae**			
Spotted dusky salamander	Desmognathus fuscus			
Southern red salamander	Pseudotriton ruber			
Mississippi slimy salamander	Plethodon glutinosus			
Southern two-lined salamander	Eurycea cirrigera			
Three-lined salamander	Eurycea longicauda			
Alligators	**Alligatoridae**			
American alligator	Alligator mississippiensis			X
Snapping turtles	**Chelydridae**			
Alligator snapping turtle	Macroclemys temminckii			X
Common snapping turtle	Chelydra serpentina	X	X	X
Musk turtles	**Kinosternidae**			
Common musk turtle	Sternotherus odoratus	X	X	X
Razorback musk turtle	Sternotherus carinatus			
Eastern mud turtle	Kinosternon s. subrubrum			
Mississippi mud turtle	Kinosternon s. hippocrepis	X		X
Mud turtle sp.	Kinosternon subrubrum	X	X	
Box and water turtles	**Emydidae**			
Ouachita map turtle	Graptemys pseudogeographica			
Mississippi map turtle	Graptemys kohnii			X
Southern painted turtle	Chrysemys picta	X		
River cooter	Pseudemys concinna			X
Red-eared slider	Trachemys scripta	X	X	X
Three-toed box turtle	Terrapene carolina	X	X	
Midland smooth softshell turtle	Apalone mutica			
Spiny softshell turtle	Apalone spinifera	X		X
Softshell turtle species	Apalone sp.	X		X

Common Name	Scientific Name	CWR	DAH	TAL
Iguanian Lizards	**Iguanidae**			
Green anole	*Anolis carolinensis*			
Northern fence lizard	*Sceloperus undulatus*			
Skinks	**Scincidae**			
Ground skink	*Scincella lateralis*		X	X
Five-lined skink	*Eumeces fasciatus*		X	X
Broadhead skink	*Eumeces laticeps*			
Southeastern five-lined skink	*Eumeces inexpectatus*			
Whiptails	**Teiidae**			
Six-lined racerunner	*Cnemidophorus sextineatus*			
Glass lizards	**Anguidae**			
Eastern glass lizard	*Ophisaurus attenuatus*			
Colubrids	**Colubridae**			
Midland water snake	*Nerodia sipedon pleuralis*		X	
Broad-banded water snake	*Nerodia fasciata confluens*		X	X
Yellowbelly water snake	*Nerodia erythrogaster flavigaster*		X	X
Diamondback water snake	*Nerodia rhombifer*	X	X	X
Mississippi green water snake	*Nerodia cyclopion*			
Graham's crayfish snake	*Regina grahamii*			
Eastern garter snake	*Thamnophis sirtalis*		X	
Eastern ribbon snake	*Thamnophis sauritus*			
Western ribbon snake	*Thamnophis proximus*	X	X	X
Midland brown snake	*Storeria dekayi*			
Rough earth snake	*Virginia striatula*			
Western smooth earth snake	*Virginia valeriae*			
Mississippi ringneck snake	*Diadophis punctatus*			
Eastern hognose snake	*Heterodon platirhinos*			
Midwest worm snake	*Carphophis amoenus*			
Northern scarlet snake	*Cemophora coccinea*			
Rough green snake	*Opheodrys aestivus*			
Western mud snake	*Farancia abacura*		X	X
Blackmask racer	*Coluber constrictor latrunculus*	X	X	

Common Name	Scientific Name	CWR	DAH	TAL
Black rat snake	Elaphe o. obsoleta			
Gray rat snake	Elaphe o. spiloides			
Rat snake sp.	Elaphe obsoleta		X	
Corn snake	Elaphe guttata			
Red milk snake	Lampropeltis triangulum			
Scarlet kingsnake	Lampropeltis triangulum			
Prairie kingsnake	Lampropeltis calligaster			
Mole kingsnake	Lampropeltis calligaster			
Speckled kingsnake	Lampropeltis getula holbrooki	X		X
Pit vipers	**Viperidae**			
Western cottonmouth	Agkistrodon piscivorus	X	X	X
Southern copperhead	Agkistrodon contortrix			
Western pigmy rattlesnake	Sisturus miliarius			
Timber rattlesnake	Crotalus horridus		X	

Note: *An 'X' in a given column means documented occurrence at the refuge indicated; CWR denotes Coldwater River, DAH denotes Dahomey, and TAL denotes Tallahatchie refuges; when no 'X' appears, it means that the species is likely or suspected to occur on the Complex, but has not yet been observed.

Appendix F: Legal Mandates

Rivers and Harbor Act (1899) (33 U.S.C. 403): Section 10 of this Act requires the authorization by the U.S. Army Corps of Engineers prior to any work in, on, over, or under a navigable water of the United States.

Antiquities Act (1906): Authorizes the scientific investigation of antiquities on Federal land and provides penalties for unauthorized removal of objects taken or collected without a permit.

Migratory Bird Treaty Act (1918): Designates the protection of migratory birds as a Federal responsibility. This Act enables the setting of seasons, and other regulations including the closing of areas, Federal or non-Federal, to the hunting of migratory birds.

Migratory Bird Conservation Act (1929): Establishes procedures for acquisition by purchase, rental, or gift of areas approved by the Migratory Bird Conservation Commission.

Fish and Wildlife Coordination Act (1934), as amended: Requires that the Fish and Wildlife Service and State fish and wildlife agencies be consulted whenever water is to be impounded, diverted or modified under a Federal permit or license. The Service and State agency recommend measures to prevent the loss of biological resources, or to mitigate or compensate for the damage. The project proponent must take biological resource values into account and adopt justifiable protection measures to obtain maximum overall project benefits. A 1958 amendment added provisions to recognize the vital contribution of wildlife resources to the Nation and to require equal consideration and coordination of wildlife conservation with other water resources development programs. It also authorized the Secretary of Interior to provide public fishing areas and accept donations of lands and funds.

Migratory Bird Hunting and Conservation Stamp Act (1934): Authorized the opening of part of a refuge to waterfowl hunting.

Historic Sites, Buildings and Antiquities Act (1935), as amended: Declares it a national policy to preserve historic sites and objects of national significance, including those located on refuges. Provides procedures for designation, acquisition, administration, and protection of such sites.

Refuge Revenue Sharing Act (1935), as amended: Requires revenue sharing provisions to all fee-title ownerships that are administered solely or primarily by the Secretary through the Service.

Transfer of Certain Real Property for Wildlife Conservation Purposes Act (1948): Provides that upon a determination by the Administrator of the General Services Administration, real property no longer needed by a Federal agency can be transferred without reimbursement to the Secretary of Interior if the land has particular value for migratory birds, or to a State agency for other wildlife conservation purposes.

Federal Records Act (1950): Directs the preservation of evidence of the government's organization, functions, policies, decisions, operations, and activities, as well as basic historical and other information.

Fish and Wildlife Act (1956): Established a comprehensive national fish and wildlife policy and broadened the authority for acquisition and development of refuges.

Consolidated Farm and Rural Development Act (1961): Authorized a major expansion of U. S. Department of Agriculture lending activities, which at the time were administered by Farmers Home Administration (FmHA), but now through the Farm Service Agency. Major loan programs include farm ownership, farm operating and emergency disaster loans.

Refuge Recreation Act (1962): Allows the use of refuges for recreation when such uses are compatible with the refuge's primary purposes and when sufficient funds are available to manage the uses.

Wilderness Act (1964), as amended: Directed the Secretary of Interior, within 10 years, to review every roadless area of 5,000 or more acres and every roadless island (regardless of size) within National Wildlife Refuge and National Park Systems and to recommend to the President the suitability of each such area or island for inclusion in the National Wilderness Preservation System, with final decisions made by Congress. The Secretary of Agriculture was directed to study and recommend suitable areas in the National Forest System.

Land and Water Conservation Fund Act (1965): Uses the receipts from the sale of surplus Federal land, outer continental shelf oil and gas sales, and other sources for land acquisition under several authorities.

National Wildlife Refuge System Administration Act (1966), as amended by the National Wildlife Refuge System Improvement Act (1997) 16 U.S.C. 668dd668ee. (Refuge Administration Act): Defines the National Wildlife Refuge System and authorizes the Secretary to permit any use of a refuge provided such use is compatible with the major purposes for which the refuge was established. The Refuge System Improvement Act clearly defines a unifying mission for the Refuge System; establishes the legitimacy and appropriateness of the six priority public uses (hunting, fishing, wildlife observation and photography, and environmental education and interpretation); establishes a formal process for determining compatibility; established the responsi-bilities of the Secretary of Interior for managing and protecting the Refuge System; and requires a Comprehensive Conservation Plan for each refuge by the year 2012. The 1997 Act amended portions of the Refuge Recreation Act and National Wildlife Refuge System Administration Act of 1966.

National Historic Preservation Act (1966), as amended: Establishes as policy that the Federal Government is to provide leadership in the preservation of the nation's prehistoric and historic resources.

Architectural Barriers Act (1968): Requires federally owned, leased, or funded buildings and facilities to be accessible to persons with disabilities.

National Environmental Policy Act (1969): Requires the disclosure of the environmental impacts of any major Federal action significantly affecting the quality of the human environment.

Uniform Relocation and Assistance and Real Property Acquisition Policies Act (1970), as amended: Provides for uniform and equitable treatment of persons who sell their homes, businesses, or farms to the Service. The Act requires that any purchase offer be no less than the fair market value of the property.

Endangered Species Act (1973): Requires all Federal agencies to carry out programs for the conservation of endangered and threatened species.

Rehabilitation Act (1973): Requires programmatic accessibility in addition to physical accessibility for all facilities and programs funded by the Federal government to ensure that anybody can participate in any program.

Archaeological and Historic Preservation Act (1974): Directs the preservation of historic and archaeological data in Federal construction projects.

Clean Water Act (1977): Requires consultation with the Corps of Engineers (404 permits) for major wetland modifications.

Surface Mining Control and Reclamation Act (1977) as amended (Public Law 95-87) (SMCRA): Regulates surface mining activities and reclamation of coal-mined lands. Further regulates the coal industry by designating certain areas as unsuitable for coal mining operations.

Executive Order 11988 (1977): Each Federal agency shall provide leadership and take action to reduce the risk of flood loss and minimize the impact of floods on human safety, and preserve the natural and beneficial values served by the floodplains.

Executive Order 11990 (1977): Executive Order 11990 directs Federal agencies to (1) minimize destruction, loss, or degradation of wetlands and (2) preserve and enhance the natural and beneficial values of wetlands when a practical alternative exists.

Executive Order 12372 (Intergovernmental Review of Federal Programs): Directs the Service to send copies of the Environmental Assessment to State Planning Agencies for review.

American Indian Religious Freedom Act (1978): Directs agencies to consult with native traditional religious leaders to determine appropriate policy changes necessary to protect and preserve Native American religious cultural rights and practices.

Fish and Wildlife Improvement Act (1978): Improves the administration of fish and wildlife programs and amends several earlier laws including the Refuge Recreation Act, the National Wildlife Refuge System Administration Act, and the Fish and Wildlife Act of 1956. It authorizes the Secretary to accept gifts and bequests of real and personal property on behalf of the United States. It also authorizes the use of volunteers on Service projects and appropriations to carry out a volunteer program.

Archaeological Resources Protection Act (1979), as amended: Protects materials of archaeological interest from unauthorized removal or destruction and requires Federal managers to develop plans and schedules to locate archaeological resources.

Federal Farmland Protection Policy Act (1981), as amended: Minimizes the extent to which Federal programs contribute to the unnecessary and irreversible conversion of farmland to nonagricultural uses.

Emergency Wetlands Resources Act (1986): Promotes the conservation of migratory waterfowl and offsets or prevents the serious loss of wetlands by the acquisition of wetlands and other essential habitats.

Federal Noxious Weed Act (1990): Requires the use of integrated management systems to control or contain undesirable plant species, and an interdisciplinary approach with the cooperation of other Federal and State agencies.

Native American Graves Protection and Repatriation Act (1990): Requires Federal agencies and museums to inventory, determine ownership of, and repatriate cultural items under their control or possession.

Americans With Disabilities Act (1992): Prohibits discrimination in public accommodations and services.

Executive Order 12898 (1994): Establishes environmental justice as a Federal government priority and directs all Federal agencies to make environmental justice part of their mission. Environmental justice calls for fair distribution of environmental hazards.

Executive Order 12996 Management and General Public Use of the National Wildlife Refuge System (1996): Defines the mission, purpose, and priority public uses of the National Wildlife Refuge System. It also presents four principles to guide management of the Refuge System.

Executive Order 13007 Indian Sacred Sites (1996): Directs Federal land management agencies to accommodate access to and ceremonial use of Indian sacred sites by Indian religious practitioners, avoid adversely affecting the physical integrity of such sacred sites, and where appropriate, maintain the confidentiality of sacred sites.

National Wildlife Refuge System Improvement Act (1997): Considered the "Organic Act of the National Wildlife Refuge System." Defines the mission of the Refuge System, designates priority wildlife-dependent public uses, and calls for comprehensive refuge planning.

National Wildlife Refuge System Volunteer and Community Partnership Enhancement Act (1998): Amends the Fish and Wildlife Act of 1956 to promote volunteer programs and community partnerships for the benefit of national wildlife refuges, and for other purposes.

National Trails System Act (1968), as amended: Mandates the Secretary of Interior and thus the Service to protect the historic and recreational values of congressionally designated National Historic Trail sites.

Appendix G: Bibliography and References Cited

Allen, J.A., B.D. Keeland, J.A. Stanturf, A.F. Clewell and H.E. Kennedy, Jr. 2001. A Guide to Bottomland Hardwood Restoration: U.S. Geological Survey, Biological Resources Division Information and Technology Report USGS/BRD/ITR-2000-0011, U.S. Department of Agriculture, Forest Service, Southern Research Station, General Technical Report SRS-40. 132 pp

Central Mississippi National Wildlife Refuge Complex. 2003. Preliminary Draft Comprehensive Conservation Plan and Environmental Assessment.

Cordell, H. Ken, J. Teasley, G. Super. August 1997. A Report for USDA Forest Service: Outdoor Recreation in the United States: Results from the National Survey on Recreation and the Environment: All Forest Service Regions. Prepared by the Outdoor Recreation and Wilderness Assessment Group, USDA Forest Service, Athens, GA, and the Department of Agriculture and Applied Economics, University of Georgia. 4 pp.

DeLong, Anita K. April 2002. Managing visitor use and disturbance of waterbirds-a literature review of impacts and mitigation measures - prepared for Stillwater National Wildlife Refuge. Appendix L (114 pp.) In Stillwater National Wildlife Refuge Complex final environmental impact statement for the comprehensive conservation plan and boundary revision (Vol. II). Department of the Interior, U.S. Fish and Wildlife Service, Region 1, Portland, OR.

Field, Libby Y. and B.A. Engle. 2002. Best Management Practices for Soil Erosion. Agricultural and Biological Engineering Department, Purdue University. http://agen521.www.ecn.purdue.edu

Fredrickson, L.H., and M.E. Heitmeyer. 1998. Waterfowl use of forested wetlands of the southern United States: An Overview. Pages 307-323 in M.W. Weller, editor. Waterfowl in Winter. University of Minnesota Press, Minneapolis, MN.

Goetz, J.C.G. 1995. A Stocking Guide for Southern Bottomland Hardwoods. Southern Journal of Applied Forestry, Vol. 19, No. 3, August 1995, pages 103-104.

Johnson, Joseph R., Herby Bloodworth, David Summers. Agricultural Land and Water Use in Mississippi, 1982-1998. Published by the Office of Agricultural Communications, a unit of the Division of Agriculture, Forestry and Veterinary Medicine at Mississippi State University. 24 pp.

Kelley, J.R., Jr. 2002. American woodcock population status, 2002. U.S. Fish and Wildlife Service, Laurel, Maryland. 16pp.

Korschgen, Carl E. and R.B. Dahlgren. 1992. 13.2.15. Human Disturbances of Waterfowl: Causes, Effects and Management. Waterfowl Management Handbook, Fish and Wildlife Leaflet 13.2.15., Washington, D.C. 8 pp.

Lawler, Mark. June 2000. Shattered Solitude/Eroded Habitat: The Motorization of the Lands of Lewis and Clark. Sierra Club Northwest/Alaska Office, Seattle, WA, and Sierra Club Northern Plains Office, Sheridan, WY. 35 pp.

Loesch, C. R., K. J. Reinecke, and C. K. Baxter. 1994. Lower Mississippi Valley Joint Venture Evaluation Plan. U.S. Fish and Wildlife Service, Lower Mississippi Valley Joint Venture, Vicksburg, Mississippi, USA.

Mississippi Development Authority. January 2003. Fiscal Year 2002 Economic Impact for Tourism and Recreation in Mississippi: January 2003. Prepared by: Mississippi Development Authority, Division of Tourism Development, Research Unit, Jackson, MS. 100 pp.

Mississippi State University. August 2002. Bird Communities in Bottomland Hardwood Restoration Sites in the Mississippi Delta. Mississippi State University, Forest and Wildlife Research Center, Department of Wildlife Fisheries Research. 3 pp.
<http://www.cfr.msstate.edu/fwrc/wildlife/bird.htm>

Mississippi State University. August 2002. Northern Bobwhite Habitat Ecology. Mississippi State University, Forest and Wildlife Research Center, Department of Wildlife Fisheries Research. 3 pp. <http://www.cfr.msstate.edu/fwrc/wildlife/bobwhite.htm>

Mississippi Wetland Management District. 1998. Mississippi Wetland Management District including: Dahomey NWR and Tallahatchie NWR. Annual Narrative. Grenada, Mississippi.

Morton, John M. 1995. Managing human disturbance and its effects on waterfowl. Pages F59 - F86 in W.R. Whitman, T. Strange, L. Widjeskog, R. Whittemore, P. Kehoe and L. Roberts (eds.). Waterfowl Habitat Restoration, Enhancement and Management in the Atlantic Flyway. Atlantic Flyway Council and DE Div. Fish and Wildlife, Dove, DE. 1114 pp.

National Invasive Species Council. January 18, 2001. Management Plan: Meeting the Invasive Species Challenge: National Invasive Species Council. Washington, D.C. 88 pp.

Natural Resources Conservation Service. 2002. Wetland Management for Waterfowl Handbook. Edited and compiled by Kevin D. Nelms, Natural Resources Conservation Service, Mississippi. 119 pp.

Natural Resources Conservation Service. November 2002. Buffer Strips: Common Sense Conservation. U.S. Department of Agriculture, NRCS.
<http://www.nrcs.usda.gov/feature/buffers/index.html>

Natural Trails & Waters Coalition. November 2002. Impacts on Soils and Plants. U.S. Department of the Interior, Forest Service.   <http://www.naturaltrails.org/>

North Mississippi National Wildlife Refuges Complex. 2003. Biological Review. U.S. Fish and Wildlife Service. Grenada, MS.

North Mississippi National Wildlife Refuges Complex. 2003. Public Use Review. U.S. Fish and Wildlife Service. Grenada, MS.

North Mississippi National Wildlife Refuges Complex. 2002. North Mississippi National Wildlife Refuges Complex including: Dahomey NWR, Tallahatchie NWR, and Coldwater River NWR: Annual Narrative, Grenada, Mississippi.

North Mississippi National Wildlife Refuges Complex. 2001-2016. Forest Habitat Management Plan. Grenada, MS.

North Mississippi National Wildlife Refuges Complex. 2000. North Mississippi National Wildlife Refuges Complex including: Dahomey NWR, Tallahatchie NWR, and Coldwater River NWR: Annual Narrative, Grenada, Mississippi.

Owen, James. March 2003. Deer Behind Britain's Great Bird Decline. Article in the United Kingdom for National Geographic News. <http://news.nationalgeographic.com>

Pierce, Marvin. March 1994. Final Survey Report on Farming Operations on National Wildlife Refuges, Region 1, U.S. Fish and Wildlife Service (No. 94-I-408). U.S. Department of the Interior, Office of Inspector General, Headquarters Audits, Arlington, VA. 11 pp.

Rankins, A. D. Shaw and M. Boyette. Effectiveness of perennial grasses as vegetative filter strips for reducing sediment and herbicide losses in surface runoff. Department of Plant and Soil Sciences, Mississippi State University.

Reinecke, K. J., R. M. Kaminski, D. J. Moorhead, J. D. Hodges, and J. R. Nassar. 1989. Mississippi Alluvial Valley. Pages 203-247 in L. M. Smith, R. L. Pederson, and R. M. Kaminski, eds. Habitat Management for Migrating and Wintering Waterfowl in North America. Texas Tech. Univ. Press, Lubbock.

Reincke, K.J. and C.K. Baxter. 1996. Waterfowl Habitat Management in the Mississippi Alluvial Valley. Pages 159-167 in 7th International Waterfowl Symposium. J.T. Ratti, Editor.

Reinecke, K. J., and C. R. Loesch. 1996. Integrating research and management to conserve wildfowl (Anatidae) and wetlands in the Mississippi Alluvial Valley, U.S.A. Gibier Faune Sauvage, Game and Wildlife 13:927-940.

Schmidt, P.R. 1993. Memorandum - Information request regarding impacts of hunting on national wildlife refuges. U.S. Department of the Interior, Fish and Wildlife Service, Office of Migratory Bird Management, Washington, D.C. 7pp.

Sweeney, Caitlin. September 2000. Public Access and Wildlife Compatibility Survey Results Report. State of California, San Francisco Bay Conservation and Development Commission, San Francisco, CA. 36 pp. <http://ceres.ca.gov.bcdc/>

U.S. Department of the Interior. November 2002. Off Road Vehicles Harm Public Lands. Bureau of Land Management and U.S. Forest Service. <http://www.americanlands.org/forestweb/off_road_vehicles.htm>

U.S. Department of the Interior. July 1999. Fulfilling the Promise. The National Wildlife Refuge System, U.S. Fish and Wildlife Service, Division of Refuges, Arlington, VA. 94 pp. http://refuges.fws.gov   Approval of Compatibility Determinations

U.S. Department of the Interior, Fish and Wildlife Service and U.S. Department of Commerce. 1996 National Survey of Fishing, Hunting, and Wildlife-Associated Recreation: Mississippi: FHW/96 MS: Issued March 1998.

U.S. Fish and Wildlife Service. 2003. Coldwater River National Wildlife Refuge. Fact Sheet.

U.S. Fish and Wildlife Service. 2003. Dahomey National Wildlife Refuge. Fact Sheet.

U.S. Fish and Wildlife Service. 2003. Tallahatchie National Wildlife Refuge. Fact Sheet.

U.S. Fish and Wildlife Service. February 2003. America's National Wildlife Refuge System: Why are hunting, fishing and trapping allowed on National Wildlife Refuges? U.S. Fish and Wildlife Service, National Wildlife Refuge System. <http://refuges.fws.gov/faqs/hunting.html>

U.S. Fish and Wildlife Service. March 2003. Hunting Statistics. Department of the Interior, U.S. Fish and Wildlife Service, Yazoo National Wildlife Refuge Complex, Hollandale, MS.

U. S. Fish and Wildlife Service. 2001. National Survey of Fishing, Hunting and Wildlife Wildlife-Associated Recreation.

U.S. Fish and Wildlife Service. 2000. Dahomey, Coldwater, and Tallahatchie National Wildlife Refuges. Brochure.

U.S. Fish and Wildlife Service. 1998. Southeast Regional Report: National Fish and Wildlife Foundation FY99 Needs Assessment. U.S. Fish and Wildlife Service, Atlanta, GA. 68 pp.

U.S. Fish and Wildlife Service. 1991. Endangered and Threatened Species of the Southeastern United States (The Red Book). Pondberry – Lindera melissifolia.

Westover, Donald E. March 1984. NebGuide: Open Burning. Published by Cooperative Extension, Institute of Agriculture and Natural Resources, University of Nebraska, Lincoln.

Yarrow, G.K. 1987. The potential for interspecific resource competition between white-tailed deer and feral hogs in the post oak savannah region of Texas. M.S. Thesis. Stephen R. Austin State University. 222 pp.

Appendix H: Public Involvement

COMMENTS ON THE DRAFT CCP-EA, AND SERVICE RESPONSES

1. **The Mississippi Department Wildlife, Fisheries and Parks (MDWFP), as a state-partnering agency with the U.S. Fish and Wildlife Service, received a courtesy copy of the preliminary draft CCP-EA for its review and comment during the Service's internal review period.** In a letter dated December 14, 2004, the MDWFP furnished comments on the internal review draft that were considered and addressed by the CCP planning team. A number of these comments and suggestions were incorporated in the Draft CCP-EA. The MDWFP did not comment formally on the May 2005 Draft CCP and EA.

2. **A reviewer from the Department of Wildlife and Fisheries at Mississippi State University, in an email dated June 17, 2005, made the following comments:**

   I served on the review team in 2002. I am delighted with the decision to adopt Alternative D – Enhanced Wildlife Management and Public Use. I believe this decision is the best course of action, particularly for wintering waterfowl that may be facing decreased availability of food in Mississippi and in the MAV [Mississippi Alluvial Valley].

   Response to Comment: Comment acknowledged. The Service is pleased that this wildlife professor and authority on waterfowl ecology and management is supportive of the preferred management alternative for the North Mississippi National Wildlife Refuges Complex.

   …our recent research has revealed abundance of waste rice in the MAV and soybean acreage in Mississippi has decreased significantly over the past 2 decades. This reduction in availability of waste agricultural seeds may be one of several important factors related to the decreased abundance of mallards and other ducks wintering in Mississippi and the MAV…. Indeed, increased intensive management of moist-soil habitat is an important strategy to mitigate decreased availability of winter food for waterfowl.

   Response to Comment: Decreasing availability of waste agricultural seeds in the Delta region is further justification for the Complex's plan to expand the acreage and increase the intensity of moist soil management.

   Regarding management of wood duck nest box program, I am delighted the team followed our recommendations, many of which were based on Dr. Brian Davis' doctoral research conducted at Noxubee NWR and along the Tenn-Tom Waterway…. The most "suitable" brood rearing habitat for wood ducks (i.e., habitat wherein ducks survived at greatest rates) was scrub/shrub.

   Response to Comments: Comment acknowledged. One of the strategies under Objective 1-2 on wood duck nest boxes does call for placing boxes close to available scrub/shrub habitat.

3. **A reviewer from the U.S. Army Corps of Engineers, in an email dated June 24, 2005, made the following comments:**

Page 72, Objective 1-7: Forest Birds – This objective states that forest habitat is highly fragmented, but I did not find a strategy that specifically addresses habitat fragmentation. I think reforesting the "focus area" shown on Figure 8 should be identified as a strategy to reduce habitat fragmentation.

Response to Comment: Objective 5-3 is specifically about focus areas within the Complex, and describes the Service's intent to protect, restore, and manage the highest priority habitats within these areas, which are shown on Figure 8 (p. 95 in the Draft CCP). Since bottomland hardwoods are the original, natural vegetative community in this area of the country, most conservation efforts would emphasize reforestation.

Page 73, Strategies – where is Table 7

Response to Comment: From the preliminary, internal review draft to the public review draft, Table 2-7 was relabeled as Table 7, and this change should have been reflected in the designation of the table in the strategy but was not. Thank you for catching this oversight.

Page 79, Strategies – suggest establishing partnerships with Delta State and Mississippi State to accomplish inventory and monitoring of refuge lands. Great opportunity to get good results with cheap labor from grad students.

Response to Comment: The Service presently has on going research and inventory efforts with DSU and will continue to expand these type activities.

Page 84, T&E – Since Dahomey NWR is across the Mississippi River from ivory-billed woodpecker habitat, Dahomey could possibly support a few IBW's. It is not too far-fetched that IBW's could expand into Dahomey; 8,126 acres of mature BLH is not too small, especially if the "focus area" located between Dahomey and the Mississipp River is reforested. Anyone looked for signs of IBW's on Dahomey?

Response to Comment: To the knowledge of Complex staff, nobody has yet looked for signs of ivory-billed woodpeckers at Dahomey refuge. At present, the refuge is still mostly isolated from other large forested areas closer to the Mississippi, and its bottomland hardwoods habitat is mostly not yet mature, which makes the presence of IBW's unlikely at this time. However, the Service acknowledges that this habitat matures and expands, it could well support IBW's in the future, especially with increasing reforestation of other lands in the focus area to the west.

General comment – Following Chapter V in the EA, does FWS include a statement that "based on the findings of the EA, there are no adverse impacts associated with the proposed action (Alternative D), therefore a FONSI is appropriate and an EIS is not warranted"?

This determination will be made by the Regional Director after his review of the final Environmental Assessment.

Good document.

Response to Comment: Comment acknowledged. The Service appreciates the Corps' input.

4. A private citizen, in an email dated June 24, 2005, commented that he generally agreed that Alternative D (the Service's preferred alternative) is the best alternative. He specifically supported the proposed expansion of hunting opportunities on the refuge that would occur under this Alternative.

Response to Comment: The Service and Complex management appreciate the strong show of support for its preferred management alternative by this member of the public.

Appendix I: Wilderness Review Summary

Wilderness Review
North Mississippi Refuges Complex
June 20, 2005

The Planning Team met at the North Mississippi Refuges Complex Office on June 20, 2005 to gather information and conduct field exams for the refuges' wilderness review. The review team included:

> Steve Gard, Project Leader
> Kimberly Hayes, Assistant Refuge Manager
> Mike Dawson, Refuge Planner
> Becky Rosamond, Wildlife Biologist
> Leon Kolankiewicz, Mangi Environmental Group

The wilderness review is a required component of the comprehensive conservation plan. The Wilderness Act defines a Wilderness Area as an area of federal land retaining its primeval character and influence, without permanent improvements or human habitation, which is managed so as to preserve its natural conditions and which:

1) generally appears to have been affected primarily by the forces of nature, with the imprint of man's work substantially unnoticeable;

2) has outstanding opportunities for solitude or primitive and unconfined type of recreation;

3) has at least 5,000 contiguous roadless acres or is of sufficient size to make practicable its preservation and use in an unimpaired condition;

4) does not substantially exhibit the effects of logging, farming, grazing, or other extensive development or alteration of the landscape, or its wilderness character could be restored through appropriate management, at the time of review;

5) is a roadless island; and

6) may contain ecological, geological, or other features of scientific, education, scenic, or historic value.

During the inventory phase of the wilderness review, the emphasis is on an assessment of wilderness character within the inventory unit. Special values (i.e., ecological, geological, scenic, historical) should be identified, but are not required. The determination to recommend (or not recommend) a Wilderness Study Area to Congress for wilderness designation will be made through the comprehensive conservation plan decision-making process.

Summary of Wilderness Inventory Findings

The wilderness review inventory team could not identify any refuge units that would meet the criteria for a wilderness study area.

Appendix J. Intra-Service Section 7 Biological Evaluation

INTRA-SERVICE SECTION 7 BIOLOGICAL

EVALUATION FORM

Division/Office: North MS NWR Complex

Refuge Manager/Phone #: Steve Gard (662)226-8286

Date: October 12, 2004   Conservation Conservation Plan

I.   **Proposed Action:** Implementation of the Comprehensive Conservation Plan.

The U.S. Fish and Wildlife Service (Service) has developed a Draft Comprehensive Conservation Plan (CCP) to provide a foundation for the management and use of the North Mississippi Refuges Complex (Complex). The plan is intended to serve as a working guide for the Complex's management programs and actions over the next 15 years.

II.   **Location (County and State/attach project area map):**

The North MS NWR Complex is comprised of three NWRs (Dahomey, Tallahatchie, Coldwater) and 128 FmHA properties in 26 counties in north MS. The Complex is headquartered in Grenada, MS.

III.   **Description of proposed action (describe in enough detail to allow proper evaluation of project impacts, attach additional pages as needed):**

The plan's overriding consideration is to carry out the purposes for which each refuge was established. Fish and wildlife are the first priority in refuge management, and public use (wildlife-dependent recreation) is allowed and encouraged as long as it is compatible with, or does not detract from, the refuge's mission and purposes.

Individual consultations will occur under Section 7 for projects related to endangered species and are not intended to be covered in this document. This CCP prioritizes wildlife and habitat management, and proposes wildlife-dependent, compatible recreational opportunities. Chapter 4 of the CCP outlines specific goals, objectives and strategies to achieve an expanded wildlife and habitat management approach, while optimizing (making the best use of) public use and environmental education opportunities. While seeking concurrences on the general management direction of the refuge, as stated previously, individual consultations will occur for projects specifically related to endangered species and critical habitat.

IV. Species and Habitats Considered:

A. List all federally endangered, threatened, proposed, and candidate species, and describe any associated critical or proposed critical habitat that may be affected by the proposed action. Make a determination of how the proposed action may affect each:

SPECIES/CRITICAL HABITAT	STATUS[1]	DETERMINATION[2]			RESPONSE REQUESTED[3]
		NE	NA	AA	
Bald eagle	T		X		
Least tern	E		X		

[1]STATUS: E = endangered, T = threatened, PE = proposed endangered, PT = proposed threatened, CH = critical habitat, PCH = proposed critical habitat, C = candidate species

[2]DETERMINATION:

NE = no effect. This determination is appropriate when the proposed action will not directly, indirectly or cumulatively impact, either positively or negatively, any listed, proposed, candidate species or designated/proposed critical habitat.

NA = not likely to adversely affect. This determination is appropriate when the proposed action is not likely to adversely impact any listed, proposed, candidate species or designated/proposed critical habitat or there may be beneficial effects to these resources.

AA = likely to adversely affect. This determination is appropriate when the proposed action is likely to adversely impact any listed, proposed, candidate species or designated/proposed critical habitat.

[3]RESPONSE REQUESTED: conference, concurrence, formal consultation

VI.

Project Leader: _Mike Dawson_   _10/12/04_
                     Signature   Date

No effect:_____

Is not likely to adversely affect:____ ✓

Is likely to adversely affect:_____

VII. Reviewing Ecological Services Office(ESO) Evaluation:

A. Concurrence ✓   Nonconcurrence ___

B. Formal Consultation Required ___

C. Conference Required ___

D. Remarks (attach additional pages if needed):

VIII. Signatory Approval:

ES Supervisor: _____   _10/12/04_
                     Signature   Date:

Note: The process ends here if the proposed action is "not likely to adversely affect".

REFUGE CHIEF : _____   _____
                    Signature   Date

ARD Ecological Services: _____   _____
                           Signature   Date

Note: These signatures are required for approval of a conference report or biological opinion.

V. Determination of effects:

A. Explanation of effects of the action: Include direct, indirect, interrelated, interdependent, and cumulative effects (attach additional pages as needed):

Definitions for Effects of the Action:

Direct Effects = are those that are an immediate result of the action.

Indirect Effects = are those that are caused by the action and are later in time but are still reasonably certain to occur. They include the effects of future activities that are induced by the action and that occur after the action is completed.

Interrelated = are those that are part of a larger action and depend on the larger action for their justification.

Interdependent = are those that have no significant independent utility apart from the action that is under consideration.

Cumulative Effects = are those effects of future State or private activities, not involving Federal activities, that are reasonably certain to occur within the action area.

The proposed CCP should benefit the listed species.

B. Explanation of actions to be implemented to reduce adverse effects:

n/a

Appendix K. Finding of No Significant Impact

North Mississippi Refuges Complex
(Dahomey, Tallahatchie, and Coldwater River National Wildlife Refuges)
Comprehensive Conservation Plan
Grenada, Mississippi

Introduction
The U.S. Fish and Wildlife Service proposes to protect and manage certain fish and wildlife resources in the northern section of the Mississippi Delta, through management of the North Mississippi Refuges Complex (Complex). An Environmental Assessment has been prepared to inform the public of the possible environmental consequences of implementing the Comprehensive Conservation Plan for North Mississippi Refuges Complex. A description of the alternatives, the rationale for selecting the preferred alternative, the environmental effects of the preferred alternative, the potential adverse effects of the action, and a declaration concerning the factors determining the significance of effects, in compliance with the National Environmental Policy Act of 1969, are outlined below. The supporting information can be found in the Environmental Assessment.

Alternatives
In developing the Comprehensive Conservation Plan for North Mississippi Refuges Complex, the Fish and Wildlife Service evaluated four alternatives: Alternatives A, B, C, and D.

The Service adopted Alternative D, the "Preferred Alternative," as the plan for guiding the direction of the Complex for the next 15 years. The overriding concern reflected in this plan is that wildlife conservation assumes first priority in refuge management; wildlife-dependant recreational uses are allowed if they are compatible with wildlife conservation. Wildlife-dependent recreation uses (hunting, fishing, wildlife observation, wildlife photography, and environmental education and interpretation) will be emphasized and encouraged.

Alternative A. No Action Alternative
Existing management and public outreach practices would be favored under this alternative. All refuge management actions would be directed towards achieving the Complex's primary purposes, including: (1) preserving wintering waterfowl habitat; (2) providing production habitat for wood ducks; (3) meeting the habitat conservation goals of national and international plans; and (4) preserving wetlands, all while contributing to other national, regional, and state goals to protect and restore migratory birds, threatened and endangered species, and resident species. Refuge management programs would continue to be developed and implemented with limited baseline biological information. Active habitat management would be implemented through water level manipulations, and moist-soil, cropland, and forest management, designed to provide a diverse complex of habitats that meets the foraging, resting, and breeding requirements for a variety of species. A summary of the current acreages by habitat type can be found in Chapter II. Complex staff would continue to restore and maintain existing wetland, open water, moist-soil, and bottomland forest habitats. Land would be acquired from willing sellers within the current 47,816-acre acquisition boundaries.

Hunting and fishing would continue to be the major focus for the Complex public use program, with no expansion of current opportunities. Current restrictions or prohibitions would remain. Environmental education, wildlife observation, and wildlife photography would be accommodated at present levels. If funding becomes available, a visitor center and headquarters office would be constructed on Highway 82 at the Povall Tract.

Alternative B.

This alternative would emphasize significantly more public recreational uses while maintaining current habitat management. Any additional staff, emphasis, and resources would be directed to allow for more public activities. Current moist-soil, cropland, forest, and wetland management would continue. Hunting and fishing opportunities would be increased as funding and personnel allow.

Auto tours, canoe trails, foot trails, interpretive trail(s), observation towers, and blinds would be added for environmental education, photography, and watchable wildlife programs. Additional staff would be used for developing and presenting both on- and off-site environmental education and interpretation programs. An outreach coordinator would be hired for the Complex.

A visitor center and headquarters office would be constructed on Highway 82 at the Povall Tract and jointly with the Private John Allen National Fish Hatchery. New sub-headquarters and visitor contact stations would be constructed at Coldwater River, Dahomey, and Tallahatchie NWRs.

Land acquisition within the current acquisition boundaries would continue with emphasis on those lands that can provide additional public use opportunities. Any additional expansions, up to 10 percent of the current acquisition boundaries, would focus on public use opportunities.

Alternative C.

Under this alternative, refuge lands on the Complex would be intensively managed to provide high quality habitat for wildlife, particularly migratory birds. Any area on the Complex with pumping capability (wells) and a water control structure would be managed for moist-soil vegetation or force-account farmed (with 100 percent of crops left standing) to benefit migratory waterfowl. Cooperative farming fields would be farmed in rice, milo, corn, or soybeans (in order of preference) and flooded during the late fall and winter.

The wood duck nest box program would be expanded on all three refuges and would extend onto Farm Service Agency tracts with suitable brood habitat. On sites with permanent water, wood duck brood habitat would be developed to promote brood survival. Boxes would be cleaned and maintained regularly to allow two and three broods per box per year.

Primary emphasis would be placed on meeting objectives of various step-down plans, providing habitat for waterfowl and shorebirds. These habitats and their use would be monitored on the Complex to ensure that goals and objectives were met. Population and habitat surveys would be conducted throughout the Complex to develop baseline data to determine initial population levels and habitat conditions. Staff would monitor changes over time.

Wildlife-dependent recreation activities would be allowed, but only where and when they would not detract from or conflict with wildlife management activities and objectives. Infrastructure on the Complex (trails, blinds, etc.) would be developed primarily to conduct wildlife management activities. A visitor center and headquarters office would be constructed on Highway 82 at the Povall Tract.

Under this alternative, the Complex would continue to seek acquisition of all willing-seller inholdings within the present acquisition boundary. Highest priority would be given to those lands adjacent to existing refuge tracts and those lands supporting unique habitats. Additionally, the Complex would concentrate all future off-refuge partnerships on promoting more intensive wildlife management on privately owned lands. Personnel priorities would include hiring a biologist and/or technician for each refuge in the Complex, as well as for the Farm Service Agency properties (considered together) in addition to a forester to conduct forest management activities at Dahomey Refuge.

Alternative D

The Service planning team has identified Alternative D as the preferred alternative. This alternative was developed based on public input and the best professional judgment of the planning team. The objectives and strategies presented in the Draft CCP were developed as a direct result of the selection of Alternative D.

Alternative D represents a combination and/or compromise between Alternative B (Public Use Emphasis) and Alternative C (Wildlife Management Emphasis). Whereas these two alternatives seek to maximize either expanded public use or expanded wildlife management opportunities, Alternative D seeks to optimize the benefits of the Complex to wildlife and people, recognizing that tradeoffs may preclude maximizing benefits to both simultaneously. In other words, Alternative D seeks the "best of both" Alternatives B and C.

Under Alternative D, refuge lands would be more intensively managed than at present to provide high quality habitat for wildlife, particularly migratory birds. Additional areas on the Complex with pumping capability (wells) and a water control structure would be managed for moist-soil vegetation or force-account farmed (with 100 percent of crops left standing) to benefit migratory waterfowl. Cooperative farming fields would be farmed in rice, milo, corn, or soybeans (in order of preference) and flooded during the late fall and winter.

The wood duck nest box program would be expanded on all three refuges and may extend onto some Farm Service Agency tracts that have suitable brood habitat. Boxes would be cleaned and maintained regularly to allow two and three broods per box per year.

Increased emphasis would be placed on meeting objectives of various step-down plans, providing habitat for waterfowl and shorebirds. These habitats and their use would be monitored on the Complex to ensure that goals and objectives were met. Population and habitat surveys would be conducted throughout the Complex to develop baseline data to determine initial population levels and habitat conditions. Staff would monitor changes over time.

This alternative would encourage more public recreational uses even while intensifying current habitat management. Additional staff, emphasis, and resources would be more or less evenly divided between enhancing public use opportunities and wildlife/habitat management. Hunting and fishing opportunities would be increased as funding and personnel allow. Moist soil, cropland, forest, and wetland management would also intensify, to the extent permitted by funding and staffing limits.

One auto tour, one canoe trail, one or more foot trail(s) and/or interpretive trail(s), one observation tower, and one or more blinds would be added for environmental education, photography, and watchable wildlife programs. Staff may be added for developing and presenting both on- and off-site environmental education and interpretation programs.

Under Alternative D, the Complex would continue to seek acquisition of all willing-seller inholdings within the present acquisition boundaries, expanding Complex acreage by up to an additional 10 percent of the current acquisition boundaries. Highest priority would be given to those lands adjacent to existing refuge tracts and those lands supporting unique habitats or offering compatible public use opportunities. Additionally, the Complex would concentrate future off-refuge partnerships on promoting more intensive wildlife management on privately owned lands.

Personnel priorities would include hiring additional law enforcement officers, an outreach coordinator for the Complex as a whole, a biologist and/or technician for each refuge in the Complex as well as for the Farm Service Agency properties (considered together), and a forester to conduct forest management activities at Dahomey Refuge.

A visitor center and headquarters office would be constructed on Highway 82 at the Povall Tract and jointly with the Private John Allen National Fish Hatchery. New sub-headquarters and visitor contact stations would be constructed at Dahomey, Tallahatchie and Coldwater River NWRs.

Selection Rationale

Alternative D is selected for implementation because it directs the development of programs to best achieve the Complex purpose and goals; emphasizes the restoration of open wetland and forest habitats; collects habitat and wildlife data; and ensures long-term achievement of Complex and Service objectives. At the same time, these management actions provide balanced levels of compatible public use opportunities consistent with existing laws, Service policies, and sound biological principles. It provides the best mix of program elements to achieve desired long-term conditions.

Under Alternatives D, refuge management actions would expand wildlife and habitat programs and enhance public use by focusing on the quality of experiences instead of a quantity of programs and facilities.

Environmental Effects

Implementation of the Service's management action is expected to result in environmental, social, and economic effects as outlined in the comprehensive conservation plan. Habitat management, population management, land conservation, and visitor service management activities on the Complex would result in increased protection for threatened and endangered species; enhanced wildlife populations; bottomland hardwood wetland restoration; and enhanced opportunities for wildlife-dependent recreation and environmental education. These effects are detailed as follows:

1. The wood duck nest box program would be expanded on all three refuges and may extend onto some Farm Service Agency tracts that have suitable brood habitat. Boxes would be cleaned and maintained regularly to allow two and three broods per box per year. If successful, this program would boost production of wood ducks by at least five-fold over present.

2. Increased emphasis would be placed on meeting objectives of various step-down plans and providing habitat for waterfowl and shorebirds. These habitats and their use would be monitored on the refuges to ensure that goals and objectives were met. Shorebirds, wading birds, and colonial nesting birds would be beneficiaries of these efforts.

3. Alternative D would encourage more public recreational uses even while intensifying current habitat management. Hunting and fishing opportunities would be augmented as funding and personnel allow. Moist-soil, cropland, forest, and wetland management would also intensify.

4. One auto tour, one canoe trail, one or more foot trail(s) and/or interpretive trail(s), one observation tower, and one or more blinds would be added for environmental education, photography, and watchable wildlife programs. In addition, both on- and off-site environmental education and interpretation programs would be expanded.

5. Under Alternative D, the Complex would continue to seek acquisition of all willing-seller inholdings within the present acquisition boundaries, expanding Complex acreage by up to an additional 10 percent of the current acquisition boundaries. Highest priority would be given to those lands adjacent to existing refuge tracts and those lands supporting unique habitats or offering outstanding wildlife-dependent public use. Additionally, the Complex would concentrate future off-refuge partnerships on promoting more intensive wildlife management on privately owned lands.

6. Educational and interpretive opportunities for the public would be expanded by the construction of one visitor center and headquarters office on Highway 82 at the Povall Tract and another visitor center with the Private John Allen National Fish Hatchery. The proposed new sub-headquarters and visitor contact stations to be constructed at Coldwater River, Dahomey, and Tallahatchie NWRs would also benefit the public.

Potential Adverse Effects and Mitigation Measures

Wildlife Disturbance

Disturbance to wildlife at some level is an unavoidable consequence of any public use program, regardless of the activity involved. Obviously, some activities innately have the potential to be more disturbing than others. The management actions to be implemented have been carefully planned to avoid unacceptable levels of impact.

As currently proposed, the known and anticipated levels of disturbance of the management action are considered minimal and well within the tolerance level of known wildlife species and populations present in the area. Implementation of the public use program will take place through carefully controlled time and space zoning such as establishment of sanctuary areas, establishment of protection zones around key sites, such as rookeries, closures of unauthorized trails, and routing of new trails to avoid direct contact with sensitive areas, such as nesting bird habitat, etc. All public use activities will be conducted within the constraints of sound biological principles and refuge-specific regulations established to restrict illegal or non-conforming activities. Monitoring activities through wildlife inventories and assessments of public use levels and activities will be utilized, and public use programs will be adjusted as needed to limit disturbance.

User Group Conflicts

As public use levels expand across time, some conflicts between user groups may occur. Programs will be adjusted, as needed, to eliminate or minimize these problems and provide quality wildlife-dependent recreational opportunities. Experience has proven that time and space zonings, such as establishment of separate use areas, use periods, and restricting numbers of users, are effective tools in eliminating conflicts between user groups.

Effects on Adjacent Landowners

Implementation of the management action should not impact adjacent or in-holding landowners. Essential access to private property will continue to be allowed through issuance of special use permits. Future land acquisition will occur on a willing-seller basis only, at fair market values within the approved acquisition boundary. Lands are acquired through a combination of fee title purchases and/or donations and less-than-fee title interests (e.g., conservation easements and cooperative agreements) from willing sellers. Funds for the acquisition of lands within the approved acquisition boundary will likely come from the Land and Water Conservation Fund or the Migratory Bird Conservation Act.

Land Ownership and Site Development

Proposed acquisition efforts by the Service will result in changes in land and recreational use patterns, since all uses on national wildlife refuges must meet compatibility standards. Land ownership by the Service also precludes any future economic development by the private sector. Potential development of beach access points, trails, and visitor parking areas could lead to minor short-term negative impacts on plants, soil, and some wildlife species. When site development activities are proposed, each activity will be given the appropriate National Environmental Policy Act consideration during pre-construction planning. At that time, any required mitigation activities will be incorporated into the specific project to reduce the level of impacts to the human environment and to protect fish and wildlife and their habitats.

As indicated earlier, one of the direct effects of site development is increased public use; this increased use may lead to littering, noise, and vehicle traffic. While funding and personnel resources will be allocated to minimize these effects, such allocations make these resources unavailable for other programs.

Implementing the comprehensive conservation plan is not expected to have any significant adverse effects on wetlands and floodplains, pursuant to Executive Orders 11990 and 11988, as actions will not result in development of buildings and/or structures within floodplain areas, nor will they result in irrevocable, long-term adverse impacts.

Coordination

The management action has been thoroughly coordinated with all interested and/or affected parties. Parties contacted include:

All affected landowners
Congressional representatives
Governor of Mississippi
Mississippi Department of Wildlife, Fisheries, and Parks
Mississippi State Historic Preservation Officer
Granada County Chamber of Commerce
Tallahatchie County Board of Supervisors
Leflore County Board of Supervisors
Mississippi Wildlife Federation
Black Bear Conservation Committee
Mississippi Fish and Wildlife Foundation
Ducks Unlimited
National Audubon Society
The Nature Conservancy of Mississippi
Local community officials
Interested citizens

Findings

It is my determination that the management action does not constitute a major federal action significantly affecting the quality of the human environment under the meaning of Section 102(2)(c) of the National Environmental Policy Act of 1969 (as amended). As such, an environmental impact statement is not required. This determination is based on the following factors (40 C.F.R. 1508.27), as addressed in the Environmental Assessment for the North Mississippi Refuges Complex:

1. Both beneficial and adverse effects have been considered and this action will not have a significant effect on the human environment. (Environmental Assessment, pages 164-170).

2. The actions will not have a significant effect on public health and safety. (Environmental Assessment, page 160).

3. The project will not significantly affect any unique characteristics of the geographic area such as proximity to historical or cultural resources, wild and scenic rivers, or ecologically critical areas. (Environmental Assessment, page 158).

4. The effects on the quality of the human environment are not likely to be highly controversial. (Environmental Assessment, pages 138-155, and page 164-170).

5. The actions do not involve highly uncertain, unique, or unknown environmental risks to the human environment. (Environmental Assessment, page 160).

6. The actions will not establish a precedent for future actions with significant effects nor do they represent a decision in principle about a future consideration. (Environmental Assessment, pages 138-155, and page 164-170).

7. There will be no cumulatively significant impacts on the environment. Cumulative impacts have been analyzed with consideration of other similar activities on adjacent lands, in past action, and in foreseeable future actions. (Environmental Assessment, page 160).

8. The actions will not significantly affect any site listed in, or eligible for listing in, the National Register of Historic Places, nor will they cause loss or destruction of significant scientific, cultural, or historic resources. (Environmental Assessment, pages 158).

9. The actions are not likely to adversely affect threatened or endangered species, or their habitats. (Environmental Assessment, pages 138-155).

10. The actions will not lead to a violation of federal, state, or local laws imposed for the protection of the environment. (Environmental Assessment, pages 157).

Supporting References

Fish and Wildlife Service. 2005. Draft Comprehensive Conservation Plan and Environmental Assessment for North Mississippi Refuges Complex, Grenada, Mississippi. U.S. Department of the Interior, Fish and Wildlife Service, Southeast Region.

Document Availability

The Environmental Assessment was Section B of the Draft Comprehensive Conservation Plan for North Mississippi Refuges Complex and was made available in June 2005. Additional copies are available by writing: U.S. Fish and Wildlife Service, 1875 Century Boulevard, Atlanta, GA 30345.

_____   _____
Sam D. Hamilton   Date
Regional Director